German Entanglements in Transatlantic Slavery

Germany has long entertained the notion that the transatlantic slave trade and New World slavery involved only *other* European players. Countering this premise, this collection re-charts various routes of German participation in, profiteering from, and resistance to transatlantic slavery and its cultural, political, and intellectual reverberations. Exploring how German financiers, missionaries, and immigrant writers made profit from, morally responded to, and fictionalized their encounters with New World slavery, the contributors demonstrate that these various German entanglements with New World slavery revise preconceived ideas that erase German involvements from the history of slavery and the Black Atlantic. Moreover, the collection brings together these German perspectives on slavery with an investigation of German colonial endeavours in Africa, thereby seeking to interrogate historical processes (or fantasies) of empire-building, colonialism, and slavery which, according to public memory, seem to have taken place in isolation from each other. The collection demonstrates that they should be regarded as part and parcel of a narrative that ingrained colonialism *and* slavery in the German cultural memory and identity to a much larger extent than has been illustrated and admitted so far in general discourses in contemporary Germany.

This book was originally published as a special issue of *Atlantic Studies*.

Heike Raphael-Hernandez is a Professor of American Studies at the University of Würzburg, Germany. Among her publications are the co-edited collection *Migrating the Black Body: The African Diaspora and Visual Culture* (2017), *Blackening Europe: The African American Presence* (2004), and *AfroAsian Encounters: Culture, History, Politics* (2006). In 2015, she was named Fellow by the American Council of Learned Societies for the collaborative research project "Visualizing Travel, Gendering the African Diaspora."

Pia Wiegmink is an Assistant Professor of American Studies at the Obama Institute for Transnational American Studies at Johannes Gutenberg University Mainz, Germany. Among her publications are *Protest EnACTed* (2011) and the co-edited collection *Approaching Transnational America in Performance* (2016). Together with Birgit Bauridl, she heads an international research network on "Cultural Performance in Transnational American Studies" (2015–2018), which is funded by the German Research Foundation.

German Entanglements in Transatlantic Slavery

Edited by
Heike Raphael-Hernandez and
Pia Wiegmink

LONDON AND NEW YORK

First published 2019
by Routledge
2 Park Square, Milton Park, Abingdon, Oxon, OX14 4RN, UK

and by Routledge
711 Third Avenue, New York, NY 10017, USA

Routledge is an imprint of the Taylor & Francis Group, an informa business

© 2019 Taylor & Francis

All rights reserved. No part of this book may be reprinted or reproduced or utilised in any form or by any electronic, mechanical, or other means, now known or hereafter invented, including photocopying and recording, or in any information storage or retrieval system, without permission in writing from the publishers.

Trademark notice: Product or corporate names may be trademarks or registered trademarks, and are used only for identification and explanation without intent to infringe.

British Library Cataloguing-in-Publication Data
A catalogue record for this book is available from the British Library

ISBN13: 978-1-138-31151-0

Typeset in Myriad Pro
by codeMantra

Publisher's Note
The publisher accepts responsibility for any inconsistencies that may have arisen during the conversion of this book from journal articles to book chapters, namely the possible inclusion of journal terminology.

Disclaimer
Every effort has been made to contact copyright holders for their permission to reprint material in this book. The publishers would be grateful to hear from any copyright holder who is not here acknowledged and will undertake to rectify any errors or omissions in future editions of this book.

Contents

	Citation Information	vi
	Notes on Contributors	viii
1	German entanglements in transatlantic slavery: An introduction *Heike Raphael-Hernandez and Pia Wiegmink*	1
2	*Sugar and slaves*: The Augsburg Welser as conquerors of America and colonial foundational myths *Julia Roth*	18
3	The right to freedom: Eighteenth-century slave resistance and early Moravian missions in the Danish West Indies and Dutch Suriname *Heike Raphael-Hernandez*	39
4	Antislavery discourses in nineteenth-century German American women's fiction *Pia Wiegmink*	58
5	Strategic tangles: Slavery, colonial policy, and religion in German East Africa, 1885–1918 *Jörg Haustein*	79
6	Catholic missionary associations and the saving of African child slaves in nineteenth-century Germany *Katharina Stornig*	101
7	Exploring race and gender in Anna Seghers's "The Reintroduction of Slavery in Guadeloupe" *Priscilla Layne*	125
	Index	147

Citation Information

The chapters in this book were originally published in the journal *Atlantic Studies*, volume 14, issue 4 (December 2017). When citing this material, please use the original page numbering for each article, as follows:

Chapter 1
German entanglements in transatlantic slavery: An introduction
Heike Raphael-Hernandez and Pia Wiegmink
Atlantic Studies, volume 14, issue 4 (December 2017) pp. 419–435

Chapter 2
Sugar and slaves: *The Augsburg Welser as conquerors of America and colonial foundational myths*
Julia Roth
Atlantic Studies, volume 14, issue 4 (December 2017) pp. 436–456

Chapter 3
The right to freedom: Eighteenth-century slave resistance and early Moravian missions in the Danish West Indies and Dutch Suriname
Heike Raphael-Hernandez
Atlantic Studies, volume 14, issue 4 (December 2017) pp. 457–475

Chapter 4
Antislavery discourses in nineteenth-century German American women's fiction
Pia Wiegmink
Atlantic Studies, volume 14, issue 4 (December 2017) pp. 476–496

Chapter 5
Strategic tangles: Slavery, colonial policy, and religion in German East Africa, 1885–1918
Jörg Haustein
Atlantic Studies, volume 14, issue 4 (December 2017) pp. 497–518

Chapter 6
Catholic missionary associations and the saving of African child slaves in nineteenth-century Germany
Katharina Stornig
Atlantic Studies, volume 14, issue 4 (December 2017) pp. 519–542

CITATION INFORMATION

Chapter 7
Exploring race and gender in Anna Seghers's "The Reintroduction of Slavery in Guadeloupe"
Priscilla Layne
Atlantic Studies, volume 14, issue 4 (December 2017) pp. 543–564

For any permission-related enquiries please visit:
http://www.tandfonline.com/page/help/permissions

Notes on Contributors

Jörg Haustein is Senior Lecturer in Religions in Africa at SOAS, University of London, UK. He is currently working on a book about colonial perceptions of Islam in German East Africa and how these influenced public debate and colonial policy. His primary fields of research are Ethiopia (especially Pentecostal and Charismatic Christianity) and Tanzania (Islam in German East Africa).

Priscilla Layne is Associate Professor in the Department of Germanic and Slavic Languages and Literatures and an Adjunct Associate Professor in the Department of African, African American, and Diaspora Studies at the University of North Carolina at Chapel Hill, USA. She works on a variety of texts from the twentieth and twenty-first centuries, primarily focusing on issues of race and gender. Her research interests include film, popular music, rebellion, social movements, (post)subculture, and postcolonial studies. She is the author of *White Rebels in Black: German Appropriation of Black Popular Culture* (2018).

Heike Raphael-Hernandez is Professor of American Studies at the University of Würzburg, Germany. Among her publications are two co-edited collections, *Migrating the Black Body: The African Diaspora and Visual Culture* (2017) and *AfroAsian Encounters: Culture, History, Politics* (2006), and *Blackening Europe: The African American Presence* (2004). In 2015, she was named Fellow by the American Council of Learned Societies for the collaborative research project "Visualizing Travel, Gendering the African Diaspora."

Julia Roth is Professor of American Studies at Bielefeld University, Germany. Her research focuses on feminist and gender studies, decolonial thinking, postcolonial studies, critical race studies, global inequalities, transnational entanglements, and interdependencies, currently with a focus on the Caribbean. She has carried out research in Argentina, the United States, Nigeria, Puerto Rico, and Cuba. Alongside her academic work, she organizes cultural–political events.

Katharina Stornig is Junior Professor of Cultural History at the International Graduate Centre for the Study of Culture (GCSC) and Justus Liebig University Giessen, Germany. Her current research focuses on the emergence and consolidation of transnational aid for children in the long nineteenth century. Her main research interests include women's and gender history, religious history, transnational history and the history of globalization, the history of photography, and the cultural history of aid and philanthropy

NOTES ON CONTRIBUTORS

Pia Wiegmink is Assistant Professor of American Studies at the Obama Institute for Transnational American Studies at Johannes Gutenberg University Mainz, Germany. Among her publications are *Protest EnACTed* (2011) and the co-edited collection *Approaching Transnational America in Performance* (2016). Together with Birgit Bauridl, she heads an international research network on "Cultural Performance in Transnational American Studies" (2015–2018), which is funded by the German Research Foundation.

German entanglements in transatlantic slavery: An introduction

Heike Raphael-Hernandez and Pia Wiegmink

ABSTRACT
This essay aims at bringing together research on Germany's colonial past and imperialist endeavors with current trends in scholarship in Atlantic history and slavery studies. While scholars of German history have begun to challenge what Jürgen Zimmerer has called the "colonial amnesia of Germans," the transatlantic slave trade and New World slavery have rarely been included in discussions about national commemorative cultural debates because Germany, it is claimed, has never directly and profitably participated in the economies of slavery. For the longest time, Germany has entertained the notion that the transatlantic slave trade and New World slavery involved only *other* European players such as England, France, Spain, Portugal, the Netherlands, or Denmark, and indeed, it seems plausible that for its own history, Germany is able to claim non-participation. Yet, the transatlantic slave trade and New World slavery were part of the earliest economic enterprises that embodied and inherently relied on global networks of trade that uprooted and relocated people in unprecedented numbers. Building on the pioneering work of scholars like Klaus Weber, Eve Rosenhaft, Felix Brahms, and Mischa Honeck, this essay re-charts the various routes of German participation in, profiteering from, as well as showing resistance to transatlantic slavery and its cultural, political, and intellectual reverberations. The essay thereby seeks to interrogate historical processes (or fantasies) of empire-building, colonialism, and slavery which, according to public memory, seem to have taken place in isolation from each other; yet, we claim that they should be regarded as part and parcel of a narrative that ingrained colonialism *and* slavery in German cultural memory and identity to a larger extent than has been illustrated and admitted so far in general discourses in contemporary Germany.

With the emergence of "the cultural turn in memory studies" in recent decades, scholars have begun to draw academic as well as general public attention to the workings of cultural memory that has been circulated and mediated within local communities and across nations via text, image, media, embodied practices, performances, and public monuments.[1] In Germany, debates about memory cultures and their public sites have focused primarily on the Holocaust. While, for obvious reasons, the Holocaust has been the most important historical event for Germany's national memory, recent years have also seen growing public demands to add other historical events to Germany's national narrative and its memory culture; one specific call for a new accounting concerns Germany's colonial past and its overseas empire that officially lasted from 1884 to 1918.[2] In cities like Munich, Hamburg, or Berlin, for example, citizens' initiatives and public campaigns have begun to demand the renaming of streets which, at present, still commemorate highly problematic colonial figures like Carl Peters, Adolf Lüderitz, or Hermann Wissmann. In a similar manner, public monuments are currently either replaced or re-contextualized by adding explanatory panels to the site.[3] Various groups and projects, such as afrika-hamburg.de, Arbeitskreis hamburg-postkolonial, Berlin Postkolonial e.V., AK Potsdam Postkolonial, or Decolonize Bremen have actively promoted postcolonial memorial practices by drawing attention to the legacy of their cities' national as well as transnational colonial history. In a different scenario, but one that insists also that Germany confronts its colonial past, members of the Ovaherero and Nama peoples in Namibia have taken Germany to court for reparation payments because of the genocide committed to their ancestors by German colonial troops from 1904 to 1908. Depending on the outcome of this court case, the decision could pave the way for other reparation claims connected to crimes committed by German colonial authorities; it could also further help catalyze Germany's changing attitude towards its colonial past and the past's place in the nation's cultural memory.

These different initiatives aim at opposing what German historian Jürgen Zimmerer has called the "colonial amnesia of Germans," which stands for a still widespread ignorance about the history of German colonialism in German public memory and for a continued denial of any colonial legacy in political discourse.[4] If one considers that Germany's era as colonial power in a variety of African and Asian regions has been well researched during the last decades, this public and political ignorance seems even more astounding. Solid academic scholarship has documented the German Empire's economic desires and its philosophical justifications, the role of its first chancellor, Otto von Bismarck, in the so-called Scramble for Africa, and the Empire's various colonial administrative rules and politics in Africa as well as Asia. One is able to find excellent publications by scholars who have focused on providing information in order to clarify revisionist and nostalgic public perceptions of German colonies and protectorates in Africa and the Pacific.[5]

While this research focuses primarily on Germany's colonial past and imperialist endeavors and inquires how this colonial past has contributed to a still persistent racism in German society to which people of African descent are exposed to on a daily basis, the transatlantic slave trade and New World slavery have rarely been included in discussions about national commemorative cultural debates because Germany, it is claimed, has never directly and profitably participated in the economies of slavery. For the longest time, Germany has entertained the notion that the transatlantic slave trade and New World slavery involved only *other* European players such as England, France, Spain, Portugal, the Netherlands, or Denmark, and indeed, it seems plausible that for its own history, Germany is able to claim non-participation. Yet, the transatlantic slave trade and New World slavery were part of the earliest economic enterprises that embodied and inherently relied on global networks of trade that uprooted and relocated people in unprecedented numbers. The publication of David Eltis and David Richardson's *Atlas of the Transatlantic Slave Trade*, which is the result of decades-long international research initiatives to document the largest forced migration in world history, visualizes the extent to which the slave trade profoundly involved the *entire* Atlantic region.[6]

As part of this awareness of the transnational character of the economies of slavery, several researchers have also begun to look more closely into different forms of potential German involvement in New World slavery and its transatlantic trade system. So far, research on German contributions to the abolition movement still figure prominently in this specific academic field,[7] whereas research on German economic participation in slavery is still in its early stages. Apart from individual approaches to specific aspects of German involvements with slavery, such as the pioneering work of the German historian Klaus Weber on German regional textile production, an encompassing and systematic study on the multiple forms of German entanglements with slavery remains to be published.[8] Felix Brahm and Eve Rosenhaft's 2016 essay collection *Slavery Hinterland: Transatlantic Slavery and Continental Europe, 1680–1850* provides a first, crucial step in this direction. Brahm and Rosenhaft illustrate the necessity to expand the study of transatlantic slavery and abolition beyond what is generally outlined as the triangular trade between Europe, Africa, and the Americas. Brahm and Rosenhaft employ the term "hinterland" to conceptualize the involvement of continental European states such as Italy, Denmark, and German-speaking countries. The hinterland although at first sight geographically detached from the enslavement and displacement of Africans, must nevertheless be considered inextricably entwined with the economies produced by the system of slavery.[9] With the essays compiled in their collection, Brahm and Rosenhaft draw attention to slavery's hinterlands, that is, in addition to the most obvious European profiteers and practitioners of slavery (for example, the British, the French, and the Portuguese) as well as the most prominent opponents of transatlantic slavery (the British and the French), they bring European countries on the radar of discourses of slavery and abolition that have thus far been thought of as detached, non-complicit, and thus irrelevant.[10] They argue that

> if these flows of people, goods, capital and indeed ideas were to be traced on a map, the resulting network would reveal itself to be something less recognizable and far more complex than the transoceanic triangle that has hitherto been an icon for the slave trade.[11]

Re-charting these various routes of German participation in, profiteering from, as well as showing resistance to transatlantic slavery and its cultural, political, and intellectual reverberations will be the subject of this collection of essays. Our focus will be twofold: First, our collection traces the encounters of Germany with slavery in the USA, the Caribbean, and South America. The first three contributions will explore how German financiers, missionaries, and immigrant writers made profit from, morally responded to, and fictionalized their encounters with New World slavery. They will demonstrate that these various German entanglements with New World slavery deem it necessary to revise preconceived ideas that erase German involvement from the history of slavery and the Black Atlantic. Second, we aim at bringing together these German perspectives on slavery with an investigation of German colonial endeavors in Africa. We see the necessity because observing that contemporary Germany still harbors strong forms of latent racism at all levels of civic society, we suggest that this demands a closer examination of its possible origins not only in the legacy of Germany's colonial past but also in Germany's much earlier economic and intellectual historical involvement with transatlantic slavery. The three remaining essays in the collection will thus look at how religious practices, political rhetoric, and East German socialist writers' fiction connected discourses of transatlantic slavery with attitudes towards colonialism in Africa in the late nineteenth and twentieth centuries. Taken together, our collection thereby seeks to interrogate historical processes (or fantasies) of empire-building, colonialism, and earlier slavery which, according to public memory, seem to have taken place in isolation from each other; yet, we claim that they should be regarded as part and parcel of a narrative that ingrained colonialism *and* slavery in German cultural memory and identity to a larger extent than has been illustrated and admitted so far in general discourses in contemporary Germany.

German involvements: A historical potpourri

The claim that Germany was not part of the history of New World slavery and its transatlantic trade is founded on the fact that Germany as a sovereign country did not exist during this time period; the German national union, the German Empire, was founded in 1871. In addition, if one turns to slave traders, financiers, shipping company proprietors, or overseas plantation owners, one indeed finds only a small group of people who were of German descent. While these traditional participatory factors are missing, one has to turn to other, at first sight more implicit forms of encounters that have served as major historical, economic, as well as intellectual influences on contemporary German society.

Any questions about German financial gains, for example, have to turn from a micro- to a macro-economic level: it is a well-established fact today that several manufacturing trades as well as trading companies, even if they were owned by single people or families, helped larger geographical areas to profit economically and to develop vital branches of domestic manufacturing. The above-mentioned work of Weber explores these forms of macro-economic participation which resulted in the industrial development of several manufacturing branches, such as textile processing and manufacturing, and in the economic strengthening of entire geographical regions such as Westphalia, Swabia, Saxony, and Silesia. Furthermore, products such as copper mined in the region of the Harz Mountains, guns from Thuringia, or glassware from Bohemia were part of a stable transatlantic trading market that allowed middle and lower class members to develop a purchasing power for goods from overseas markets. The manufacturing of and trade in these products might not have implied an immediate involvement in slavery's economy, but, as Weber argues, should be seen in the larger, macro-economic context of a steady financial improvement of entire regions and their populations.[12]

If one searches for any economic entanglement of individual German entrepreneurs with slavery, one has to turn to trading companies and their participations as sales and trading powers as well as financiers. Already among the early Atlantic players, one is able to find German companies that were well known and successful during their own era such as the Welser and Fugger families, both from Augsburg, a city in the southern part of today's Germany, and the Ehinger family from Konstanz, a southern city as well. Their members became important partly because they helped finance the Portuguese slave trade in the early 1600s, as the Fuggers did, or, held economic titles to slave plantations in today's Venezuela, as the Welser did. The financial participation, often more in forms comparable to public holding companies, emerged again during the late seventeenth century; large sums came from the Baring brothers in the city of Bremen, for instance, who were partners in the Company of Merchants Trading to Africa; the Duke

Johann Friedrich von Württemberg and Konrad von Rehlingen, a financier from Augsburg, were both shareholders in the Dutch West India Company; Johann Abraham Korten, a trader in textile goods from the city of Elberfeld, held shares from the South Sea Company.[13] Eventually, in 1682, after the earlier Fugger and Welser companies, another German trading company entered the market: by the order of the Prussian Duke Friedrich Wilhelm, the Brandenburgisch-Afrikanische Compagnie (Brandenburg African Company) was founded first and foremost for the purpose of participating in the transatlantic slave trade.[14] Otto Friedrich von der Groeben, a German aristocrat, became the duke's representative in West Africa; because of his efforts, in 1682 and 1683, the company was able to establish two trading posts in West Africa, Fort Groß-Friedrichsburg and Fort Dorothea (which became Dutch in 1690), and a base on the Danish West Indian island of St. Thomas. It is estimated that from 1682 until 1717, the Compagnie brought about 19,000 captured Africans to the Caribbean.[15] When Germans began to dream of their own colonial empire at the end of the nineteenth century, Emperor Wilhelm II rediscovered the Prussian Duke Friedrich Wilhelm I as a worthy colonial forefather in Africa. What is remarkable here is that Wilhelm II – in an earlier instance of what Zimmerer later calls "colonial amnesia" – plays down the duke's participation in the slave trade because the dominant rhetoric of the time in regard to any colonial expansion in Africa emphasized Germany's humanitarian mission with its fight against the inner-African slave trade.[16] Several years later, in 1896, in the context of a colonial exhibition in Berlin, a bank of the river Spree in Berlin was named after the company's most involved representative, Otto von der Groeben. It took until 2011 for a public initiative to fight for the renaming of the area and to replace the colonial name with that of May Ayim, an Afro-German writer and activist. Interestingly, the public debate about the act of renaming the riverbank was sparked off because several politicians and historians had refused to consider von der Groeben a persona that figured prominently in the slave trade.[17] The legacy of von der Groeben in public memory and the refusal to establish a direct link between him, German entrepreneurship, and the slave trade serves as just one example of a still missing larger discourse on German entanglements with the transatlantic slave trade and resulting New World slavery.

The majority of German participation in slavery, however, happened via individual traders. In her research on traders in eighteenth- and nineteenth-century London, historian Margrit Schulte Beerbühl found that about five hundred of them were of German descent. According to Schulte Beerbühl, the majority of these traders were not directly involved in the actual trafficking of Africans, but more in the business of trading goods that were part or product of the transatlantic slave plantation economy.[18] Several German entrepreneurs became financially involved only after their relocation to London; two trading families from Hamburg, the Rückers, one of the city's leading senator families, and the Schröders, founders of the successful bank Henry Schröder & Co. in London, can serve as examples here. Probably the financially most successful German who built his family's wealth via his multiple entanglements in the slave trade as well as in the plantation economy was Heinrich Carl von Schimmelmann (1724–1782). Born into a financially rather humble trading family in Mecklenburg-West Pomerania, he rose to such financial success during his appointment as the financial counselor to the Danish monarch Frederick V that he was considered at that time to be one of the richest people in Europe. After moving to Hamburg, he began his trading by shipping

German manufactured goods such as cotton, weapons, and alcohol to West Africa where he bought captured Africans destined for the slave market in the Americas; his returning ships brought goods produced by slave labor such as sugar and tobacco to Europe. In addition, he himself owned large plantations with more than a thousand slaves in the Danish West Indies. Remarkably, in 2006, the city of Hamburg included him in a group of former citizens who had brought wealth and fame to the city by dedicating busts in one of the city's central places to them, thus testifying once more not only to a public amnesia with regard to Germany's colonial past but also to Germany's entanglements with slavery. Similar to the civic engagement that led to a revision of the memorialization of von der Groeben in Berlin, the Schimmelmann bust had to be removed due to fierce public protest.[19]

In addition to these economic and material entanglements throughout several centuries, the eighteenth and nineteenth centuries saw another encounter: the German intellectual elite, writers, and a reading public were very much influenced by travelers, among them scholars, missionaries, adventurers, sailors, doctors, and business men, who offered narratives of these faraway places overseas. Their reports about slavery and black people in the Americas sparked a widespread interest among Germans, ranging from a general public, who enjoyed rather sensationalist accounts of the New World, to German intellectuals, who publicly debated the economic and moral consequences of the slave trade and slavery. One representative of a German progressive thinkers' critical assessment of slavery was Matthias Christian Sprengel (1746–1805), a professor of history at Göttingen and Halle, who in 1779 chose the transatlantic slave trade and the involvement of the British colonies in America in this trade as the topic of his inaugural lecture at the university in Halle. He became a fierce opponent of slavery throughout his entire career.[20]

The probably best-known traveler who brought factual details and judgmental evaluations about slavery to the general German public was the Prussian natural scientist Alexander von Humboldt (1769–1859). His extensive travels throughout the Americas, where he observed slavery first hand, turned him into an outspoken opponent of the institution; the brutality on Cuban slave plantations he had observed during his visits to the island in 1800 and 1804 led him to declare that slavery is "possibly the greatest evil ever to have afflicted humanity" in his book *Essai politique sur l'isle de Cuba* in 1826.[21] Humboldt's clear antislavery stance and his meticulous thoughts on the economic and political necessity to abolish slavery resulted not only in a ban of the Spanish translation of this publication in colonial Cuba but – perhaps a less known fact in English-speaking countries – also turned him into a cause célèbre for American abolitionists when he criticized, for example, Massachusetts' senator Daniel Webster's support for the Fugitive Slave Act of 1850.[22] Humboldt's popularity among opponents of slavery in the USA is attested to by numerous reports about him in antislavery newspapers.[23] This popularity stems first and foremost from his protest against an 1856 translation of his essay on Cuba by John Sidney Trasher, a pro-slavery advocate and promoter of the annexation of Cuba. Despite the explicit critique of slavery inherent in the work, Trasher, in what he presented as merely an act of translation, omitted the chapter which contained most of Humboldt's arguments against the slave economy from the *Essay on the Island of Cuba* and subsequently used Humboldt's work as evidence for his pro-slavery agenda.[24]

However, travel narratives such as Humboldt's that openly and forcefully condemned the institution of slavery were seldom. The German reading public was rather presented with narratives like the one by Baron Albert von Sack (1757–1829). In his function as a chamberlain to the Prussian king, von Sack traveled to Suriname and North America from 1805 to 1807. As a scientist and explorer, his mission was to report not only about the flora and fauna of Suriname, but also about local customs and public life. In his narrative, he offers very detailed impressions of the slaves' daily living conditions, which he mixes with his own personal thoughts about the institution of slavery. Addressing his own initial doubts about the institution, he is able to put any misgivings to rest by employing the argument of the good vs. the bad master. He writes:

> I confess, that the result of my observations has greatly diminished the prejudice which I brought with me from Europe, in respect to the situation of the negroes in the colonies. It must, indeed, be acknowledged, that the fate of the negro depends entirely on the temper and disposition of the master; for, while I have found the negroes happy on some plantations, I have at times, in my rural walks, seen, and still heard more of, the severe correction of others.[25]

Utilizing the "bad vs. good master"-rhetoric, he sprinkles his text with plenty of examples of his encounters with the enslaved who allegedly assure him that they are better off in slavery as long as they have a good master; one reads, for instance,

> Mastera, when we have good master, we find ourselves more happy that those free negroes are, and when we see one of them, we make him hear this, for they live upon nothing but mackarel, whilst we other negroes have plenty of different provisions on the plantations.[26]

Von Sack's account of slavery in Suriname and his repeated emphasis on the need for the "good master" would be taken up again by the German Empire's colonial rhetoric at the end of the nineteenth century. These so-called first-hand impressions of slavery which did not condemn the institution of slavery as a moral wrong, but merely criticized "bad masters" helped lay the ideological groundwork for German colonial actions against people in Africa. The exploitation of the colonized was camouflaged with the discourse of offering a morally better institution: while the German colonial system still required a master, albeit a good one, because Africans would benefit or even prefer such a system, it also could bring civilization to the supposedly uncivilized Africans. As historian Andrew Zimmerman points out, it was precisely at the moment when Germans began to create colonial state institutions and large-scale colonial trade businesses in Africa towards the end of the nineteenth century that they also:

> began to reconceptualize their colonial subjects as "Negroes" (*Neger*), rather than *Naturvölker* or natives (*Eingeborene*). Central to this new racial concept was the project, as many colonial thinkers put it, of "educating the Negro to work" (Erziehung des Negers zur Arbeit). […] The supposed naturalness of Africans and other colonized societies gave way to a supposed capacity for obedience and agricultural labor that could be realized only through authoritarian, but ostensibly benevolent white rule.[27]

The ascribed naturalness of enslaved and colonized peoples was used as a trope which justified their exploitation with the argument that manual labor and rigid governance are forms of education and thus civilization.

Von Sack's narrative also serves as an important historical document for another ideological construct. Many of the writings that seemingly pretended to be taken aback by the institution of slavery portrayed people of African descent, without any inhibitions, in the most racist ways. By employing all forms of racial stereotypes, travel narratives such as von Sack's nurtured already prevalent notions of white European superiority with statements like "for even the free negroes in the colony [Suriname] possess but little humanity"[28] or "our method of reasoning respecting the negroes is often mistaken."[29] Often, he describes the enslaved Africans as easily satisfiable with small offers of entertainment; one reads, for example:

> [...] a good and sensible master will never fail to allow these dances to his negroes, as they are very fond of the diversion, and it gives them fresh life and activity to go cheerfully to work again; at those plantations which I have visited, the negroes receive each of them a glass of rum, on their return in the evening from their work.[30]

Presentations like this testify to the fact that widespread German intellectual interest in slavery might have been concerned with the institution, but otherwise did not see any contradiction in simultaneously harboring racist attitudes towards black people that perceived them admittedly as fellow human beings, but nevertheless as inferior, helpless, childlike, and uncultured. These so-called first-hand impressions contributed to a strengthening of philosophical and pseudo-scientific reasoning regarding notions of racial superiority; German philosophers and natural scientists like Immanuel Kant (1724–1804), Johann Friedrich Blumenbach (1752–1840), Georg Wilhelm Friedrich Hegel (1770–1831), or Friedrich Nietzsche (1844–1900) were able to build their racist theories on such historical "testimonial" material.[31]

Racist stereotypes and notions of white superiority were also disseminated by several popular German writers who brought the excitement of traveling to faraway places via fiction to the reading public at home. Balduin Möllhausen (1825–1905) and Friedrich Gerstäcker (1816–1872), to name just two prominent examples, were widely read, well-known authors. Möllhausen and Gerstäcker collected their material for their much-loved, self-styled ethnographic adventure novels during their own extensive travels to North America. While the purpose of their texts was the playful invitation to travel, at least fictitiously, to these places in the New World, their writings either employed already well-established white supremacist attitudes or nurtured new notions of superiority. In his travel diary, Möllhausen, for example, while on a Mississippi steamboat, writes enthusiastically about the landscape along the riverbanks and the wonderful economic opportunities this part of America would offer to any enthusiastic entrepreneur; during his "economic bliss" ramblings, he does not mention slavery at all. Yet, he is very well aware of the existence of the institution because he also marvels about the wonderful dinner atmosphere on the steamboat which, according to him, is even further enriched by accompanying music of enslaved black men who do their job with "grinning joy."[32] With small, interspersed remarks such as these, writers could claim that they had not intended any stereotyping of black people, nevertheless depictions like these inevitably contributed to the image of the childlike, always happy, even in unfree circumstances, black person as long as he or she could play some music.

Even writers such as Mathilde Anneke (1817–1884), who became ardent critics of slavery when they emigrated to the USA, were not devoid of employing racial stereotypes.

In her 1866 novella *Uhland in Texas*, for instance, she depicts German immigrants, due to their innate humanism, as model citizens of the New World, who inevitably also attack slavery as an inhuman institution and moral wrong. Although German American antislavery authors like Anneke at times come up with unconventional inclusions such as a Black Columbia or interracial marriage, her black characters, however, do not feature as prominently as her German immigrants, but function rather as supporting cast for the German lead characters. Her works, ultimately, serve to celebrate German moral, cultural, and intellectual superiority. Unfortunately, many of the assumptions and racial constructs delivered in these texts are still widely accepted in contemporary Germans' attitudes towards people of African descent.[33]

Our argument for this collection is that to begin charting the history of German colonialism, one cannot neglect the important precursors to this discourse, namely Germany's early economic entanglement in slavery in the Americas and the genealogies of pre-colonial German intellectuals' participation in the creation and dissemination of racial stereotypes. It is this entanglement of slavery and colonialism that needs to be examined more thoroughly in German (colonial) history. For this entanglement, utilized by the German Empire for the justification of its entry into its own colonial era, a variety of German travelers played a crucial part; as so-called explorers, they traveled to different parts of Africa to test economic possibilities for Germany. In their reports, one is able to repeatedly detect that American slavery is used as an ethical reference point for an ideological justification for the German entry into colonialism; America with its unfree labor system is a "bad master" whereas Germany would never introduce such a labor arrangement in their colonies, thus being the "good master."[34] One of these travelers, Carl Peters (1856–1918), first a traveler and then himself a colonial landowner, became one of the prime movers for the ideological and economic foundation for the German Empire's entry into East Africa as colonial power. Already in one of his early reports, the myth of the "good German master" is utilized when he writes that "the difficulty was to replace slavery with a contract between employer and employee that was in accordance with our European ethical sense of right and wrong." ["lag die Schwierigkeit darin, an die Stelle der Sklaverei das unserem europäischen sittlichen Rechtsbewußtsein entsprechende Kontrakts-Verhältnis zwischen Arbeitgeber und Arbeiter treten zu lassen."][35] Yet, while he propagates the self-perception of the ethical "good" German, he also outlines the capitalist system of colonial exploitation:

> The cheapest results were achieved by Mr. Hermes from Petershöhe in Useguha, who temporarily managed to drop wages to 20–25 cents. The secret solution for the labor question according to the sense of the contract lies in the rise of necessities of the black population […] Since the black person gets nothing at this market without cash, he has to enter a wage contract. […] If we can retain the workforce with cheap conditions, we can assume – considering the general fertility of this area – that the same thing would be feasible and able to compete on the global market.
>
> [Die günstigsten Resultate erzielte wohl Herr Hermes auf Petershöhe in Useguha, welcher die Lohnsätze zeitweilig bis auf 20–25 Pf. herabzudrücken vermochte. Das Geheimnis für die Lösung der Arbeiterfrage im Sinne des Kontraktverhältnisses liegt im Anwachsen der Bedürfnisse der schwarzen Bevölkerung […] Die Begehrlichkeit der Schwarzen richtet sich vornehmlich auf Toilette = Gegenstände und Geräthschaften [sic] verschiedener Art […] Da der Schwarze ohne Baarzahlung [sic] auf diesem Markt nichts erhält, so bequemt er sich eben dazu, in ein Lohnverhältnis zur Gesellschaft zu treten. […] Wenn wir die Arbeitskräfte zu so

billigen Preisen erhalten können, so läßt sich bei der allgemeinen Fruchtbarkeit des Gebiets berechnen, daß dasselbe auf dem Weltmarkt konkurrenzfähig ist.][36]

Peters' suggestions to the imperial court in Berlin remind us of Zimmerman's thesis which claims that

> [a]s German interaction with its colonial empire moved from the distance of trade to the close contact of colonial state formation and the capitalist organization of labor, German authorities borrowed ideologies developed by older racially segregated states and economies, especially the United States.[37]

What once more comes to the fore here and what shall be further explored in this collection is how inextricably entwined discourses of slavery and colonialism have been in German economic, political, and intellectual history.

Structure of contributions to this collection

The essays in this collection aim at tracing intellectual, political, and literary entanglements of Germany with slave economies in the transatlantic world. The first three essays examine the economic, religious, and cultural points of contact German traders, missionaries, and immigrants had with New World slavery in the seventeenth, eighteenth, and nineteenth centuries. Taken together, the essays refute the still prevalent notion that Germans had little or nothing to do with the trade of captured Africans, that Germans had so few points of contact with the institution of slavery that they could not have had any substantial knowledge of the undertakings overseas, and that Germans did little to help end both the slave trade and the institution of slavery.

Julia Roth's essay on the two mercantile Augsburg families, the Welser and the Fugger, who were influential financiers during the Holy Roman Empire, examines how deeply involved these two trading families and their businesses were in the Spanish conquest of the New World. The financial endeavors of the Welser and Fugger, Roth shows, were not only pivotally entangled with the Spanish conquest of the Americas, the subjugation and enslavement of Amerindians, and the flourishing of the transatlantic slave trade, but they also became much-admired founding figures for German colonial fantasies at the end of the nineteenth century and during the Nazi regime. While the Welser and Fugger are still idealized as exemplary global business players, the structures of conquest, exploitation, and enslavement that enabled their financial success is to the greatest extent still omitted in German public memory today.

Heike Raphael-Hernandez addresses another facet of German entanglements with New World slavery. In her essay, she retrieves the complex and at times contradictory attitudes of Moravian missionaries, a Protestant group from Saxony, towards enslaved Africans. For her investigation, she singles out the Moravian missionary endeavors in the early eighteenth-century Danish West Indies and Dutch Suriname. She claims that, in their mission-related contacts during this very short, specific period, both groups, the enslaved Africans and the German missionaries who, at that time, mostly came from the lowest classes of their home regions, would receive glimpses of secular possibilities for future societies which eventually would help bring changes to their own specific secular settings. She demonstrates this with three aspects: the missionaries' approach to literacy for the enslaved, their encouragement of the enslaved to implement verbal and even legal protest, and, probably the most empowering tool, their invalidation of white people's assumed God-given superiority in the eyes of black people. The nexus of these three aspects, very likely contributed to each group's vision of a society-to-come, which, in turn, must have led more to an ideological insistence on the human right to freedom with all its different implications than has been noted in scholarship thus far.

While Roth and Raphael-Hernandez focus on German involvements with slavery in the Caribbean and South America, Pia Wiegmink turns to North America. In her essay, she analyzes antislavery fiction by two nineteenth-century German immigrant women writers, Therese Albertine Louise von Jakob Robinson's novel *The Exiles* (1852) and Matthilde Franziska Anneke's post-bellum novella *Uhland in Texas* (1866). Wiegmink discusses how the intersecting discourses of antislavery, Americanization, and womanhood are negotiated in nineteenth-century German-American women's fiction. She illustrates how these two writers expanded the repertoire of US American antislavery literature by strategically using the immigrant's insider-outsider perspective to provide an ethnically distinct, yet effective critique of slavery for a North American audience.

These three essays on New World slavery are complemented by two essays that turn to East Africa. The essays by Jörg Haustein and Katharina Stornig are contributions to a field that has been little studied to date.[38] Both essays draw attention to the ways in which antislavery politics and activism in Europe became inextricably entwined with German colonial endeavors in East Africa.

Jörg Haustein examines the antislavery rhetoric with which Germans justified the occupation of Tanganyika in 1889. In his analysis, Haustein illustrates the highly strategic employment of this rhetoric by German colonizers and explores how it was built on the complex and at times contradictory relationship of German colonization with slavery and Islam. With regard to Tanganyika, Haustein's essay demonstrates how the issue of slavery became part and parcel of strategic concerns that comprised government politics, missionary work, and economic decision-making. While German colonizers at first presented slavery as a "Muslim" institution and emphasized Germany's (Christian) civilizing mission, once they established their rule in the colony, political affiliations changed and antislavery arguments became enmeshed in a discussion of labor shortage.

Katharina Stornig adds another facet to the relation of Germans with slavery and colonial efforts; in her essay she examines transnational Catholic associations and their confession-based activism in German-speaking Europe in the late nineteenth century. Stornig shows that these associations, as part of a transnational network of antislavery benevolent and missionary work which operated within and between Catholic Europe and parts of Africa, drew on a variety of forms of gendered antislavery organizations as well as on rhetoric that had already been proven successful in North America's abolitionist movement. Her essay brings to the fore how the idea of the African child slave that had to be rescued by Catholics in Germany became a central reference point in Catholic benevolent work; Stornig shows how these particular practices of Catholic antislavery work not only became part of everyday life activities of German Catholics, but also decisively contributed in the dissemination of general representations of Africans, such as the innocent child that depends on Christian guidance.

The last essay in this collection turns to post-World War II Germany and asks some much-needed questions about East Germany's socialist self-perception of owning a *tabula rasa* in regard to any prior, historical German colonial endeavors or white supremacist attitudes. With her analysis of one of East German author Anna Seghers' Caribbean novellas, *The Reintroduction of Slavery in Guadeloupe* (*Wiedereinführung der Sklaverei in Guadeloupe*, 1949), Priscilla Layne examines whether Seghers succeeds in presenting a postcolonial narrative that envisions collective cross-racial revolutionary action. To support her endeavor, Layne adopts an intersectional approach and presents a nuanced reading of the affiliations of race, class, gender, and nationality in Seghers' novella. Layne's assessment shows that ultimately, and despite Seghers' attempts to present a socialist vision of solidarity, the novella is not able to cut across the racial and gendered alliances the text wants to overcome and instead remains trapped in the legacy of European colonialist thinking.

The six essays in this collection re-chart the diversity of German contact zones and entanglements with slavery in the Americas and its subsequent colonial legacy in Africa. They examine a broad variety of practices that connected German entrepreneurs, missionaries, politicians, aid organizations, and writers with the trade in captured Africans, the plantation economies of the Caribbean, the peculiar institution in the USA, and German colonial politics in Africa. Furthermore, the essays examine not only how those historical players involved in these entanglements reflected upon their own, respective societies, but also how contemporary Germany has remembered and continues to remember these German participants. The research presented in these essays provides evidence of how these past entanglements still profoundly shape contemporary German cultural memory and its hesitant willingness towards any racial discourse. It is our hope that with this collection, a discourse that has already been started will continue to thrive in the academic as well as in the public arena.

Notes

1. Tamm, "Semiotic Theory of Cultural Memory," 127.
2. During its duration from 1884 to 1918, the German Empire's overseas colonies consisted of German East Africa (Tanganyika, Ruanda-Urundi, Wituland), German South-West Africa (present-day Namibia), German West Africa (Cameroon, Togoland), several southern Pacific islands (Solomon Islands, Marshall Islands, Caroline Islands), German New Guinea, Micronesia, and German Samoa.
3. Similar initiatives have been taken place in other European countries such as the Netherlands and Great Britain; see, for example, Kardux, "Monuments"; Rice and Kardux, *The Slave Trade's Dissonant Heritage*.
4. Zimmerer, "Kolonialismus und kollektive Identität," 9.
5. See, for example, Brian, "Beasts Within and Beasts Without"; Conrad, *Globalization and the Nation in Imperial Germany*; Geulen, "World Order and Racial Struggles"; Kundrus, *Moderne Imperialisten*; Osterhammel, *Die Verwandlung der Welt*; Sobich, *Schwarze Bestien, Rote Gefahr*; Steinmetz, *The Devil's Handwriting*; Zimmerer, ed., *Kein Platz an der Sonne*; Zimmerman, "Race and World Politics"; and Zimmerman, *Anthropology and Antihumanism in Imperial Germany*. A very recent endeavor to revise public perceptions about German colonialism was the exhibition *German Colonialism: Fragments Past and Present* which opened in 2016 at the German Historical Museum (Deutsches Historisches Museum) in Berlin and was accompanied by a comprehensive exhibition catalogue. See Stiftung Deutsches Historisches Museum, *German Colonialism*.
6. Eltis and Richardson, *Atlas*.
7. See, for example, Honeck, *We Are the Revolutionists*; Diedrich, "From American Slaves to Hessian Subjects"; Jones, "'On the Brain of the Negro'"; Levine, "'Against All Slavery'"; Paul, "German Reception of African American Writers"; Paul, "Cultural Mobility Between Boston

and Berlin." Collections such as McBride, Hopkins, and Blackshire-Belay, eds., *Crosscurrents* and Honeck, Klimke, and Kuhlmann, eds., *Germany and the Black Diaspora* can be seen as vanguard collections because their essays address encounters of Germans with African Americans or Africans in a variety of political and cultural settings throughout several centuries.

8. See, for instance, Weber, "Deutschland," 37–67.
9. Brahm and Rosenhaft, "Introduction," 6.
10. In their compelling research, some of the contributors to *Slavery Hinterlands* explicitly focus on the multifaceted entanglements of German society with the system of slavery; Anka Steffen and Klaus Weber bring evidence of these entanglements via their research in the Prussian textile industry; Rebekka von Mallinckrodt inquires the mutual impact of the system of slavery and other forms of forced labor, such as serfdom; and Daniel Hopkins' essay shows how the work of German scientists, in particular that of the botanist Julius Philip Benjamin von Rohr (1737–1793), was inextricably connected to the economic matrix of slavery that encompassed not only the cotton and sugar plantations in the New World but also conducted agricultural research that aimed at transplanting cotton production to Africa. See Steffen and Weber, "Spinning and Weaving"; Mallinckrodt, "No Slaves in Prussia?"; and Hopkins, "Julius von Rohr."
11. Brahm and Rosenhaft, "Introduction," 13.
12. Weber, "Deutschland," 54.
13. For more information, see Weber, "Deutschland," 37–67.
14. See Koslofsky and Zaug, "Ship's Surgeon," 28; Kopp, "Mission Moriaen," 2.
15. For more information, see van der Heyden, *Rote Adler*. See also Kopp, "Mission Moriaen," 2–7. We would like to thank Dorothea Fischer-Hornung who alerted us to the existence of Fort Dorothea in Ghana and shared relevant information about its history with us; see the entries for Fort Groß-Friedrichsburg and Fort Dorothea on the website of the Ghana Museums and Monuments Board, "Forts and Castles."
16. Kopp, "Mission Moriaen," 7.
17. Ervedoza, "May-Ayim-Ufer," 432–437.
18. See Schulte Beerbühl, *Deutsche Kaufleute in London*.
19. Krieger, "Heinrich Carl von Schimmelmann," 319. Although the controversy over the bust is an indicator of a growing public awareness about Germany's past entanglements with slavery, historian Martin Krieger rightly observes that while the legacy of Schimmelmann and in particular his profits from his plantations in the Caribbean have been critically researched and made public in Denmark in the latter half of the twentieth century, "we can only wish that projects like those [in Denmark] will function as inspiring models for Germany." The German original reads: "es bleibt zu wünschen, dass derartige Projekte auch in Deutschland eine Vorbildfunktion entfalten" (our translation). Ibid., 321.
20. Dippel, *Germany and the American Revolution*, 52. See also Ratzel, "Sprengel, Matthias Christian," 299–300.
21. Humboldt, *Political Essay*, 144.
22. Walls, *The Passage to Cosmos*, 207.
23. For example, the *National Anti-Slavery Standard*, the official mouthpiece of the American Antislavery Society, paid tribute to the German naturalist and explorer by reprinting his writings in two issues in 1858 and 1859. For further information, see Foner, *Humboldt on Slavery*, 10, 26. His popularity among abolitionists is also attested by memorabilia like wallet-size cards which were given to Union soldiers during the Civil War. The Boston Public Library holds one of these wallet-sized cards. As historian Laura Dassow Walls explains, the card consists of a reprint of a letter Humboldt had written to a New Yorker in which he expressed his adoration for the city of New York and his despise for Daniel Webster. The card was given away as a token of support for wounded soldiers. See Walls, *The Passage to Cosmos*, 198.
24. Remarkably, it was not even a decade ago and due to the meticulous research by historian Vera Kutzinski that translations of Humboldt's *Essay* into English, Spanish, and German were examined more thoroughly. See Kutzinski, "Translations of Cuba." In 2010, a more accurate translation of Humboldt's original essay became available in English. As historians Vera

Kutzinski and Ottmar Ette, who provided the translation, observe:

> It is of little surprise, then, and highly ironic given Humboldt's recorded feelings and writings on the subject [slavery], that postcolonial critics from the English-speaking world have targeted Humboldt as an apologist for European colonialism and even for slavery in the Americas. See Kutzinski and Ette, "Inventories and Inventions," xxxiii.

Incidents like this demonstrate the need to re-examine the material archives and to carefully scrutinize the scholarly discourse about German entanglements with slavery.

25. Sack, *Narrative*, 109.
26. Ibid., 114.
27. Zimmerman, "Race and World Politics," 364.
28. Sack, *Narrative*, 105.
29. Ibid.
30. Ibid., 109.
31. For further information, see Eigen and Larrimore, *The German Invention of Race*.
32. Möllhausen, *Tagebuch*, 1.
33. The following, very recent example from the city of Heidelberg, Germany, can serve as perfect example for the claim that widespread latent racism toward people of African descent is still very much part of contemporary German civil society. Since the summer of 2015, Germany has become host country to a larger number of refugees than ever before in its history. While the majority of refugees are not from sub-Saharan African countries, but from Middle Eastern countries such as Iran and Syria, complaints against refugees often utilize the stereotypes of black people. Because of its world-famous university and its large body of international researchers, students, and faculty, Heidelberg loves to present itself as a liberal, racist-free, welcoming, inclusive place. As late as 13 May 2017, the daily newspaper that is still widely read, wrote about local residents who do not feel safe anymore because of the refugees in their neighborhood, citing one resident, Ernst B., who stated that many of the refugees would drink and yell and in general completely misbehave. The explanation could be, so Ernst B., that people from Africa simply display different social behavior in public places. In subsequent letters to the editor, many readers were outraged about such a negative statement about refugees. In their rescue mission of the refugees' and Heidelberg's reputation, not one person addressed the racial scapegoating of people of African descent. See Hörnle, "Busbahnhof," 3.
34. For further information on German self-perception of being the "good" colonialists, especially shortly before the outbreak of World War I, see Kundrus, *Moderne Imperialisten*.
35. Peters, *Die deutsch-ostafrikanische Kolonie*, 39. Our translation.
36. Ibid., 40, 44. Our translation.
37. Zimmerman, "Race and World Politics," 363.
38. Brahm and Rosenhaft make this compelling point that so far scholarship has paid little attention to the fact that towards the end of the nineteenth century "a phenomenal burst of anti-slavery sentiment and engagement can be observed in several continental European countries […] and it became closely linked to European colonial politics." Brahm and Rosenhaft, "Introduction," 20–21.

Acknowledgements

We would like to express our deep-felt thanks to our contributors as well as to our reviewers for their superb work, their cooperation, and their endurance in putting together this collection. Furthermore, we owe many thanks to the editors of *Atlantic Studies: Global Currents* for their support during the completion of this collection; especially Dorothea Fischer-Hornung and David Lambert were a great team to work with throughout the entire process.

Disclosure statement

No potential conflict of interest was reported by the authors.

Bibliography

Brahm, Felix, and Eve Rosenhaft. "Introduction: Towards a Comprehensive European History of Slavery and Abolition." In *Slavery Hinterland: Transatlantic Slavery and Continental Europe, 1680–1850*, edited by Felix Brahm and Eve Rosenhaft, 1–23. Woodbridge: Boydell Press, 2016.

Brian, Amanda M. "Beasts Within and Beasts Without: Colonial Themes in Lothar Meggendorfer's Children Books." *German Studies Review* 37, no. 2 (2014): 253–274.

Conrad, Sebastian. *Globalization and the Nation in Imperial Germany*. Cambridge: Cambridge University Press, 2010.

Diedrich, Maria I. "From American Slaves to Hessian Subjects: Silenced Black Narratives of the American Revolution." In *Germany and the Black Diaspora: Points of Contact, 1250–1914*, edited by Mischa Honeck, Martin Klimke, and Anne Kuhlmann, 92–111. New York: Berghahn Books, 2013.

Dippel, Horst. *Germany and the American Revolution 1770–1800*. Wiesbaden: Franz Steiner, 1978.

Eigen, Sara, and Mark Larrimore, eds. *The German Invention of Race*. New York: SUNY Press, 2006.

Eltis, David, and David Richardson. *Atlas of the Transatlantic Slave Trade*. New Haven: Yale University Press, 2010.

Ervedoza, Clara. "Das May-Ayim-Ufer in Berlin." In *Kein Platz an der Sonne: Erinnerungsorte der deutschen Kolonialgeschichte*, edited by Jürgen Zimmerer, 424–441. Bonn: Bundeszentrale für politische Bildung, 2013.

Foner, Phillip S. *Alexander von Humboldt on Slavery in the United States*. Berlin: Humboldt-University, 1984.

Geulen, Christian. "World Order and Racial Struggles: The Ideological Matrix of Colonialism." In *German Colonialism: Fragments Past and Present*, edited by Stiftung Deutsches Historisches Museum, 33–41. Berlin: Deutsches Historisches Museum, 2016.

Ghana Museums and Monuments Board. "Forts and Castles." *Ghana Museums and Monuments Board*. Accessed August 6, 2017. http://www.ghanamuseums.org/forts/forts-castles.php

van der Heyden, Ulrich. *Rote Adler an Afrikas Küste: Die brandenburgisch-preußische Kolonie Großfriedrichsburg in Westafrika*. Berlin: Selignow, 2001.

Honeck, Mischa. *We Are the Revolutionists: German-Speaking Immigrants and American Abolitionists after 1848*. Athens: University of Georgia Press, 2011.

Honeck, Mischa, Martin Klimke, and Anne Kuhlmann, eds. *Germany and the Black Diaspora: Points of Contact, 1250–1914*. New York: Berghahn Books, 2013.

Hopkins, Daniel. "Julius von Rohr, an Enlightenment Scientist of the Plantation Atlantic." In *Slavery Hinterland: Transatlantic Slavery and Continental Europe, 1680–1850*, edited by Felix Brahm and Eve Rosenhaft, 133–160. Woodbridge: Boydell Press, 2016.

Hörnle, Micha, "Ist der Busbahnhof ein neuer Angstraum?" *Rhein-Neckar-Zeitung*, May 13, 2017, 3.

Humboldt, Alexander von. *Political Essay on the Island of Cuba. A Critical Edition*. Edited and translated by Vera M. Kutzinski and Ottmar Ette. Chicago: University of Chicago Press, 2010.

Jones, Eileen Jeannette. "'On the Brain of the Negro': Race, Abolitionism, and Friedrich Tiedemann's Scientific Discourse on the African Diaspora." In *Germany and the Black Diaspora: Points of Contact, 1250–1914*, edited by Mischa Honeck, Martin Klimke, and Anne Kuhlmann, 134–152. New York: Berghahn Books, 2013.

Kardux, Johanna C. "Monuments of the Black Atlantic: Slavery Memorials in the United States and the Netherlands." In *Blackening Europe: The African American Presence*, edited by Heike Raphael-Hernandez, 87–105. New York: Routledge, 2004.

Kopp, Christian. "Mission Moriaen – Otto Friedrich von der Gröben und der brandenburgisch-preußische Sklavenhandel." *berlin-postkolonial*. Accessed May 3, 2017. http://www.afrika-hamburg.de/PDF/kopp_groeben.pdf

Koslofsky, Craig, and Roberto Zaugg. "Ship's Surgeon Johann Peter Oettinger: A Hinterlander in the Atlantic Slave Trade, 1682–1696." In *Slavery Hinterland: Transatlantic Slavery and Continental Europe, 1680–1850*, edited by Felix Brahm and Eve Rosenhaft, 25–43. Woodbridge: Boydell Press, 2016.

Krieger, Martin. "Heinrich Carl von Schimmelmann." In *Kein Platz an der Sonne: Erinnerungsorte der deutschen Kolonialgeschichte*, edited by Jürgen Zimmerer, 311–322. Bonn: Bundeszentrale für politische Bildung, 2013.

Kundrus, Birthe. *Moderne Imperialisten: Das Kaiserreich im Spiegel seiner Kolonien*. Köln: Böhlau, 2003.

Kutzinski, Vera M. "Translations of Cuba: Fernando Ortiz, Alexander von Humboldt, and the Curious Case of John Sidney Thrasher." *Atlantic Studies* 6, no. 3 (2009): 303–326.

Kutzinski, Vera M., and Ottmar Ette. "Inventories and Inventions: Alexander von Humboldt's Cuban Landscapes." In *Political Essay on the Island of Cuba by Alexander von Humboldt. A Critical Edition*, edited by Vera M. Kutzinski and Ottmar Ette, vii–xxxiii. Chicago: University of Chicago Press, 2010.

Levine, Bruce. "'Against All Slavery, Whether White or Black': German-Americans and the Irrepressible Conflict." In *Crosscurrents: African Americans, Africa, and Germany in the Modern World*, edited by David McBride, Leroy Hopkins, and C. Aisha Blackshire-Belay, 65–81. Columbia: Camden House, 1998.

von Mallinckrodt, Rebekka. "There Are No Slaves in Prussia?" In *Slavery Hinterland: Transatlantic Slavery and Continental Europe, 1680–1850*, edited by Felix Brahm and Eve Rosenhaft, 109–131. Woodbridge: Boydell Press, 2016.

McBride, David, Leroy Hopkins, and C. Aisha Blackshire-Belay, eds. *Crosscurrents: African Americans, Africa, and Germany in the Modern World*. Columbia: Camden House, 1998.

Möllhausen, Balduin. *Tagebuch einer Reise vom Mississippi nach den Küsten der Südsee*. Leipzig: Hermann Costenoble, 1858.

Osterhammel, Jürgen. *Die Verwandlung der Welt: Eine Geschichte des 19. Jahrhunderts*. München: C.H. Beck, 2009.

Paul, Heike. "Cultural Mobility Between Boston and Berlin: How Germans Have Read and Reread Narratives of American Slavery." In *Cultural Mobility: A Manifesto*, edited by Stephen Greenblatt, 122–171. Cambridge: Cambridge University Press, 2009.

Paul, Heike. "The German Reception of African American Writers in the Long Nineteenth Century." In *Germany and the Black Diaspora: Points of Contact, 1250–1914*, edited by Mischa Honeck, Martin Klimke, and Anne Kuhlmann, 115–133. New York: Berghahn Books, 2013.

Peters, Carl. *Die deutsch-ostafrikanische Kolonie in ihrer Entstehungsgeschichte und wirtschaftlichen Eigenart*. Berlin: Verlag von Walther & Apolant, 1889.

Ratzel, Friedrich. "Sprengel, Matthias Christian." In *Allgemeine Deutsche Biographie* (Vol. 35), 299–300. München: Historische Kommission bei der Bayerischen Akademie der Wissenschaften, 1893.

Rice, Alan, and Johanna C. Kardux, eds. *The Slave Trade's Dissonant Heritage: Memorial Sites, Museum Practices, and Dark Tourism.* Special Issue of *Atlantic Studies* 9, no. 3 (September 2012).

Sack, Albert von. *A Narrative of a Voyage to Surinam; of a Residence There During 1805, 1806, 1807; and of the Author's Return to Europe by the Way of North America.* London: G. and W. Nicol, 1810.

Schulte Beerbühl, Margrit. *Deutsche Kaufleute in London: Welthandel und Einbürgerung (1660–1818).* München: De Gruyter Oldenbourg, 2007.

Sobich, Frank Oliver. *"Schwarze Bestien, rote Gefahr": Rassismus und Antisozialismus im deutschen Kaiserreich.* Frankfurt am Main: Campus, 2006.

Steffen, Anka, and Klaus Weber. "Spinning and Weaving for the Slave Trade: Proto-Industry in Eighteenth-Century Silesia." In *Slavery Hinterland: Transatlantic Slavery and Continental Europe, 1680–1850,* edited by Felix Brahm and Eve Rosenhaft, 87–107. Woodbridge: Boydell Press, 2016.

Steinmetz, George. *The Devil's Handwriting: Precoloniality and the German Colonial State in Qingdao, Samoa, and Southwest Africa.* Chicago: The University of Chicago Press, 2007.

Stiftung Deutsches Historisches Museum, ed. *German Colonialism: Fragments Past and Present.* Berlin: Deutsches Historisches Museum, 2016.

Tamm, Marek. "Semiotic Theory of Cultural Memory: In the Company of Juri Lottmann." In *The Ashgate Research Companion to Memory Studies,* edited by Siobhan Kattago, 127–143. London: Routledge, 2015.

Walls, Laura Dassow. *The Passage to Cosmos: Alexander von Humboldt and the Shaping of America.* Chicago: University of Chicago Press, 2009.

Weber, Klaus. "Deutschland, der atlantische Sklavenhandel und die Plantagenwirtschaft der Neuen Welt." *Journal of Modern European History* 7 (2009): 37–67.

Zimmerer, Jürgen, ed. *Kein Platz an der Sonne: Erinnerungsorte der deutschen Kolonialgeschichte.* Bonn: Bundeszentrale für politische Bildung, 2013.

Zimmerer, Jürgen. "Kolonialismus und kollektive Identität: Erinnerungsorte der deutschen Kolonialgeschichte." In *Kein Platz an der Sonne: Erinnerungsorte der deutschen Kolonialgeschichte,* edited by Jürgen Zimmerer, 9–38. Bonn: Bundeszentrale für politische Bildung, 2013.

Zimmerman, Andrew. *Anthropology and Antihumanism in Imperial Germany.* Chicago: University of Chicago Press, 2001.

Zimmerman, Andrew. "Race and World Politics: Germany in the Age of Imperialism, 1878–1914." In *The Oxford Handbook of Modern German History,* edited by Helmut Walser Smith, 359–377. Oxford: Oxford University Press, 2011.

Sugar and slaves: The Augsburg Welser as conquerors of America and colonial foundational myths

Julia Roth

ABSTRACT

In her 1883 collection of biographies of the most famous *conquistadores* of the Americas, Colombian writer Soledad Acosta de Samper noticeably included two German representatives of the Augsburg-based Welser trading company. Her depictions demonstrate that German finance and investment has been constitutive for the early colonial endeavor in the Americas of which the enslavement of Amerindians and the trade in enslaved Africans formed an integral part from the outset. This essay pursues a twofold aim: Firstly, it employs Acosta de Samper's account of the Augsburg traders as a lens for elaborating on the little-studied German activities in the Spanish colonies. Secondly, the essay is interested in how early colonial endeavors such as the Welser's have been serving as a showcase example for German colonial fantasies ever since. Both arguments refute the dominant discourse of the "late" or "insignificant" German role in the colonial enterprise, the transnational slave trade, and the trade in enslaved Amerindians. This essay will pursue and promote a perspective that focuses on the entangled histories and processes of conquest and colonialism, thus broadening the claim of the structural involvement of German-territorial actors such as the Welser company whose activities were transnational in scale to begin with. A relational entanglement perspective brings into view the transnational flows of capital, goods, people, and ideas; the essay thereby raises questions concerning the acknowledgement and confrontation of a German responsibility for colonization and enslavement.

The Colombian journalist, novelist, historiographer, and defender of women's rights Soledad Acosta de Samper (1833–1913) was the first woman to write about the *conquistadores*, and also the first author to include the early German colonizers of the Americas. In her introduction to the *Biografías de Hombres Ilustres ó Notables* (Biographies of Famous or Notable Men), Acosta de Samper collected around 300 biographies of the most famous "discoverers," *conquistadores*, and missionaries to the Americas. In the section "discoverers," she emphasizes the decisive role the Welser traders from Augsburg and their representatives, so-called factors, played in the conquest of the Americas. Acosta de Samper traces the Welser's motivations for the conquest by reconstructing their routes to the most significant part of the German colonization in what is today Venezuela and Colombia. She writes:

> Unfortunately, the initiated colony (of Venezuela) was only a year old, when emperor Charles V had to take the fruit from her to fill his royal till, emptied because of the wars he kept up against most of the European kings. With the objective to obtain the jingly money that a company of rich Flemish traders (the Rothschilds of the sixteenth century) offered him, brought them, as a feud of the crown, all the territory of Venezuela, from Cabo de la Vela to Maracapana, with the right to conquer the land, and under the condition to found two cities and three forts. They were under the mandate of a governor or *adelantado* who was nominated by the company that was called the *Welzares* or *Belzares* of Augsburg.[1]
>
> [Por desgracia, apenas tenía un año de vida la iniciada Colonia [de Venezuela], cuando el Emperador Carlos V tuvo á también sacar fruto de ella para llenar sus arcas reales, vaciadas por las guerras que sostenía contra la mayor parte de los reyes europeos. Con el objeto de conseguir el dinero sonante que le ofrecía una compañía de ricos comerciantes flamencos (los Rothschild del siglo XVI), cedió á éstos, como feudo de la corona, todo el territorio de Venezuela, desde el Cabo de la Vela hasta Maracapana, con derecho á conquistar en la tierra adentro, y con la condición de fundar dos ciudades y tres fortalezas bajo el mando de un Gobernador ó Adelantado, que nombraría a la compañía que llamaban de los Welzares ó Belzares de Augsburgo.]

Through the prominent inclusion of two early German conquerors in her book, Acosta de Samper's account hints at the German partaking in the conquest of the Americas: Southern German trading houses like the Fugger and the Welser played a central role as financers and traders during the economic expansion in and network building in and with actors in the Americas since the fourteenth century.[2] Being one of the wealthiest and most influential traders of the Renaissance, the Welser company became an interesting trading partner for Emperor Carl V. who was financing the Spanish conquest through foreign investment. Enjoying privileges based on their financial support for the ruling houses, these companies gained great impact in the political proceedings of the then Holy Roman Empire of the German Nation(s) as financers and experts.[3] Today, Germany is usually held to have played a comparatively insignificant role in the conquest of the Americas, in early colonialism, and in the transatlantic slave trade. However, the episode of the company of the Welser, and, to a lesser extent, the Fugger, during the early phase of the conquest reveals that German capital and expertise was indeed crucial for the colonial endeavor, even though German engagement might have been smaller in numbers than that of other European powers. Moreover, the Welser episode has been crucial with regard to German self-fashioning ever since, thus increasing the Welser's symbolic and epistemic impact to a larger extent than their actual historical influence might have been. This essay is particularly interested in this symbolic and epistemic significance for later German colonial discourses.

The use of the term "German" for the time period during which the Welser was active in the Americas is debatable since the German Reich was founded later. However, the different kingdoms, princedoms, etc., being part of the Holy Roman Empire of the German Nation (ruled by the Habsburg monarchy, Catholic Austria, and Lutheran Prussia), I refer to the "Germans" in accordance to numerous of my sources.[4]

This essay focuses on the entangled character of global interrelations based on the notion that German actors, capital, and ideas have from the outset formed an integral part of the conquest and colonization of the Americas. It pursues a relational perspective for a current reading of the Welser which highlights the transnational character of different actors beyond national borders and different regions, when it comes to colonization and the German involvement in the slave trade. Shalini Randeria has coined the notion of "entangled histories of uneven modernities" as a historical concept of transcultural relations. Due to its historical dimension and the attention to historically produced and persistent colonial asymmetries, her concept provides a helpful frame.[5] The concept goes back to Sidney Mintz's elaboration on the history of sugar.[6] Based on the idea of a "shared and divided" history, Randeria's notion of "entangled histories of uneven modernities" focuses on the intertwined but unequal interrelations and exchanges between the regions of the world, while accentuating that not only the colonizing countries had an impact to the colonized regions, but that the transfer has been happening vice versa as well, even so under structurally highly uneven terms. The concept aims at rendering problematic the notion that Europe/the West would have developed independently from the "rest" of the world.

Accordingly, rather than presenting a marginal and negligible aspect in the colonial endeavor as many studies still have it, a relational perspective reveals the ways in which the Welser have served as an example and reference for German colonial endeavors and fantasies ever since. Making the German participation in the colonization process visible enables another perspective on the German involvement in global entanglements and structures of inequality. Unlike dominant accounts of German history, which locate German colonialism solely in the "big" German colonies in Africa in the late nineteenth century, such a perspective shows that German actors, labor, and capital have formed an active part in the colonial process from the outset and opens the view toward transnational entanglements. In a second step, building on Susanne Zantop's work on German colonial fantasies, the essay examines examples of colonial fantasies coming up during the imperial-colonialist expansion of the nineteenth century in Germany. These fantasies were often based on foundational myths from the early phase of the conquest. In the nineteenth century in particular, the example of the Welser (and, to a lesser extent, the Fugger) served as such a powerful myth and as a reference point for those who supported colonialism and dreamed of a "place at the sun" for Germans.

Germans in the conquest

In accordance with Acosta de Samper's account, Charles V. financed the conquest with private capital. When in the early sixteenth century, it became probable that the Habsburgs would also inherit Spain, South German merchants, who maintained close relations with the Habsburg monarchy, saw their chance to profit from the expansion into the Americas. Already in 1508, the Welser owned large lands on the Canary island of Tenerife and soon a sugar plantation with a mill on the island of La Palma, thus becoming very active in the European sugar market.[7] In 1519, the Welser and Fugger houses granted considerable large loans for the election of King Charles V. as emperor.[8] In return, the traders were granted privileges – such as licenses for trading enslaved Africans and partaking in the conquest of certain American regions – hardly any other actor enjoyed. These privileges were fixed in the Contract of Madrid from 12 February 1528. Together with the

Asiento contract of 28 March 1528 granting the Welser a secure colonial staging point in Venezuela, they are also being referred to as "Welser Contracts."[9] By that time, the conquest of "Las Indias Occidentales" – as Europeans also called the Americas until the nineteenth century, referencing Marco Polo's term – was at its peak. Montezuma's realm in Mexico had already been overthrown, fueling heretofore-unimagined fantasies among the conquerors from Europe about riches through the discovered gold treasures.[10] Meanwhile, the conquest of South America was just beginning.

Although the South American territories were actually closed to foreign colonial interests, the Welser company was allowed to conquer, re-colonize, and exploit large parts of what is today Venezuela and parts of Colombia. The company of Bartholomäus (V.) Welser senior (1484–1561) held the governorship of "Little Venice" (Venezuela) from 1528 until 1556. During this time, his governors carried out seven larger expeditions in the region, the so-called *entradas*, covering a distance of more than 20,000 kilometers. Several hundred (Christian) Europeans who set out to find local civilizations rich enough to be plundered usually carried out the *entradas*. The Welser are even referenced as creators of the myth of the gold city of El Dorado based on a Colombian legend in the sixteenth century.[11] The German governors conquered Cundinamarca and founded New Granada. For the Welser, the colonial foundation provided a secure staging-post for their trade in the Americas, first under the governance of Ambrosius Alfinger (1529–1533), who in 1530 handed the authority over Venezuela in form of a letter of attorney to his vice governor Nicolas Federmann. Later governors were Georg Hohermuth von Speyer (1533–1540), and Philipp von Hutten (1540–1546). In what is today Colombia and Venezuela, the Welser built, or participated in, the foundation of several cities such as Coro Maracaibo and Bogotá under Alfinger. Until 1554, the Welser company exploited minerals at the Venezuelan coast, hoping to find great amounts of gold. When Federmann and Alfinger did not discover gold, they captured, enslaved, and sold Amerindian inhabitants.[12] The assassination of Philipp von Hutten and Bartholomäus Welser (VI.) junior in 1546 near Quíbor during an expedition in search for El Dorado terminated their governance of Venezuela. With the death of Charles V. in 1556, the trading rights expired. After the conquest was completed, the Spanish crown ended the private financing of the colonial project.[13]

The Spanish crown had hoped to gain the Welser financiers' support for the colonial holdings because the privileges the crown granted the Welser company for the conquest in the Caribbean region promised the Germans profits from various businesses, including the trade in enslaved Africans. As German Studies scholar Susanne Zantop emphasizes: "The wealthy financiers would thus help the Spaniards expand and secure their colonial holdings, while doing some colonizing and profiteering on the side."[14] Since the conquest was an insecure endeavor, the Welser were granted the "safeguarding through a net of rights and contracts."[15] Most importantly, this "safeguarding" consisted in receiving the monopoly of the trade in enslaved Africans, which provided them the most profitable source of income during their involvement in the conquest.[16] Other sectors the Welser were participating in and profiting from, such as the sugar production and copper mining industries, also relied on enslaved labor. Hence, from the outset, a broad range of investment, production, and trading activities accompanied the Welser's conquering activities in the Americas.

Products and profits: The Welser in the Caribbean

Despite a growing number of studies and publications dealing with the Welser and the Fugger and other early German colonizers in the conquest of the Americas, the aspect of their partaking in the transnational slave trade is seldom elaborated on.[17] In an early study of 1962, economic historian Enrique Otte claimed that "the chapter on the slave trade is one of the least satisfying of the hitherto existing research on the Welser," ["(d)as Kapitel über den Sklavenhandel ist eines der unbefriedigensten der bisherigen Welserforschung."] and his dictum can still be considered paradigmatic for the dominant German discourse on the Welser.[18]

In 1526, the Welser governors Jörg Ehinger and Ambrosius Alfinger founded an overseas trading establishment in Santo Domingo on the island of Hispaniola (today Dominican Republic and Haiti). Already in 1523, the trading house of the Welser had started to grow sugar cane in Santo Domingo for producing sugar, the first colonial mass product of the global economy.[19] In 1532, the company purchased the sugar mill Santa Bárbara in the department of San Juan de la Maguana through the Welser's overseas agent Sebastian Renz from Ulm for the price of 3427 Pesos, 202 Arrobas sugar, and 4 slaves.[20] With 11 kettles, Santa Bárbara was one of the largest mills on the island, where sugar production was becoming the main industry.[21] In general, the work on the sugar mills was carried out by enslaved Africans, and the list of inventories of the sugar mill Santa Bárbara provides insightful proof thereof.[22] The bill of sale for the sugar mill Santa Bárbara from 1530 lists "a gin trap for the 'negros' with chains." ["(U)n cepo de los negros con su cadenado y telera."][23] In contrast to some of the animals of the mill, the enslaved African workers are not mentioned by name. Between "the following oxes" which are listed by name, and "the following beasts" ["los bueyes siguientes" and "las bestias siguientes"], which are partly listed by name, the bill also lists "up to 14 'negros' and other absent ones, which would be up to 16." ["La gente de negros que hay en él, hasta catorze negros presentes e otros dos absentes, que serían hasta diez e seys."][24] On the one hand, such listings provide evidence for the well-known, but often neglected fact that enslaved African workers constituted an integral part of the sugar industry in the Caribbean long before enslaved labor became the backbone of the US-American tobacco and cotton industries. On the other hand, listing them in the same category as the animals points at the dehumanized and disenfranchised status of the enslaved workers. As mentioned above, as part of the privileges granted to them by the Spanish crown, the Welser held the monopoly for the import of slaves, a much-needed unpaid workforce after the extinction of the autochthonous populations of the Antilles.[25] Already in 1526, Heinrich Ehringer and Hieronymus Sailer had bought licenses for the trade in enslaved Africans from the Genovese Tomás and Domingo de Forne (for 85 enslaved Africans licensed by the governor Lorenzo de Gorrevod), and in 1527 from the Spanish Antonio de Medina and Diego de Zárate licenses for a total of 155 enslaved Africans. Most of the licenses were soon to be re-sold.[26] A contract from 12 February 1528 granted them the license to import 4000 enslaved Africans to the Americas over the following four years.[27] For this license, the Welser company had paid the Spanish crown 20,000 ducats to be paid back over four years. In turn, they were freed from all further tolls for sale or import, which opened for them a profit opportunity of 80,000 ducats.[28] Besides the trade in luxury goods such as cloths, sugar, gold, pearls, vine, and medical products like guaja wood (a treatment against syphilis) and the increasing export of sugar, the slave trade provided the company's major source of income.[29]

For the years between 1532 and 1538, Otte bemoans an "imprecise state of sources" ["ungenaue Quellenlage]" regarding the number of enslaved Africans imported by Germans.[30] The only documents he could find are the fragmentary and incomplete Dominican Almorjarifazgo lists which state 10 transports of enslaved Africans by Germans, 2 at a time for the years 1532, 1533, 1537 and 1538, 1 for 1534 and 1536.[31] Otte estimates that in each case supposedly 150–200 enslaved Africans were "delivered" to the Americas.[32] He further mentions the decree of Spanish Empress Isabella from September 1532, in which she permits the Germans to "again send their overseas governors to America in order to transfer and sell the rest of the 4,000 slaves." ["(die Kaiserin Isabella stellte den Welsern die Erlaubnis aus,) erneut ihre Faktoren nach Amerika zu senden, um den Rest der 4.000 Sklaven zu überführen und zu verkaufen."][33] Other known licenses he lists are the ones from 30 May, 1535, by the Emperor Charles V. to Heinrich Ehinger and Albert Cuon (who was not a Welser) for 200 enslaved Africans as compensation for their pastel and saffron treaty, which they sold to Juan Glavarro already on 21 June, and in July 1529 a license for the export of 800 slaves to the Welser (whom they, again, re-sold).[34]

Besides the use of enslaved labor as part of their sugar production, the Welser company also invested and participated in the exploitation of minerals such as silver in the Mexican mines of Sultepec and copper discovered around 1538 near Cotuy.[35] Copper became a much-sought-after mineral in the Caribbean colonies for the pots and pans needed for the booming sugar production[36] Up until this point, these pots were imported from Europe, in particular from Nuremberg. When copper mines were discovered in Cuba, the Fugger and Welser saw their bargain here as well since they had experience in mining. The Spanish crown was eager for the export in experienced miners and, again, granted the agents of the Welser company these privileges. Arriving in Cuba in 1540, the patrician and mining expert Johann Tetzel, to whom German historian Theodor Gustav Werner refers as "the first 'montane entrepreneur' of the 'New World,'" bought the copper mine El Cobre near Santiago de Cuba with the financial support of Lazarus Nürnberger (from whom he received 500 gulden in 1546) and others.[37] Tetzel made efforts to find new ways of extracting copper and attempted to return to Cuba with mining experts. Therefore, in the *asiento* of 11 January 1546 on the exploitation of the copper mines in Cuba, signed in Madrid, Charles V. granted "Hans Tetzel from Nürnberg" the right to start running "first 10 and later more" copper mines and to erect the necessary buildings.[38] Furthermore, during the first 10 years the crown freed Tetzel from customs for the material and equipment necessary for the mines and for the produced copper.[39]

German capital unquestionably had a decisive impact during this early epoch of European colonization. Cuban historians Álvarez Estévez and Guzmán Pascual highlight that the "sense and orientation" of the German traders furthermore helped to facilitate the import of many German products – such as equipment for copper mining or, later, for building railways – to the Cuban market.[40] Their economic and financial power further enabled them to establish close contact with the colonial government in Cuba as well as with the highest levels of politics and society on the island, granting them special privileges such as trading licenses, good conditions for the purchase of land and mills, and even privileged citizenship rights.[41] Regardless of the small role and episode of Tetzel's activities in Cuba, Álvarez Estévez and Guzmán Pascual see the arrival of Tetzel and his team as the island's first contact with international finance capital; they argue that Tetzel's limited exploitation of these copper mines which started in 1530

> contributed to the fact that Cuba found itself [...] for the first time in contact with the big financial powers of the world, represented by the German houses of the Fugger and the Welser of Augsburg, of the Ehingers of Constance, of the Hochstaetters etc.[42]

In a similar way, German historian Theodor Gustav Werner considers the Tetzel mine in Cuba and the implementation of such enterprises in general as the "seed" for an industrial development in the Americas which required an entrepreneurial spirit, experience, good planning, equipment, and production means as well as a respective number of workers and enslaved unpaid workers.[43] German historian of slavery, Michael Zeuske, emphasizes that by ensuring the factual monopoly of the captive and slave trade between Africa and the Americas in 1528, the Welser actually exercised "the first monopoly control of the Atlantization between the West African and the Caribbean sugar enclaves."[44] He argues that Germans from different locations actively participated in the trade in enslaved workers, bringing many traders "wealth and standing."[45] According to Zeuske, such German slave traders contributed to "new stages of capitalism" marked by the intertwining of mass slave trade and financial, scientific, technical as well as technological dynamics.[46] Thereby, the influence of most of the magnate merchants and bankers shifted increasingly from Africa to the Atlantic and the Americas. German colonial engagement in the Americas did, of course, not end with the Welser episode – there are numerous other examples of German traders making profit in the region.[47] These investments usually included the exploitation of slave labor, and German merchants continued to be actively involved in the trade in enslaved African workers.[48]

In addition to examining the national dimension of involvement in the slave trade, which is still rarely done in German public discourse an inter-relational focus brings into view the transnational flows and entanglements of capital, goods, people, and ideas. As Zeuske shows, it is worthwhile to analyze the processes of conquest, colonization, and enslavement also as structural, relational, and entangled phenomena, not solely as national endeavors. A relational perspective helps to make more visible also the impact of actors such as the Welser, who were not citizens of one of the major colonizing nations and are therefore often marginalized or omitted in historical accounts on or representations of the period. The newly built "Fugger und Welser Erlebnismuseum" (Fugger and Welser Adventure Museum) in Augsburg provides a recent example of a revision of this tendency. The museum presents Augsburg as a metropolis of European trade and the Fugger as the "first global players" as can be read on a stand-up display at the museum's entrance. The partaking in the trade in enslaved Africans and the enslavement of Amerindians is briefly mentioned on two displays of the exhibit, but there is no mentioning of the role of the exploitation of slave labor for the increase in affordable luxury goods in Europe and the accumulation of wealth while the exhibit as a whole follows a positivistic representation of the Fuggers' and Welsers' activities as a progress and success story, which each year still attracts numerous tourists to the Bavarian town. The magazines by the Augsburg tourism agency available at the museum praise the Fugger and Welser as "geniuses of commerce,"[49] these publications depict Anton Fugger as "the wealthiest man of the world" and present him as a role model for doing business today."[50]

While today the Welser and Fugger are thus romanticized as progressive first "global players," their activities historically functioned as a romanticized colonial foundational myth and as an important reference point for later colonial endeavors and cultural texts. The Welser's colonial involvement as financers, factors, mining experts, and conquerors has served as an important trope in numerous German self-narrations on colonial and imperial power until later phases of German colonial and imperial expansion and came to function as a model for later colonial German engagement.

In a cursory glance at the discourse about the German colonizers, the following section thus focuses on the interpellation and interpretation of the Welser enterprise by the friar Bartolomé de Las Casas in the sixteenth century and by the writer Soledad Acosta de Samper in the nineteenth century as two very opposite readings and as discursive landmarks of the Germans' activities in the colonies. A relational perspective proposes to digress from the focus on nation states, on only the "biggest" colonial players, and on one-dimensional (moral) evaluations of such historical actors. It shifts the focus instead toward the discursive effects their representations had as well as for their impact for uncovering entangled histories beyond national, cultural, and ideological boundaries. Both Las Casas' and Acosta de Sampers' text reference the entwined character of different histories (for instance by pointing at the active German partaking in the conquest) and simultaneously justify European colonialism and persistent unequal power structures, since both do not question the righteousness of colonial domination and support the missionary (in Las Casas' case) and imperial (in Acosta de Sampers' case) project.

Black legends and colonial foundational myths

When it comes to the reception of the German partaking in the conquest, German historian Jörg Denzer makes out "two major trends" initiated by the early chroniclers that have marked the interpretation of the epoch of the German conquerors until today: first, a rather positive evaluation of the German enterprise as introduced in the chronicles by the Spanish chronicler Oviedo y Valdés, and, second, a tradition of historiography coined by Dominican friar Bartolomé de Las Casas' polemic referred to as the German Black Legend.[51] This tradition depicts the Welser epoch as the darkest chapter of the Spanish conquest of the Americas, and it was employed anew in different historical contexts such as the Nazi dictatorship.[52] Originally, the Black Legend (*leyenda negra*) referred to the negatively connoted cruel behavior of the Spanish conquerors and colonizers in the Americas as described by Las Casas. In his *Brevísima relación de la destrucción de las Indias* (An Account, Much Abbreviated, of the Destruction of the Indies, 1542), Las Casas had indicted the Spaniards for their brutality against the Amerindian inhabitants. Actually being addressed to the Spanish crown in order to stop the crimes the Spanish conquerors committed against the Amerindian populations, Las Casas' account has become one of the most controversial texts concerning the conquest of the Americas and its aftermaths.[53]

Notably, in line with this argument, defenders of a pro-Spanish position have referred to Las Casas' *Account, Much Abbreviated*, by promoting the Germans as the most brutal colonizers, regardless of the predominating accusations of the Spanish atrocities in the colonies.[54] The so-called German Black Legend Las Casas interpellates in this argumentative piece served to blame the Germans for having been the worst conquerors, and indeed more cruel than the Spaniards. Las Casas further used the arguments of his book in the famous theological and philosophical debate of Valladoid he had with Ginés de Sepulveda on whether the indigenous population had souls and thus should be granted human rights. The Black Legend is based on Las Casas' depiction of the Germans in his chapter "On the kingdom of Venezuela" in an equally accusatory manner in the same text as "those German, or animal, tyrants,"[55] and he denounces the Germans' capturing and enslavement of the Amerindians as extremely brutal.[56] Aiming at convincing the king to become active against the cruelties committed in the Americas, Las Casas' text is highly polemic and full of exaggerations; for instance, he uses extremely high numbers such as of victims of the colonizers' cruelties. While Las Casas dedicated a relatively small part of several paragraphs to the German participation in the conquest, Acosta de Samper's *Biographies of Famous or Notable Men* three centuries later gave a more differentiated view of the German colonizers.[57] Acosta de Samper's depiction of the Welser draws a manifold picture of the Augsburg colonizers and traders in the Americas. She describes Ambrosius Alfinger, the Welser governor and colonizer of parts of what is today Venezuela, as a monstrous creature devoid of human feelings. The way she depicts Alfinger seems to be in line with Las Casas' one-sided depiction of Germans, Acosta de Samper compares Alfinger to the Hun ruler Attila and portrays him as a monster who treated the Amerindian with pure cruelty when claiming: "Fortunately for the indigenous of the plateau of Bogota, it was not their fate to have Alfinger as their first discoverer, since *this new Attila* would have destroyed them." ["Felizmente para los indígenas de las mesetas de Bogotá, no tocó Alfinger ser su primer descubridor, pues aquél nuevo Atila las hubiera dejado asoladas."][58] Already in her introduction to the book, Acosta de Samper depicts Alfinger in negative terms, particularly in comparison to her appraisal of Christopher Columbus' "heroic" achievements as "this soldier of faith and knowledge":

> the first is DISVCOVERY. It necessarily begins with Columbus' life and continues with the narration of the most notable discoverers, from OJEDA to this monster that was called Alfinger.[59]
>
> [ese soldado de la Fe y de la Sabiduría. [...] La *primera* es el DESCUBRIMIENTO. Ésta empieza por necesidad con la vida de Colón, y continúa con la relación de los *descubridores* más notables, desde OJEDA hasta aquel monstruo que se llamó Alfinger.]

However, in contrast to her negative description of Alfinger as a brute monster, which seems to cater to the German Black Legend, Acosta de Samper describes Nicolaus Federmann in essentially positive terms, thereby pointing at the diverse and manifold characters and ways of behavior of early German conquerors:

> It was *Nicolás de Federmann, a man of such good and courteous manners*, that the chroniclers reference that he was never heard to utter broken words, and he was so friendly, compassionate and merciful with his inferiors that these adored him. *He has never been accused of being grabby, nor cruel, and his enemies could never mention a bloody or pervert deed by him.*[60]

Acosta de Samper refers to Federmann's ambition in the conquest and his consequent disobedience to his governor Alfinger in a more balanced tone than Las Casas and others.[61] Her depiction illustrates that German conquerors were, for one, as common as conquerors of other origins and thus deeply intertwined with the colonial endeavor, including the trade in slaves.[62] Secondly, Acosta de Samper's portraits show that their conduct in the colonies also differed just as much as among the conquerors of other groups. Besides their necessarily partial and context-bound viewpoints, both Las Casas' and Acosta de

Samper's texts provide insightful sources for the active involvement and participation of German financiers, merchants, adventurers, mercenaries, and slave traders in the colonization and exploitation of the Americas already in the sixteenth century. By portraying them as presenting a range of characters, Acosta de Samper's account suggests a certain normality, or even banality of the German conquerors who were neither monsters, nor heroes. Acosta de Samper's portraits hence contradict the aforementioned widespread blaming of the German Welser traders as the worst conquerors of the Americas in order to deviate attention from Spain based on Las Casas' account. A relational perspective which focuses on the entangled character of global interrelations, as I would like to promote for a current reading of the Welser, brings a more complex picture into focus. Rather than making a moral statement, such a perspective seeks to uncover the ways in which German actors, German capital, and German ideas have been part and parcel of the European colonial expansion into the Americas from the start, and the Welser continuously served as a crucial point of reference for colonial endeavors, as the following section demonstrates. They thus represent a showcase example of the entangled histories of different actors, spaces which helped producing uneven structures or, following Randeria and Conrad, "modernities." A respective relational approach implies that, on the one hand, German actors, ideas, and money formed an active part in colonialism since the sixteenth century. On the other hand, such a focus reveals that, vice versa, the Americas were also constitutive for European, and also German, wealth, political, economic, and epistemic influence and expansion as well as for self-narrations and projections concerning colonial power. Today, the partaking in the colonial enterprise is still mostly played down in German public discourse, particularly after the horrible crimes committed by Germans in the name of imperialism and racial superiority during the Nazi regime. The conviction to represent a more "progressive," "developed" culture and political system and be in possession of superior forms of knowledge, civilization, religion, etc., persists, and is often justified precisely with the argument of the presumed absence of a "real" colonial history (the Nazi dictatorship excluded). Examining the Welser from a relational point of view thus serves to shift the focus to the continuities of colonial/modern engagement in and with the colonies as a structural (rather than exceptional) phenomenon, as a view on the discursive site of the nineteenth century illustrates.

The Welser as nineteenth-century German colonial foundational myth

Particularly in the nineteenth century in the context of European imperial colonialism, the Welser episode has served a completely opposite function to that of the Black Legend, transforming the Welser into heroic figures onto which foundational myths of German eligibility as conquerors and later colonial fantasies could be projected. These myths reveal another decisive aspect of the impact and the discursive function of the earlier German conquerors. It is characteristic for German historical and social discourse that, while the crimes of the Holocaust are being dealt with extensively, little attention has been paid to the entanglements and continuities of racist and colonial practices and politics since 1492.[63]

In the years 1770–1870, colonial fantasies gained momentum in German territories. It was a phase marked by the re-emergence of two thematic strands within colonial discourses: on the one hand the narrative of the failure of the Welser's enterprise, and, on the other hand the emphasis on their violent behavior as fueled by accounts such as Las Casas' which led to the German Black Legend. These strands were increasingly complemented with narratives that rejected the guilt and the formation of a German peculiarity. Zantop describes this phase as being marked by a "national character" related to a "distinct colonial cult."[64] Following Zantop, particularly the notion of the "missed opportunity" and the lack of larger colonial possessions of colonial power and wealth as incorporated by the Welser functioned as a basis for new German dreams and ambitions, thus serving first and foremost as substitute practices rather than as excuses for committed colonial brutalities: "not so much as an ideological smokescreen or cover-up for colonial atrocities or transgressive desires, but as *Handlungsersatz*, as substitute for the real thing, as imaginary testing ground for colonial action."[65]

In accordance with such a perspective, the Welser myth provided a sort of foundational myth of German colonial fantasies. References to the Welser episode can be traced continuously in German discourses of colonialization, for example, when a new competition for the Caribbean islands was under way in the late eighteenth century, Zantop makes out a number of German texts, reports on the political situation, and dramatic plays expressing colonial fantasies.[66] It seems noteworthy that these texts often make reference to South America, even though German colonial endeavors of that time focused on Africa and the Pacific. On the basis of popular literary, dramatic, journalistic, and political texts as well as children's books, Zantop's study demonstrates how references made to the early German conquerors and colonizers in these texts became a sort of "origin myth" or "foundational myth" for German colonialism. Zantop also shows that counter-narratives, which were critical toward the colonial and imperialist spirit, were not broadly received. Examples of such counter-narratives are the poem "Vitzliputzli" (1848) by German poet and dramatist Heinrich Heine or the famous long poem "Die Berlocken" (The Trinkets, 1881) by Swiss novelist and poet Gottfried Keller. Politically, both Heine and Keller remained marginal figures, "who could not defend themselves against the wave in popular writings that catered to psychic needs and not to reason or understanding and accommodated the desire for superiority, control, and possession."[67]

Tellingly, in an exemplary manner for the *zeitgeist* at the peak of German imperial and nationalist-fascist expansionism, the introduction to the 1938 publication *Deutsche Konquistadoren in Südamerika* (*German Conquerors in South America*) includes a reprint of Nicolaus Federmann's *Indianische Historia*. The motto to this book is an appraisal to the "noble German blood" in form of Johann Filchardt's 1573 poem "Ernstliche Vermahnung an die lieben Teutschen" (Serious Exhortation to the Dear Germans). German historian Arnold Federmann's introduction is titled "Forgotten Germans" and praises the Germans – and the Welser and Fugger in particular – as important patrons first of the trade with Portugal and Spain, and, later also as sponsors of the "journey West" and the conquest of Venezuela and parts of Ecuador.[68] He laments, however, that while Columbus, Pizarro, or Cortés are well-known, the names of these German conquerors are hardly mentioned:

> It thus remained unknown to the widest German circles that Germans not only took great part in the journeys of the Spanish and Portuguese to the East Indian territories, but that the Germans played the main part also in the allotment of Venezuela.[69]

He thus dedicates the book to the endeavor to make up for this "injustice done to the German names through the concealment even if it may be only silence."[70] How much this edition is appropriated to the nationalist spirit of the Nazi dictatorship becomes even more obvious in the following paragraph, which draws a completely unrealistic picture of a German unity or character of the time of the Welser: "May from now on remain unforgotten in the conscience of the people what these Germans some day achieved during yearlong campaigns of conquest, daily endangering their lives – in the honor of themselves and the German name!"[71] Even Adolf Hitler referred to the Welser and instrumentalized them for his endeavor to create a "new Germany" in Brazil in 1940, by arguing "the Fugger and Welser have had their possessions here."[72]

Notably, while in Nicolaus Federmann's account only the enslavement of captured Amerindians is mentioned, in his introductory description of the conquest of Venezuela, Arnold Federmann extensively describes the transatlantic trade in enslaved Africans. He refers to the privileges granted to the Welser in the contracts of 1528, including,

> that the owner of privileges should have the right to import 4,000 negro slaves to the West Indian colonies and sell them for no more than fifty ducats per negro. [...] The more frail characters among the conquerors and first colonists participated with pleasure in the slave trade or squeezed their bondservant Indians through excessive work. [...] The drop out of Indian work forces was now in these American colonies substituted by negro slaves with which there was a roaring and lucrative trade.[73]

> [daß die Privileginhaber das Recht haben sollten, 4000 Negersklaven nach den Westindischen Kolonien einzuführen und für nicht mehr als fünfzig Dukaten pro Neger zu verkaufen. [...] Denn die anfälligen Charaktere unter den Konquistadoren und ersten Kolonisten beteiligten sich selbst gerne am Sklavenhandel oder preßten ihre leibeigenen Indianer durch übermäßige Arbeit aus. [...] Der Ausfall an indianischen Arbeitskräften wurde nun in diesen amerikanischen Kolonien unbedenklich durch Negersklaven ersetzt, mit denen man einen schwunghaften und gewinnbringenden Handel betrieb.]

Arnold Federmann's framing of Nicolaus Federmann's account demonstrates that while many Western European writers appropriated the Americas in cultural texts for different interests, for many Germans, these territories served the specific function of making up for a missed opportunity and a loss. This loss could be overcome through new efforts serving the construction of a Western superiority, or Occidentalism. As Zantop emphasizes:

> The New World's Southern hemisphere was not only the first object of German colonial desire, it remained the German colonialist dream even after the German Empire actively supported settlement in Africa. The continued fascination with things South American [...] produced what I would call in analogy to Said's Orientalism, a German Occidentalism.[74]

Colonial activities in South America and Occidentalist projections thereof were omnipresent in German national self-fashioning. Postcolonial approaches and decolonial activism are nevertheless only slowly gaining momentum in German academic and political discussions. Respectively, it remains symptomatic for the German historic discourse to play down the colonial periods as well as the intellectual colonization of and implementation of epistemic Occidentalism in the Americas in which Germans played indeed a decisive part.[75] Similarly, for a long time, little work has been done on the German involvement in the slave trade and the profits Germans made from enslaved labor. However, in recent years, the amount of singular events and projects addressing German colonialism and its legacies began to increase.[76] As the mentioned examples of German colonial activities illustrate, structural forms of German colonial engagement provide a rule rather than a negligible exception.

Outlook: Competitive memories and claims for reparations

Acosta de Samper's two very different portraits of early German conquerors of the Americas first and foremost show that German conquerors were as common as conquerors of other origins and that they were also structurally involved in the colonial endeavor and the trade in slaves. Acosta de Samper's depictions illustrate that the German colonizers, just like the colonizers of all other nationalities, participated in, profited from, and also failed in the colonial enterprise and the slave trade. Secondly, in contrast to earlier, more generalizing depictions, her portraits show that the Germans' conduct in the colonies cannot be generalized, but that different colonizers behaved very differently, just like the conquerors of other groups.

From a relational perspective, Germans have been no exception, neither as latecomers nor as negligible actors, regardless of the number, size, or duration of actual German colonies. The case of the Welser shows that neither "Western" nor German wealth and "modernization" developed independently from other world regions. On the contrary, Western expansion and economic and financial growth were highly dependent on the exploitation of the colonized spaces, the labor of the colonized, the resources of the colonies, and imported enslaved work force. Since an entanglement perspective focuses on the structural dimension(s), it shows the ways in which German capital, goods, knowledge, and ideas have been involved in colonial expansion at least since the Welser's participation in the conquest of the Americas. Furthermore, it illustrates that the Welser have played a central part in the transatlantic slave trade and they profited from resources and luxury products produced by slave labor. From such a relational perspective, unequal global entanglements and persistent asymmetrical colonial power structures can be examined not as a recent phenomenon, but as having been a reality and a structural fact for more than 500 years. Situating German colonialism only in the nineteenth century is just part of the story. The perspective this essay proposes brings the interrelations and continuities into view and shows how German actors, capital, and knowledge have been part and parcel of colonization and the slave trade. German wealth was based on the exploitation of the resources and (cheap or unpaid/enslaved) labor in the colonies and was thus part in the production of global colonial inequalities that partly persist and are revived until today.

Furthermore, up until the culmination of racist imperialist crimes during the Nazi dictatorship the foundational myths of earlier conquerors like the Welser have fueled German colonial fantasies and the desire to make up for the "missed opportunity" of not having played a more significant role in the colonial contest. It is thus time to resuscitate these silenced memories and the claims for reparation and decolonization related to these memories and take responsibility for the German participation in enslavement, oppression, exploitation, and genocide. As German journalist and ethnologist Wolfgang Lieberknecht, for instance, puts it:

> The slave trade, for which the Europeans were responsible, had of course been abolished when the German Reich was founded. But in the past centuries, Germans participated in the activities of the different European slave trading nations [...]. And it has, like most

other European countries, not produced a movement for the abolition of the slave trade [...]. Thus, there are good reasons to ask also in this part [of the world] for the historical-moral responsibility for the slave trade and for the necessary consequences.[77]

Seen from this angle, later German colonial, imperial, and finally fascist engagement can no longer be treated as solely an outcome of the nineteenth-century European imperialist expansionist spirit isolated from earlier proceedings, interrelations, and continuities. Rather this spirit can also be read as a perceived late chance of making up for continuously disappointed dreams. Currently, an increasing number of activists and critical scholars in Germany confront this neglected part of history. One of their claims are reparations for the German genocide of the Nama and Herrero in what is today Namibia, and for stopping the denial of a meaningful German colonial history before the Holocaust.[78] Others address persistent racist street names and the government's plan of a museum called Humboldt Forum, which shall contain collections received under questionable conditions from colonized spaces. Against the backdrop of the marginalized long history of German colonial practices and fantasizing, these claims appear in a different light as well.

Notes

1. Acosta de Samper, *Biografías de hombres ilustres ó notabes*, 79. My translation.
2. The Welser was an important trading house provided with international links and lots of capital. The company was therefore involved in political contexts and provided for example public housing in Augsburg. The Welser and Fugger families developed the first balance sheet and used their expertise to oversee the financial transactions for the Roman Curia, or Council, gaining the family increasing political power. These activities in combination with maintaining strong business relations to the Habsburg Royal Family and owning trading centers in Venice and Nuremberg helped to further increase the family's wealth and political influence. Over time, the Fuggers functioned as bankers for popes, emperors, and kings while maintaining their interests in the trade of goods, such as copper and newspapers.
3. While the English translation uses the singular form (Holy Roman Empire of the German Nation), in German, "nations" is used in the plural form (Heiliges Römisches Reich Deutscher Nationen).
4. See for example Las Casas' account from 1542 who uses the term "German" in a general, all-encompassing way, referring to the conquerors (particularly Alfinger) from the German-speaking regions. See also the section on Las Casas in this essay.
5. Randeria, "Entangled Histories."
6. Mintz, *Sweetness and Power*.
7. Zeuske, *Handbuch Sklaverei*, 508.
8. The Fugger, another wealthy Augsburg-based trading enterprise, received contracts securing them the use of the American colonies and the rights to exploit the Spanish copper and quicksilver mines as an insurance and acquittance for their credits. Products from the transnational slave trade entered the trading network of the Fugger and the Welser alike. However, unlike the Welser, the Fugger's actual time in the Americas was limited: their endeavor to conquer what is today Chile was soon abandoned due to the region's less central geographical position and Pizarro's influence in the Andean region. Denzer, *Die Konquista*, 55.
9. Denzer, *Die Konquista*, 28.
10. Ibid., 12.
11. Ibid., 14–15.
12. Ibid., 20–24.
13. Ibid., 26.
14. Zantop, *Colonial Fantasies*, 19–20.
15. Denzer, *Die Konquista*, 53.

16. Lieberknecht, "Der Sklavenhandel." The original reads: "Wir geben euch Erlaubnis, dass ihr oder wer eure Vollmacht hätte, 4000 Negersklaven (aus Afrika), davon wenigstens ein Drittel weiblichen Geschlechts, nach den genannten Inseln (Haiti und Puerto Rico) und dem Festland bringen und dort verteilen könnt." [We give you permission that you, or who might have the letter of attorney, to bring 4000 negro slaves (from Africa), of which at least one third female, to the mentioned islands (Haiti and Puerto Rico) and the mainland and distribute them there.]
17. See, for example, Otte, "Die Welser;" Schmitt, *Konquista als Konzernpolitik*; Simmer, *Gold und Sklaven*; Denzer, *Die Konquista*. For a particular focus on the enslavement of Amerindians, see Schmitt, *Konquista als Konzernpolitik* and Simmer, *Gold und Sklaven*.
18. Otte, "Die Welser," 128; footnote 85. My translation.
19. Mintz, *Sweetness and Power*; Ortíz, *Cuntrapunteo Cubano*.
20. Arroba (from Arabic al-rub) is an old Spanish weight unit still used in Mexico equal to about 25 pounds (or 9.5 kilograms). It is also an old Portuguese unit of weight still used in Brazil equal to about 32 pounds or 12 kilograms ("Arroba," Merriam Webster; "Arroba," Dictionary.com).
21. Otte, "Die Welser," 126.
22. The following numbers are based on the list elaborated on by Otte ("Die Welser"). Otte points out that the original price was "16 enslaved Africans" ("Die Welser," 126).
23. See Otte's transcript in "Die Welser," 153. My translation.
24. Ibid., 154. My translation.
25. Ibid., 132. According to Otte, the Welser were already involved in the slave trade, when Charles V. offered them to take over the commerce. The first transport in enslaved Africans reached Santo Domingo in December 1528 with 250 enslaved Africans on board.
26. Ibid.
27. Ibid., 133. Otte elaborates on the "advantageous sales and payment conditions" for the German traders, for instance, the highest price per enslaved. He mentions acts of resistance by the American subjects against the privileges for the Welser.
28. Denzer, *Die Konquista*, 53.
29. Otte, "Die Welser," 139. Otte's study demonstrates that the trade in enslaved Africans formed an integrated part for the German traders' colonial conquest. According to Otte, Lazarus Nürnberger also traded in slaves and at the end of 1544 bought a license for 25 enslaved Africans whom he thought to deliver to America from the entrepreneurs Jácome and Juan Bautista Botti. In April 1544, Nürnberger let the register of the Casa de la Contratación confirm him to buy twenty male and five female slaves at the Cape Verde Islands and ship them to the Americas.
30. Ibid. My translation.
31. Ibid. The *almorjarifazgo* was a tariff applied to exports and imports of goods imposed by the governor Lope García de Castro.
32. Ibid. Otte emphasizes that these numbers do not coincide with the declaration of the Audiencia Real of Santo Domingo from the end of July of 1535.
33. Ibid., 140. My translation. Following Otte, the fiscal of the Indian Council, Juan de Villalobos, criticized the quality of the enslaved Africans delivered by the Germans.
34. Ibid., 143.
35. Denzer, *Die Konquista*, 50.
36. Werner, *Das Kupferhüttenwerk*, 20.
37. Ibid., 19.
38. Ibid., 317. The *asiento* in the history of slavery refers to the permission the Spanish government gave to other countries between the years 1543 and 1834 to sell people as slaves to the Spanish colonies.
39. Ibid., 471–472.
40. Álvarez Estévez and Pascual, *Alemanes en Cuba*, 23.
41. Ibid., 24, 25.
42. Ibid., 44.
43. Werner, *Das Kupferhüttenwerk*, 465.

44. Zeuske, *Handbuch Sklaverei*, 504.
45. Ibid., 512.
46. Ibid., 514.
47. The German administration of the island of Tobago from the 1630s until 1659 and a commercial settlement in St. Thomas from 1685 until 1731 provide further examples of German activities in the colonies worth mentioning. Other endeavors, such as the attempt of Friedrich Wilhelm and his successors to purchase or occupy islands like Tobago, St. Croix, or St. Eustache for their trade in enslaved workers, failed. The Bavarian-Dutch and French-Bavarian joint colonial projects in Guyana (1664) were not concluded, neither was the colonial contract between the Duke of Hanau and the Dutch West-Indian Compagnie over a colony referred to as "Hanau-Indien" (Hanau-India, 1669), located between the Orinoco and Amazonas rivers (Zantop, *Colonial Fantasies*, 33). In the seventeenth century, inspired by Dutch traders, the elector of Brandenburg Friedrich Wilhelm participated in colonial endeavors on the African West coast. An expedition in 1681 to the so-called Gold Coast resulted in the foundation of the Brandenburg-African Compagnie (brandenburgisch-afrikanische Kompagnie) for the triangular overseas trade with West Africa, which held the Brandenburg monopoly over the African trade in pepper, ivory, gold, and enslaved Africans for 30 years. In 1687, the Compagnie built the fort Groß-Friedrichsburg and a settlement in Arguin, both of which primarily served for the trade in enslaved Africans. During its existence (between 1450 and 1867), the company sold about 19,000 enslaved Africans who had survived the Middle Passage from Africa to America. Over 17,000 enslaved Africans per year were sold to the Caribbean (Zantop, *Colonial Fantasies*, 38).
48. Ibid., 19. Cuba provides numerous examples of how, particularly in the eighteenth and nineteenth century, German capital was regularly invested in the Americas. Since slavery in Cuba was only abolished in 1886, German investments on the islands usually included the exploitation of slave labor, and German merchants continued to be actively involved in the trade in enslaved African workers. Tellingly, the German sugar export association (*Deutscher Zuckerexportverein*) existed until 1886, the very year when slavery was finally abolished in Cuba (Álvarez Estévez and Guzmán, *Alemanes en Cuba*, 30). See in this context also the study by Schulte Beerbühl and Frey on the cigar merchant Uppmann from Bielefeld, "Die H. Upmann Zigarre."
49. Wallenta, "Die Handelsgenies," 11–15.
50. Kluger, *The Wealthy Fuggers*, 7, 13.
51. Denzer, *Die Konquista*, 26.
52. See, for example Arciniegas, *Germans in the Conquest*.
53. Brog, *In Defense of Faith*, 101.
54. Denzer, *Die Konquista*, 22.
55. Las Casas, *An Account*, 68. Las Casas engages in some wordplay in Spanish, irreproducible in English: Germans (*alemánes*) are paraphrased with the similar sounding term for animals (*animales*), he thus speaks about "these German, or beastly, tyrants." For more information on the German black legend, see Zantop, *Colonial Fantasies*, 24.
56. Las Casas, for instance, refers particularly to Alfinger whom he holds to be a Lutheran; therefore, he as a Catholic has to denounce him ("The German governor, this tyrant and also, we believe, heretic, for he neither heard mass nor allowed many others to hear it either, with other signs of Lutheranism that we found out)" (Las Casas, *An Account*, 66). However, Las Casas originally did not "single out" the Germans, since he stated that they were just as bad as other conquerors:

> [S]ince they entered into these lands […] they have sent many ships loaded and shipped with Indians over the sea to be sold for slaves in Santa Marta and on the island of Hispaniola and Jamaica and the island of San Juan. […] There is no reason to make all these Indians into slaves save perverse, blind, and stubborn willfulness, in obedience to the insatiable greed for gold and those exceedingly avaricious tyrants, like all others in all the Indies have always done, taking and sizing those lambs and sheep from their homes and taking alike their women and children in the cruel and

nefarious ways that we have spoken of, and shackling them in the king's irons to sell them for slaves. (Las Casas, *An Account*, 68)

57. In the appendix to her biographies, titled "Otros conquistadores de segundo y tercer orden" (Other conquerors of second and third order), Acosta de Samper lists Juan Nicolás de Aleman without further detail than the note that he came to the Americas with Federmann and established himself in Tocaima, and that one of his daughters was later married to a Flame called Matías Esporquil (Acosta de Samper, *Biografías de hombres ilustres ó notabes*, 393).
58. Ibid., 83. My translation.
59. Ibid., 4. My translation. Emphasis in the original.
60. Ibid., 97. My translation.
61. Ibid. Acosta de Samper even depicts Federmann as physically attractive, which is an unusual perspective for a woman of her time: "He had a white and beautiful face, was of elevate stature, a red and thick beard and was skilled in all physical exercises."
62. The only account by a German conqueror himself is the *Indianische Historia* by Nicolas Federmann which he wrote about his trip in 1531. Federmann's main interest was to find gold, and he justified the submission of the Amerindians through the endeavor to bring them the Christian faith and baptize them and to either make them become his "friends" and be exploited as guides and carriers or destroy their lands, capture them, enslave them, and rob their children and wives. In his introduction to the 1965 edition to Federmann's account, anthropologist and historian Juan Friede describes the practice of literally enslaving Amerindians as follows: "Above all prisoners were used as carriers. They were forged iron rings around the neck, which were then connected through a chain. This system allowed them to be used as baggage carriers and avoid their escape" (Friede, "Einführung," xvii). The German original reads: "Als Träger wurden vor allen Dingen auch Gefangene benutzt. Man schmiedete ihnen eiserne Ringe um den Hals, die dann durch eine Kette verbunden wurden. Dieses System erlaubte es, sie als Troßträger zu benutzen und ihre Flucht zu verhindern." Federmann, *Indianische Historia*, 23. Federmann's account also provides evidence of what Rubin has referred to as the "traffic in women" practiced between colonizing and colonized men. Rubin, "The Traffic in Women." At one instance, Federmann describes a "dwarf woman" he is given by a cacique (indigenous leader or noble man in Caribbean Taíno language). Federmann, *Indianische Historia*, 30.
63. The works by Zimmerer and Zeller, eds., *Völkermord in Deutsch-Südwestafrika*; Zimmerer and Peraudin, eds., *German Colonialism*; Zimmerer, ed., *Verschweigen–Erinnern–Bewältigen* and *Von Windhoek bis Auschwitz?*; Eckert, *Kolonialismus*; Conrad, *Deutsche Kolonialgeschichte*; Randeria, Römhild, and Conrad, *Jenseits des Eurozentrismus*, the recent (2016–2017) exhibition "German Colonialism: Fragments Past and Present" shown at the German History Museum in Berlin, etc., indicate a slow change of discourse. Numerous interventions and studies by People of Color have for decades been claiming a critical revision of Germany's colonial past and its present continuities, see Eggers et al., *Mythen, Masken und Subjekte*; Guitiérrez-Rodríguez and Steyerl, *Spricht die Subalterne Deutsch?*; Ha, Lauré al-Samarai, and Mysorekar, *Re/Visionen*. For an early account of German colonial history and the Welser, see also Opitz, Oguntoye, and Schultz, *Showing Our Colors*.
64. Zantop, *Colonial Fantasies*, 2.
65. Ibid., 16.
66. Ibid., 31–33.
67. Ibid., 209.
68. Federmann, *Deutsche Konquistadoren*, 7.
69. Ibid., 7–8.
70. Ibid., 9.
71. Ibid.
72. Kommunikation und Kaffee Augsburg quoted in Rauschnig, *Gespräche mit Hitler*, 61.
73. Federmann, *Deutsche Konquistadoren*, 23. My translation.

74. Zantop, *Colonial Fantasies*, 10. According to Fernando Coronil, the concept of Occidentalism describes

> the ensemble of representational practices that participate in the production of conceptions of the world, which (1) separate the world's components into bounded units; (2) disaggregate their relational histories; (3) turn difference into hierarchy; (4) naturalize these representations; and thus (5) intervene, however unwittingly, in the reproduction of existing asymmetrical power relations. (Coronil, "Beyond Occidentalism," 57)

Elaborating on this idea for the German context, in "Critical Whiteness", Gabriele Dietze has formulated the need for a self-critical examination of Western domination and its parameters in order to outclass naturalized hierarchical power asymmetries. Dietze transfers the self-critical stance of the concept of Critical Whiteness Studies to the specific German context as expressed in her concept "kritischer Okzidentalismus" [Critical Occidentalism], a "figure of thinking in a way critical of hegemony as a condition of possibility for a politics that seeks to avoid power asymmetries." Dietze, "Critical Whiteness," 239 (my translation).

75. The period of the brandenburgisch-afrikanische Kompagnie or the Berlin-based so-called Africa Conference (or Kongo Conference) of 1884 is also inadequately studied and taught.
76. See, for example, the Kreuzberg Museum in Berlin, which dedicates part of a room of its permanent exposition to the brandenburgisch-afrikanische Kompagnie as part of the city's history. In 2014, several subcultural Berlin institutions like the "post-migrant" theater Ballhaus Naunynstrasse and the art space "Savvy Contemporary" organized events memorizing the Berlin-based Africa conference of 1884 during which the European colonial powers divided the African continent among themselves. The project "Denkwerk" in Bremen, initiated by university professor Sabine Broeck, makes high-school students research the city's slavery past. Furthermore, there are numerous "postcolonial" city tours organized by initiatives like "Bielefeld postcolonial" or "Hamburg postcolonial."
77. Lieberknecht, "Der Sklavenhandel."
78. Namibian, Afro-German, and international activists are claiming financial, cultural (e.g., turning back a collection of skulls from the genocide on the Nama and Herrero), and intellectual (rewriting of history, canons, school curricula) reparation for the crimes committed in the colonies.

Acknowledgements

The author would like to thank a number of people for ongoing discussions about the topic of colonial entanglements, slavery, and Germany, especially Sabine Broeck, Manuela Boatcă, Claudia Rauhut, Carsten Junker, Gabriele Dietze, Alanna Lockward, Walter Mignolo, Roberto Zurbano, Anke Lucks, and Thomas Krüger, as well as Annika McPherson for accompanying me to the Welser museum in Augsburg. I am also grateful to the BMBF project "The Americas as Space of Entanglements" at the Center for InterAmerican Studies at the University of Bielefeld, which has supported my research abroad, part of which served as the basis for the current article, to the Ibero-American Institute in Berlin for providing important sources and library space, and to the editors of this volume for the opportunity of being part of this necessary project.

Disclosure statement

No potential conflict of interest was reported by the author.

ORCID

Julia Roth ⓘ http://orcid.org/0000-0003-4233-3527

Bibliography

Acosta de Samper, Soledad de. *Biografías de hombres ilustres ó notabes. Relativos á la época del Descubrimiento, Conquista y Colonización de la parte de América denominada actualmente EE.UU. de Colombia*. Bogotá: Imprenta de la Luz, 1883.
Álvarez Estévez, Rolando, and Marta Guzmán Pascual. *Alemanes en Cuba (siglos XVII al XIX)*. Havana: Editorial de las Ciencias Sociales, 2004.
Arciniegas, Germán. *Germans in the Conquest of America: A Sixteenth Century Venture*. New York: The Macmillan Company, 1943 (first published under the title: *Alemanes en la Conquista de América*. Buenos Aires, 1941).
"Arroba." *Merriam Webster Online Dictionary*. Accessed 7 April 2017. www.merriam-webster.com/dictionary/arroba.
"Arroba." *Dictionary.com*. Accessed 7 April 2017. www.dictionary.com/browse/arroba.
Brog, David. *In Defense of Faith: The Judeo-Christian Idea and the Struggle for Humanity*. New York: Encounter Books, 2010.
Conrad, Sebastian. *Deutsche Kolonialgeschichte*. München: C.H. Beck, 2012.
Coronil, Fernando. "Beyond Occidentalism: Toward Nonimperial Geohistorical Categories." *Cultural Anthropology* 11, no. 1 (1996): 51–87.
Denzer, Jörg. *Die Konquista der Augsburger Welser-Gesellschaft in Südamerika 1528–1556*. München: C.H. Beck, 2005.
Dietze, Gabriele. "Critical Whiteness und Kritischer Okzidentalismus. Zwei Figuren hegemonialer Selbstreflexion." In *Weiss – Weißsein – Whiteness: Kritische Studien zu Gender und Rassismus*, edited by Jana Hussmann-Kastein, Daniela Hrzán, and Gabriele Dietze, 232–250. Stuttgart: Peter Lang, 2006.
Eckert, Andreas. *Kolonialismus*. Frankfurt: Fischer, 2006.
Eggers, Maisha, Grada Kilomba, Peggy Piesche, et al., eds. *Mythen, Masken und Subjekte. Kritische Weißseinsforschung in Deutschland*. Münster: Unrast, 2005.
Federmann, Nicolaus. *Indianische Historia. Mit einem Vorwort von Juan Friede*. München: Klaus Renner, 1965.
Federmann, Arnold. *Deutsche Konquistadoren und Südamerika*. Berlin: Reimar Hobbing, 1938.
Friede, Juan. "Einführung." In *Indianische Historia. Mit einem Vorwort von Juan Friede*, edited by Nikolaus Fendermann, vii–xx. München: Klaus Renner, 1965.
Guitiérrez-Rodríguez, Encarnación, and Hito Steyerl, eds. *Spricht die Subalterne Deutsch? Migration und Postkoloniale Kritik*. Münster: Unrast, 2003.
Ha, Kien Nghi, Nicola Lauré al-Samarai, and Sheila Mysorekar, eds. *Re/Visionen. Postkoloniale Perspektiven von People of Color auf Rassismus, Kulturpolitik und Widerstand in Deutschland*. Münster: Unrast, 2007.
Heyden, Ulrich van der. *Rote Adler an Afrikas Küste. Die brandenburgisch-preußische Kolonie Großfriedrichsburg in Westafrika*. Berlin: Selignow, 2001.

Kluger, Martin. *The Wealthy Fuggers. Pomp and Power of the German Medici in Golden Augsburg of the Renaissance*. Augsburg: Regio Augsburg Tourismus GmbH, 2016.

Kommunikation und Kaffee Augsburg. "Welser und Fugger und der deutsche Imperialismus." *KoKa, Kommunikation und Kaffee*, 2014. Accessed 20 January 2016. http://koka-augsburg.net/welser-fugger/.

Las Casas, Fray Bartolomé de. *An Account, Much Abbreviated, of The Destruction of the Indies* [1524], edited with an introduction by Franklin W. Knight and translated by Andrew Hurley. Cambridge: Hackett, 2003.

Lieberknecht, Wolfgang. "Eingebrannt: C AB C (Churfürstlich-Afrikanisch-Brandenburgische Compagnie). Der Sklavenhandel und die Deutschen." *Journal Ethnologie* 087/264 (2004). Accessed 20 January 2016. http://www.journal-ethnologie.de/Deutsch/Schwerpunktthemen/Schwerpunktthemen_2004/Sklaverei/Eingebrannt:_C_AB_C/index.phtml.

Mintz, Sidney. *Sweetness and Power. The Place of Sugar in Modern History*. New York: Viking Press, 1985.

Opitz, May, Katharina Oguntoye, and Dagmar Schultz, eds. *Showing Our Colors. Afro-German Women Speak Out*. Amherst: University of Massachusetts Press, 1992.

Ortíz, Fernando. *Contrapunteo Cubano del tabaco y el azúcar*. Havana: Editorial de Ciencias Sociales, 1983.

Otte, Enrique. "Die Welser in Santo Domingo [1962]." In *Von Bankiers und Kaufleuten, Räten, Reedern und Piraten, Hintermännern und Strohmännern. Aufsätze zur atlantischen Expansion Spaniens*, edited by Günter Vollmer and Horst Pietschmann, 117–159. Stuttgart: Franz Steiner, 2004.

Otte, Enrique. "Jakob und Hans Cromberger und Lazarus Nürnbger, die Begründer des deutschen Amerikahandels [1963]." In *Von Bankiers und Kaufleuten, Räten, Reedern und Piraten, Hintermännern und Strohmännern. Aufsätze zur atlantischen Expansion Spaniens*, edited by Günter Vollmer and Horst Pietschmann, 161–197. Stuttgart: Franz Steiner, 2004.

Randeria, Shalini, Sebastian Conrad, and Regina Römhild, eds. *Jenseits des Eurozentrismus. Postkoloniale Perspektiven in den Geschichts- und Kulturwissenschaften*. Frankfurt/Main: Campus, 2014.

Randeria, Shalini. "Entangled Histories of Uneven Modernities: Civil Society, Caste Solidarities and Legal Pluralism in Post-colonial India." In *Civil Society – Berlin Perspectives*, edited by John Keane, 213–242. New York: Berghahn, 2006.

Rauschnig, Hermann. *Gespräche mit Hitler*. Zürich: Europa, 1940.

Rubin, Gayle. "The Traffic in Women: Notes on the 'Political Economy' of Sex." In *Toward an Anthropology of Women*, edited by Rayna Reiter, 157–210. New York: Monthly Review Press, 1975.

Schmitt, Eberhard. *Konquista als Konzernpolitik: Die Welser-Statthalterschaft über Venezuela 1528–1556*. Bamberg: Kleine Beiträge zur europäischen Überseegeschichte, 1992.

Schulte Beerbühl, Margit, and Barbara Frey. "Die H. Upmann Zigarre – Der Bielefelder Hermann Dietrich Upmann und die Schaffung einer Weltmarke." In *Forschen – Verstehen – Vermitteln. Festschrift zum 100. Jahrestag des Historischen Vereins für die Grafschaft Ravensberg*, edited by Johannes Altenberend and Reinhard Vogelsang, 243–279. Bielefeld: Verlag für Regionalgeschichte, 2015.

Simmer, Götz. *Gold und Sklaven: Die Provinz Venezuela während der Welser-Verwaltung (1528–1556)*. Berlin: Wissenschaft und Technik, 2000.

Tatendrang, ed. *Fugger und Welser. Museum, Historie, Marketing*. Augsburg: Liquid Agentur für Gestaltung, 2015.

Wallenta, Wolfgang. "Die Handelsgenies. Die Fugger und Welser in Augsburg." In *Fugger und Welser. Museum, Historie, Marketing*, edited by Tatendrang and Das Magazin, 11–15. Augsburg: Liquid Agentur für Gestaltung, 2015.

Werner, Theodor Gustav. *Das Kupferhüttenwerk des Hans Tetzel aus Nürnberg auf Kuba (1545–1571) und seine Finanzierung durch europäisches Finanzkapital*. Wiesbaden: Franz Steiner, 1961.

Zantop, Susanne. *Colonial Fantasies: Conquest, Family, and Nation in Precolonial Germany, 1770–1870*. Durham, NC: Duke University Press, 1997.

Zimmerer, Jürgen, ed. *Verschweigen–Erinnern–Bewältigen. Vergangenheitspolitik in globaler Perspektive*. Special Volume of *Comparativ* 14, no. 5/6 (2004).

Zimmerer, Jürgen, and Michael Perraudin, eds. *German Colonialism and National Identity*. New York: Routledge, 2011.

Zimmerer, Jürgen, ed. *Von Windhuk nach Auschwitz? Beiträge zum Verhältnis von Kolonialismus und Holocaust*. Münster: LIT, 2011.

Zimmerer, Jürgen, and Joachim Zeller, eds. *Völkermord in Deutsch-Südwestafrika. Der Kolonialkrieg in Namibia (1904–1908) und die Folgen*. Berlin: Christoph Links, 2003.

Zeuske, Michael. *Handbuch Geschichte der Sklaverei. Eine Globalgeschichte von den Anfängen bis zur Gegenwart*. Berlin: de Gruyter, 2013.

The right to freedom: Eighteenth-century slave resistance and early Moravian missions in the Danish West Indies and Dutch Suriname

Heike Raphael-Hernandez

ABSTRACT
The essay retrieves the complex and at times contradictory encounters of Moravian missionaries, a Protestant group from Saxony, with enslaved Africans. For my investigation, I will single out both groups' contact in the early eighteenth-century Danish West Indies and Dutch Suriname. I claim that, in their mission-related contacts during this specific period, both groups would receive glimpses of secular possibilities for future societies which eventually would help bring changes to their own specific secular settings. For the enslaved Africans, it implied an insistence on freedom from the misanthropic institution of New World slavery; for the Germans, it implied a maturing of progressive ideas in regard to the still existing secular estates system. This could happen only because these first missionaries often operated with means that were not part of any official mission directives. I will demonstrate this with three aspects: the missionaries' approach to literacy for the enslaved, their encouragement of the enslaved to verbal and even legal protest, and, probably the most empowering tool, their invalidation of white people's assumed God-given superiority in the eyes of black people. The nexus of these three aspects very likely contributed to each group's vision of a society-to-come, which, in turn, must have led more to an ideological insistence on the human right to freedom with all its different implications than has been noted so far in scholarship.

In an essay on the "Self-Liberation Ethos of Enslaved Blacks," written in 1988, historian Hilary McD. Beckles took slave resistance scholarship to task: he acknowledged that historians of slavery had identified different local acts of day-to-day resistance of the enslaved, the large numbers of unsuccessful plots and slave revolts, and the successful rebellions that included such occurrences as long-term marronage in, for example, Jamaica and Suriname, as well as the revolution in Haiti. Yet, Beckles still saw the need for more research into the details of the enslaved Africans' political and ideological culture. For him, a major concern for scholars, when they depict the different forms of revolts and protests, should be to ask about specific ideological choices that led to a "maturing political consciousness" and were part of a larger, transatlantic resistance movement.[1] Two decades later, in 2009, recognizing that this scholarship was still missing for the most part, historian Vincent

Brown echoed Beckles's earlier insistence on locating a resistance ideology and called on scholars to not just "prioritize the documentation of resistance over the examination of political strife in its myriad forms."[2] Brown argued that scholars "should begin from a different point of departure, highlighting instead particular meanings as situational guides to consequential actions – motivations, sometimes temporary, that are best evaluated in terms of how they are publicly enacted, shared, and reproduced."[3]

My essay builds on Beckles's and Brown's insistence of locating specific historical contexts that show how such an ideologically inspired "maturing political consciousness" could have taken place. For my discussion, I will turn to the Caribbean and will focus on the encounter of enslaved Africans with early eighteenth-century Moravian missionaries, a German evangelical group from Herrnhut, Saxony. I will single out the very first Moravian missionaries who started their work among enslaved Africans in the Danish West Indies and in the Dutch colony of Suriname in the 1730s and will offer the idea that both groups, the early Moravian missionaries and the enslaved Africans, in their mission-related contacts, inspired each other toward attitudes that contributed to a maturing political consciousness for both groups. For the enslaved Africans, it implied a growing ideological insistence on an all-encompassing freedom from the misanthropic institution of New World slavery; for the Germans, it implied an awakening of progressive ideas in regard to the secular estates system, which still held many Germans in either serfdom or other forms of civil bondage.

The early period between the 1730s and 1760s differed from all subsequent periods of Moravian missionary presence in the Caribbean because the majority of the first Moravian missionaries to the Caribbean and Suriname came from Germany's lowest classes. Among their listed job descriptions, one finds an overwhelming number of potters, carpenters, tailors, blacksmiths, brick layers, and shoemakers. The idea of sending such tradespeople was a pragmatic one because the missionaries had to be financially independent from Europe and had to support themselves through the work they could find in the island communities in which they settled. Craftsmen seemed to have a better chance of finding employment than trained scholars of theology, who were usually members of higher classes. This fact helps to understand why the home community at the headquarters in Herrnhut did not have problems with sending the non-scholars to the mission field, that is, the "plain" and uneducated brothers and sisters, who were to carry out one of the most important tasks of Moravian theological essence – taking God's word to all corners of the world.

Germany, at that time, was arranged into a *Ständegesellschaft*, which meant that individuals belonged to groups that were determined mainly by birth and were organized around a hierarchy of prestige that was arranged according to legal and social criteria.[4] While I do not imply that the living conditions of the lower classes in the German territories can be compared to the inhumane suffering of the enslaved people in the Caribbean, for my thesis it is important to note that the German system included forms of unfreedom that were based on hereditary subjection, which, among other factors, limited a person's rights to move, marry, or do certain kinds of work.[5] The early missionaries' secular class belonging might have caused them to find more of a common ground with the enslaved than with their own, often aristocratic Moravian church leaders back at home. It is with these two rather incomparable groups, the lower class German missionaries and the enslaved Africans, that I detect a critical nexus of spiritual matters with secular empowerment that carried an ideological potential for both groups.

Such a mutual, ideological inspiration could have happened because, without abandoning or disregarding official theological matters, the early missionaries in the West Indies and Suriname unofficially seemed to have taken St. Paul's spiritual statement of "There is neither Jew nor Gentile, neither slave nor free, nor is there male and female, for you are all one in Christ Jesus" from Galatians 3:28 to the secular realm. As part of their group's theology, Moravians practiced a Christian ideal that was based on the New Testament, but for their time, it was unusual and rather radical: inside their church community, all Moravians, regardless of class, gender, or race, were of equal standing and treated each other with the same respect. Outside their church community, however, Moravians in the mission field were supposed to observe the social arrangements in regard to the class and racial divisions of plantation societies.[6] Yet, as I will show, quite a few of these early missionaries were siding with black people against white people in matters that were not related to theological aspects or church work. I will call this their "spiritual-cum-secular" attitude. As a consequence of this transfer of spiritual equality to the secular realm, both groups afforded each other, even if this was only temporarily, a vision of the *not yet*, a term the German Marxist philosopher Ernst Bloch coined.[7] Visions of alternative futures, even if an individual is able to only see fragments of the *not yet*, can serve as ideological empowerment. In their contact with each other during this particular time and place, the Moravian Germans and the enslaved Africans must have seen such fragments of the *not yet*, of possibilities of an alternative future. This could happen because the missionaries often operated with means that were not part of any official mission directives. I will demonstrate this with three aspects: the missionaries' approach to literacy for the enslaved, their encouragement of the enslaved to verbal and even legal protest, and, probably the most empowering tool, their invalidation of white people's assumed God-given superiority in the eyes of black people. The nexus of these three aspects, very likely, contributed to each group's vision of a society-to-come, which, in turn, must have led more to an ideological insistence on the human right to freedom with all its different implications than has been noted so far in scholarship.

Historical background

To understand the growing secular awareness of the right to freedom by enslaved people via the early Moravians and vice versa, one has to start with the Moravians' historical and spiritual background. The Moravians were a Protestant group that traced their spiritual origins back to the Czech reformer Jan Hus (1369–1415). Because of their open theological opposition to state church doctrines, they were branded as heretics in their home territory of Moravia. In 1722, when they fled from Moravia to Saxony to escape religious persecution, Count Ludwig von Zinzendorf gave them refuge on his estate in Herrnhut in Upper Lusatia, which was part of Saxony, Germany. Since Zinzendorf was raised in the spirit of German Pietism and had a strong interest in foreign evangelism, he chose this group of refugees to found the *Herrnhuter* community; in English they are known as the Moravians to emphasize their older connection to Jan Hus and Moravia. The group's international missionary attempts began with their Caribbean mission in the Danish West Indies in 1732. This was later followed by additional missionary activities in Suriname, Berbice,

Greenland, Jamaica, South Africa, Siberia, Sri Lanka, and Labrador. In addition, they worked among Native Americans in Pennsylvania and in New York State, among enslaved Africans in Salem, North Carolina, and among Jews in Amsterdam in the Netherlands.[8]

The Caribbean mission began in 1732 when two men, Leonard Dober, a potter, and David Nitschmann, a carpenter, arrived on the island of St. Thomas.[9] By that time, slavery was already a well-established, large institution in the Caribbean and several European nations participated as global players in its transatlantic economy. Christian theology presented an integral tool for this institution; a variety of the different state churches participated fully in the maintenance of slavery by preaching submission and acceptance of fate to the enslaved, but otherwise did not care at all for them as fellow human beings. Since the two Moravian missionaries wanted to bring a different Christian message to the enslaved, but a personal, unsupervised contact with the enslaved seemed impossible because of the rigid plantation system and its stringent regulations, the two men tried to sell themselves into slavery soon after their arrival. Although this attempt failed because, as they were told, slavery would not be a system for white people, it also gained them an immediate reputation of being religious troublemakers and rebels. In addition, their action resulted in violent hostility toward them, not only from white planter society, but also from white working-class members – a hostility and violence that many subsequent missionaries also had to face as part of their daily lives in the Danish West Indies. Despite these problems, or perhaps also because of them, the two men were able to slowly gain the enslaved people's trust; in their *diaria*, one finds many entries that report about visits with slaves on a variety of plantations as well as visits the missionaries received from the enslaved in their own home.[10] Two years later, in 1734, two more missionaries, Friedrich Martin and Matthäus Freundlich, joined Dober and Nitschmann and extended the mission to the island of St. John. Later that year, 18 additional Moravians, 14 men and four women, arrived, but went immediately to the island of St. Croix to start an additional mission. Over the following decades, many more Moravians arriving from Saxony joined these early missionaries. From the very start, these Moravians had to deal with tremendous poverty, physical violence, and adverse climatic conditions in all the islands – factors that contributed to an exceptionally high rate of mortality among their members. For example, of the initial group of 18 members that started the missionary work in St. Croix in 1734, 11 died during the first year from malnutrition and diseases that they had no means of curing. Many others got lost at sea during the voyages from Europe to the West Indies. Yet despite all these obstacles, by 1738, the missionaries could already count some 600 converts in St. Thomas alone.[11]

The mission in Suriname began with a small group of Moravians in 1735.[12] Unlike their counterparts in the Danish West Indies, this group's initial intention for their travel was not the start of another missionary outpost. Instead, Suriname was rather a geographical compromise because their leader, Count von Zinzendorf, had been expelled from Herrnhut in Saxony, and the group had to find a new place where they eventually could settle as a religious community. Since missionary activities overseas had already become a priority at that time, Suriname was one of several places they discussed as a potential home for the new Herrnhut, and the arriving small group can be considered a "scouting group" for a future residential consideration.

By the 1730s, Suriname was infamously known for its large slave community and the planters' exceptional brutality toward the enslaved.[13] Because of this brutality and

Suriname's geographical opportunities with its partly inaccessible, mountainous interior, Suriname's population included also a recognizably large group of run-away slaves, also known as maroons. By 1750, the number of maroons was estimated to be about 6000; many of their members had already been born in marronage.[14] After their arrival in 1735, the first Moravians intended their missionary tasks to take place only among the indigenous people; the growing missionary activity among the enslaved Africans happened rather as a side effect. Later, in the 1760s, they also began missionary work among the different maroon communities.[15] Soon after their first small missionary successes, they were officially asked to accept a variety of postmaster positions, which were go-between positions that were supposed to help establish peaceful relations between the Dutch local government and the maroons.

Intertwined maturing political consciousness and visions of the *not yet*

The Moravian Christian influence on the enslaved Africans' cultures of resistance has been well researched. The scholarship of Jon Sensbach, Armando Lampe, Sylvia Frey, and Betty Wood testify to this fact.[16] Sensbach, for example, maintains that while planters in early slave societies generally dreaded Christianity's potential to destabilize the social order, it was the Pietist version of the German Moravians in particular that "furnished thousands of colonized people with a new belief system to reckon with their subjugation."[17] My approach complements the already existing scholarship by adding the claim of the mutually inspiring influence of both groups on each other.

If one turns to the Moravian archival material, hoping to locate any easily recognizable, spelled-out ideological statements and evidence of an intertwined growing political consciousness of the two groups, one will not find any texts that offer such ideological messages. After all, the majority of these texts are part of missionary reports to their headquarters; they were written to let the congregation at home know about the successful work in the mission field.

To locate the two groups' mutual inspiration toward specific political visions of freedom, one can turn to the above-mentioned theory of the *not yet* by the German philosopher Ernst Bloch. As explained earlier, according to his theory, visions of possible alternative futures, of societies-to-come, even if an individual is able to see only fragments of the *not yet*, will serve as ideological empowerment for the individual. Since Bloch does not have the desires of an individual and his or her limited wish fulfillment in mind, but the liberation of the whole human race, he adds the *collective existence* to this political vision. Glimpses of the *not yet* will, for example, cause a hungry person to not only search for food for him- or herself, but to also seek changes to the situation that caused hunger in the first place for the entire community, a motivation Bloch refers to as *revolutionary interest*.[18] Revolutionary interest coupled with the individual's glimpses of the *not yet* serve as *pre-appearance*, which differs from illusion because an illusion is removed from reality whereas the foundation for Bloch's *pre-appearance* is an individual person's reality; the person will be able to begin to act in his or her reality As humans, in difference to the divine, we are not able to envision or anticipate the future in its fullest, only in fragments or glimpses. But even these fragments of the *not yet* are powerful enough to let a person experience an ideologically empowered hope and help him or her begin to change his or her respective present circumstances.[19]

To locate such fragments of the *not yet* for both groups in their interaction with each other, one needs to look at two important arenas: their interactions inside and outside the church community. Inside the church, all members, regardless of their class, gender, race, or social status, were equal. Moravians based their idea on St. Paul's above-mentioned premise that there would be "neither slave nor free" because all would be "one in Christ." This was not just a secret favorite verse of some missionaries, but one of the main doctrines of Moravian theology. Throughout their own history, Moravians have tried to practice this divine call to equality. It meant that Afro-Moravians belonged as equals to the larger community of all "mankind" via the smaller community of the Moravian church. And indeed, African members, free and enslaved, held a variety of administrative and theological positions in their congregations; slaves became deacons, elders, and helpers in mixed-race communities. In fact, theirs was the first Christian church that provided equality to women; Rebecca Protten, a free black woman from St. Thomas, for instance, became a leader for white women in Germany.[20] To not only rhetorically pretend to consider every human being equal in the eyes of God, but to actually assign honorable positions to their African-descended members testifies to the Moravians' deeply felt sincerity of returning human dignity to the enslaved.

The practiced cross-racial and cross-class equality inside their church community can also be seen in the way they addressed each other. Moravians, white as well as black members, expressed their respect for each other by addressing each other with "Brother" and "Sister." They write about "Br. Petrus," "Br. Abraham," "Br. Johannes," and "Br. Cornelius." In the few letters the archives hold that were written by black members, the writers sign with these brotherly and sisterly titles of love, respect, and belonging; they, as "Br. Cornelius" does, send their greetings to "Br. Nathaniel" and "Br. Johan."[21] Afro-Moravian "Isaac and his Rebecca, Nathanael, Jacob, Paulina, Anna Louisa" send "their affectionate greetings" to all brothers and sisters in the church community.[22] When white missionaries write about them in reports and letters, they always include them with "dear" such as in "our dear black sisters of the Peter de Winth plantation,"[23] or "it is a blessing to work among the dear black people."[24] When one considers that black men still protested their address as "boy" and carried signs that stated "I AM A MAN" during the Civil Rights Marches of the twentieth century, one can only guess how influential these respectful titles and addresses alone must have been for a secular empowerment. African American theologian Albert J. Raboteau hints at this empowerment when he states that:

> Anglo-Americans feared the precise ethos that the slaves quickly recognized and valued in Christianity: the incorporation of Africans into the church community changed the relationship of master and slave into one of brother and sister in Christ, a relationship that inevitably contradicted the racist belief in black inferiority upon which slavery depended.[25]

It is important to note that this "inside" their church community equality did not only serve their Afro-Moravian members as visions of the *not yet*; simultaneously, the presence of their black members was of essential importance to white Moravians too because for the very first time, white people, even if this was only limited to the Moravian community, learned to practice cross-class and cross-racial interaction. For both sides, one can see here the potential of the *not yet* that helped to create and nurture a secular political imagination.

During the eighteenth century, it is indeed the singularity of the Moravian community to have broken the class and racial division inside their church community. However, when turning to the secular setting, one finds a different side, too. For example, the Moravian church archives hold also several letters of Countess Dorothea von Zinzendorf, an active Moravian member herself, which she had written to a local judge in Saxony, asking that he would find and return peasant men and women who were under her jurisdiction, but had left Herrnhut without her permission.[26] Her tone is clearly that of a class-entitled person who is irritated about such illegal behavior of her lower class German subjects. Among these documents about German "run-aways," one finds also a letter concerning a black man, Samuel Johannes, who had been given into her custody as an eight-year-old boy. Trying to legally justify her property rights to this young man, she unhesitatingly uses phrases that one would rather expect in documents referring to slavery: She claims that he was given to her personally as a gift, so he would be her property. Since she provided not only room and board over the years, but allowed him to learn two different trades, she concludes that:

> based on this information, it goes without saying that I am the only one, in addition to God, who can claim any legal rights to ownership and usage of this person, in fact, one will not find another person anywhere in the entire world but me who will be able to claim any proper rights to this person.[27]

Considering that the Zinzendorfs were Moravian Christians, her attitude comes a bit as a surprise. One could argue that while Moravians were able to practice equality for all people inside their community, they were not able to do this outside the church due to the social constraints of their specific societies. However, as the example demonstrates, her reasoning as well as her linguistic choices for justifying her ideas were only partially caused by societal constraints; personal assumptions about race and class played an important part, too. Her secular class background was the ultimate deciding factor in her attitude toward human bondage.

It is important to note that although a lower class status alone does not provide one with a racist-free attitude, but as members of a society that still practiced serfdom in everyday circumstances, the early missionaries must have seen themselves as being closer to the enslaved Africans than to higher class Germans. Their social background might have helped them, for example, to regularly visit the enslaved in their quarters where they shared their food with them – a practice that infuriated white people in the islands from the very start, as it seriously disrupted commonly understood race relations between white and black people. In addition, these early missionaries – and those of the first decade, the 1730s in particular – were often so poor that they themselves were frequently suffering from starvation. In their reports and letters, one finds several examples of the missionaries' misery becoming so acute that the slaves shared their own food with them.[28] However, despite their constant hunger and economic misery, they repeatedly turned down offers for free room and board on a variety of plantations because these offers came with the obligations of working as overseers. Leonard Dober, among the first group arriving in St. Thomas, writes in a letter that although he was so miserable, he would not accept such an offer, simply so that nobody should later say that he made the slaveholder rich.[29] One can also read about such a refusal in a letter by one of the missionaries in Suriname, Brother Lawatsch, who writes to Leonard Dober that the governor wanted to pay them a small salary for the missionary work they had started among the maroons, yet they turned down the offer because they feared that the salary would come with partial obligations to the Dutch colonial government.[30] Over the years, they kept refusing offers of room and board or small salaries, as tempting as they might have been, in order to not be obligated to white society in various ways.

With the examples, one recognizes the opportunities of the *not yet* to help create and nurture a secular political imagination. The glimpses of the *not yet* inside the church community and outside in secular everyday settings provided the ideological tool for activating resistance against what Orlando Patterson has called the "social death" of the enslaved; the Moravian cross-racial and cross-class community afforded the enslaved a "social existence outside the realm of the master."[31] Indeed, both groups granted each other glimpses of the *not yet* as empowerment for the secular world to be "outside the realm of the master." When one reads the available documents critically, one is able to detect a specific secular resistance, which I call their "spiritual-cum-secular" attitude that was practiced together by white missionaries and black enslaved people. I will show this with three aspects.

Literacy as weapon

One example of an aspect that began with spiritual intentions but turned into secular empowerment can be seen in the slaves' and missionaries' joint attitude toward literacy and its application in rather subversive agendas. The missionaries, who often had only rudimentary levels of literacy themselves,[32] taught the enslaved to read and write – admittedly with the primary goal of studying holy scripture – because according to Pietist notions, one has to be able to read the Bible oneself in order to engage with God's word regularly in small weekly discussion groups. While this idea implies that it should go without saying that every Moravian should be able to read, granting this right to the enslaved in St. Thomas was rather the singular idea of one of the early missionaries, as Moravian scholar Helen Richards explains:

> In order to gain the slaves' confidence, Friedrich Martin, the zealous and creative new mission leader, decided soon after his arrival in 1736 that it was time to try a new approach. Acting on what he knew to be a yearning on the part of the slaves to plumb the literary secrets that they believed held the key to white power, he designed a plan that would expand the missionary program to include regular lessons in reading and writing.[33]

However, with their idea of enabling the slaves to read and write the missionaries came into conflict with the official Danish slave code for the islands that forbade literacy for enslaved people; the planter society knew all too well that Bible-reading slaves would become aware of white Christian hypocrisy. In addition, it is important to note that while the missionaries' acts might not have violated Moravian theology, they definitely acted against the secular rules their leader Count von Zinzendorf had set up for the mission field. This becomes obvious by his reaction to their idea: in a letter of 1736 to another missionary group, the Moravian missionaries to the Samoyed in Siberia, Zinzendorf wrote,

> Under no circumstances involve yourself in external affairs other than work. The Brethren on St. Thomas are teaching the Moors to write, we disapprove of this completely. One can arouse the anger of the authorities with such a small thing.[34]

In a later nineteenth-century text, Frederick Douglass, a former American slave, reports about the slaves' own awareness of the empowerment that reading could provide for them. Douglass recalls that he gave pieces of bread to hungry white children so that they would teach him how to read which leads him to exclaim, "The more I read, the more I was led to abhor and detest my enslavers."[35] In the Moravian documents, we learn about much earlier instances of slaves' very strong desires to become literate.[36] One repeatedly finds in the letters and diaries of the missionaries that many slaves seem only to be coming to the Christian meetings in order to learn to read and write.[37] They will not sit still and listen when they learn about the blood that Christ sacrificed for them, it is reported, but instead seem to want to hurry the missionaries up to get to the part where they teach them how to spell. The missionaries' reaction shows that most of them were rather torn between their support of the slaves' desire and their own wish to bring first and foremost the Christian message to them. In their texts, the missionaries frequently express their concern that many slaves seem to be interested in literacy only for secular gains. One measure introduced to prevent this problem was moving the spelling instructions to the latter part of the evening after Bible instructions, hoping that this would deter all but the very sincere from attending. At a certain point, the missionaries even tried limiting these spelling lessons to those who were close to being converted.[38] Yet all this was to no avail; the enslaved indeed had discovered the secular power of literacy.

The belief that literacy was to hold the key to secular white society's power structure could also be observed in Suriname. The archival material for Suriname includes several reports about maroon chiefs who asked the Moravian missionaries to educate their children, but otherwise showed no interest at all in the missionaries' Christian work.[39]

Still, even if several missionaries worried that they were taken advantage of by the enslaved, and even if many enslaved and maroons saw that they were being lured into Christianity via literacy, both groups, in obvious cooperation, used literacy for secular empowerment in their respective circumstances. This claim can be illustrated with the example of the slaves' use of passes during slave revolts. While official Moravian church policies urged their members not to get involved in protests or even in revolts, the written discourse about these events allows one to speculate about how a creative protest could have taken place. In the documents one reads repeatedly about slave uprisings or about rumors of slave revolts, and about planters who, in panic, forbade slaves from leaving their plantations. Together with white Moravians, the enslaved Moravian members often asked for "exception passes" so that they would be able to attend church meetings. Especially evening meetings that would cause slaves to return after dark were regarded as suspicious activities by plantation owners. Being fully aware of the planters' fears, Moravians wrote passes for hundreds of slaves, and one can only speculate that they were not used exclusively for attending evening church gatherings in town. In one planter's diary, one is able to find a report about a particular incident when slaves were not allowed to leave their plantations because of the rumor of an imminent slave revolt; nevertheless, as the planter records, he saw at least 200 black people on their way to Posaunenberg, the Moravian church in St. Thomas.[40] In the *Historie der caribischen Inseln,* written by the visiting German Moravian member Christian Oldendorp, one finds an example that proves the collaboration between the white missionaries and the slaves. In his report for the year 1750, Oldendorp wrote about several slave revolts in St. Thomas and a subsequent ban on leaving plantations after dark. Concerned that their members would not be able to participate in church meetings, the missionaries were able to get an exception to this order for all slaves who would show passes with Moravian signatures. One of their Afro-Moravian members, Mingo, was then tasked to write and also sign these passes. Furthermore, the report notes that during subsequent times of revolts and rumors of rebellions, the white missionaries simply left it to Mingo to write and sign these passes without checking on him.[41]

In another document, a letter from 1739, seven slaves even write to the Danish king, Christian VI.[42] In their letter, written in the name of 650 black scholars of Jesus Christ, they protest about the continued harassment and mistreatment of the Moravian missionaries by plantation owners along with recounting how plantation owners have burned the slaves' spelling books and how some slaves have even had their ears and feet cut off as a punishment for reading the Bible. Seven slaves specifically object to the incarceration of two white missionaries and ask the king to show his mercy and grace by interfering with their imprisonment.

Here, one can observe par excellence the "spiritual-cum-secular" intertwining rebellious attitude of both groups. Considering that all international Moravian missionary communities regularly received Zinzendorf's written instructions for the mission field, the missionaries in St. Thomas and Suriname must have known about Zinzendorf's disapproval.[43] Yet, despite their frustration about the disinterest of many slaves and maroons in the Christian message, they nevertheless ignored Zinzendorf's orders and supported instead the empowering appeal of literacy among the enslaved and maroons. This fact alone, to ignore the orders of a secularly higher ranking person, even if they were equal members in the church community, can already be considered an indicator for a growing political consciousness among the missionaries.

Encouragement to protest

The secular class/race division seems to also have led the early group of lower class missionaries to combine their daily missionary work with secular advice for the enslaved about how and when to protest.[44] In their documents, the missionaries do not openly write about this, but in some seemingly unrelated material, one is able to repeatedly detect secular siding with the slaves against white society. Johannes Wilhem Zander, one of the first missionaries to Suriname, for example, reports in one of his letters in 1742 that he visits the enslaved on a regular basis in their slave quarters, thus hoping to establish some form of friendly relationship. He writes that in general daily circumstances for the enslaved are so bad that one can only lament about their situation; their misery would be so horrible that it is no wonder but understandable that no black person would trust any white person because they constantly expect some severe abuse by white people.[45] In later letters, one learns that some of the missionaries, despite the official order of not getting involved in any secular activities that would antagonize Suriname's officials as well as plantation society, got actively involved in helping enslaved people to legally protest their harsh treatment. In one of the *diarium* entries, one reads, for example, that Missionary Forkel, who worked on two plantations as a carpenter, encouraged several enslaved people to file a legal action against their plantation director Geerke because of his inhumane and excessive brutality. When questioned by the judge why he, as a white man, had encouraged black people to file this action, he answered that they were also human beings who were loved by God like every other person.[46]

Because of the excessive physical brutality executed by slaveholders in Suriname, it was common that enslaved people ran away in hope of joining one of the maroon tribes in the mountains. As a consequence, the colonial government together with the plantation directors passed a law that anyone who was able to catch one of these run-aways and return him or her, dead or alive, to his so-called owner would get a financial reward. The incentive must have been substantial because maroons themselves returned run-aways on a regular basis, not only to show their willingness to work together with the colonial authorities, but to also use these run-away returns as a steady source of income. Likewise, the indigenous people in Suriname used the return of run-aways for their financial gains. In their letters, the Moravian missionaries repeatedly express their fierce opposition to this practice. As one of their interventions to this practice, they try to tell converted members that a person who loves God should not participate in such acts at all. For example, in a letter to Leonard Dober, missionary Lawatsch writes that he would like to see the indigenous people he is working with stop this practice, but he also knows that he is encouraging them to disobey the local laws of the planter society. He, therefore, concludes: "We have to be careful that it does not come across as if one forbade them to do so because when our local authorities learned about this, we could get into real trouble and might even be exiled."[47] These examples demonstrate that the missionaries were very much aware of the fact that they operated outside any mission-only tasks and severely interfered in secular matters instead.

Likewise, the missionaries in St. Thomas did not see their tasks solely in spiritual encouragement. For example, it is clear from an exchange of letters between the headquarters in Herrnhut, Saxony and Bethlehem, Pennsylvania and the missionaries in St. Thomas that the missionaries regularly met with Afro-Moravian members during the night. While, in all likelihood, these meetings were intended for Christian worship and instructions, the missionaries knew very well that the planters regarded these night meetings also as potentially subversive activities for slave revolts. Since they did not stop these meetings despite the Moravian leaders' concerns, it cannot be ruled out that the missionaries were very much aware of their part in providing an opportunity for some other, rather subversive activities. Bishop Spangenberg raised this issue in a letter sent to Georg Weber, one of the missionaries in St. Thomas, asking him: "Are you sure that you need to gather during the night? Would you not be blamed when indeed a night revolt would take place?"[48]

Especially with one of the missionaries, Brother Michler, it is possible to see how West Indian missionaries must have understood their relationships with the enslaved. It is important to note that Michler was not an outcast or a troublemaker among the missionaries, but someone who took his task of bringing Christianity and God's love to the enslaved people very seriously. In fact, the Moravian leaders very much appreciated his work, especially among the children; in one of his letters, Spangenberg writes about him: "I was very pleased with Michler's children *diarium*. I can see that he is hardworking, and that the children are well-acquainted with him."[49] Yet, Michler also repeatedly addresses the brutality of slave owners in his reports and in his *diarium*.[50] It seems that he must have asked several times about Moravian support for the protests by the enslaved because in one letter, Bishop Spangenberg writes to Georg Weber:

Among other things, Brother Michler reminds one of the negroes' complaints about the ruthlessness of their masters. In this regard, great carefulness is necessary, and St. Paul answers: Servants, be obedient toward those who are your masters, not only to the kind and the benevolent, but also to the whimsical.[51]

Yet, it seems that Michler must have ignored the advice about sharing the message about obedience with the slaves because, in addition, one learns that Michler, together with some slaves, has started to build a meeting house on one of the plantations although they had not received any permission for doing so. Bishop Spangenberg asks Georg Weber whether he knew about this and whether Weber had agreed with this action and, what made matters even worse, if the other missionaries actually had known about the action, why nobody had written a single word about this to the headquarters.[52] With such attitudes, however, the missionaries knowingly defied Zinzendorf's rules for the mission field. As the examples of Michler and Weber in the West Indies and Forkel, Zander, and Lawatsch in Suriname show, the early Moravians not only offered the spiritual foundation of "You are all one in Christ," but both groups, the missionaries as well as the enslaved, utilized secular protest together, thus encouraging each other to some larger awareness of their secular empowerment – a fact they themselves must have been very well aware of when they wrote their reports to the Moravian leadership.

Eternal slavery and the invalidation of white superiority

One of the best examples for the missionaries' "spiritual-cum-secular" conduct that must have contributed tremendously to a vision of the *not yet* can be observed with the missionaries' attitude toward sinning. Their raging about spiritual matters in regard to sinning must have caused something that was of essential importance to a growing secular political awareness among enslaved people: white Moravians took away white people's assumed God-given superiority, thus taking away white people's unimpeachable invulnerability in the eyes of black people.

For the missionaries, St. Paul's words, "neither slave nor free [...] you are all one in Christ Jesus," implied that to sin or not to sin was a concern that applied equally to blacks as well as whites. One can see this with the example of how the missionaries handled dancing, drumming, and promiscuous behavior. The missionaries were often very angry with the enslaved because they considered these activities forms of sin that separated a person from God. In their letters and diaries, the missionaries constantly lament that even slaves who have been baptized and are now Afro-Moravian members go back to their old ways and enjoy dancing and drumming on Saturday nights. According to the missionaries, slave dances were part of African heathen cultures. In their *diaria*, one reads about many incidents in which the missionaries punished members by placing them on "probation," thus excluding them from communion and even expelling those who did not show remorse for their action after a certain period of time. In later years, it became obvious that the missionaries lost innumerable potential as well as actual members among the enslaved, simply because of their religious zeal against dancing, drumming, and everything else they considered to be sins of the flesh.

However, it is of crucial importance that they also showed the same zeal when telling black people about white people's behavior and sin. They often were viciously raging against white planters' sinful behavior and repeatedly told enslaved black people that these free white people would be damned to eternal slavery in hell for their adultery and sexual exploitation of black women. Already the very first two missionaries, Leonard Dober and David Nitschmann, told the enslaved they came into contact with that white plantation owners who call themselves Christian, but leave their wives behind in Europe and force slave women into sexual relationships with them, would not belong to Christ, but to the devil.[53] One repeatedly finds texts that report how enslaved women complained to the missionaries about their sexual exploitation by plantation owners and white workers, and the missionaries clearly took a stance against white people in these cases, openly declaring that these white men will be judged for their sins, as God does not differentiate between "slave or free" in making his judgment. They even encouraged enslaved women to use this thought as a spiritual weapon against their tormentors. One finds such an example in an *diarium* entry for St. Thomas in 1737; one reads that a slave woman, about to be sexually violated by one of the plantation overseers pulled out a Bible and read to him about his sin and the eternal punishment he would receive by the laws of the white man's – that is, *his* – religion. According to the report, her act caused him to relent.[54]

Such rhetorical encouragements as these might not have been in conflict with the Moravians' official policy of non-involvement in any secular politics, yet they must have caused something else that was of essential importance to slave resistance and rebellion: they took away white people's spiritual and mental superiority in the eyes of black people. This fact cannot be emphasized enough because after all, both groups were still part of a historical period in which religious beliefs were fundamental, and one's assumed individual judgment by God could still cause existential fears.

Conclusion

Beginning in the 1770s, Moravian missionaries slowly began to give up their initially radical attitudes and moved instead toward friendly cooperation with the planter class. Instead of breaking bread with the slaves in their huts or inviting them into their homes to share their own food with them, as the first missionaries had practiced, they now dined at the master's table. In later missionary reports from Suriname, one can often read about incidents when missionaries acted as the henchmen of plantation directors by telling slaves to obey their masters' orders to work on Sundays, the only day that was work-free for slaves.[55] In addition, quite a few of the later missionaries also discovered a secular taste for slavery's profits, thus sacrificing religious zeal to monetary gain and greed. It is a well-known fact that Moravian missionaries of later decades were siding more with plantation owners than with the enslaved people; quite a few of them became ardent slave holders themselves. During the later decades until emancipation, the Moravian narrative of earlier ideals of dignity, respect, and equality abandoned acquires a tragic overtone.[56]

For the early group, however, as I argue, I see a missionary modus operandi that I call "spiritual-cum-secular" that later groups did not offer anymore. One can safely assume that when the early missionaries started their assignments, they had not developed secular oppositional stances toward slavery because their leader, Count von Zinzendorf, would not have endorsed their call to the mission field. The missionaries' secular consciousness grew while working together with the enslaved; a maturing political consciousness happened therefore to both groups in mutual encouragement. Because of their Pietist theology and radical forms of practiced Christianity in secular settings, wittingly as well as unwittingly, the early Moravians and the enslaved inspired each other, thus contributing to a political consciousness and offering visions of the *not yet* that would eventually lead to their insistences on an all-encompassing and unconditional human right to freedom in their respective societies.

Numerous enslaved Africans who came into contact with the Moravian missionaries over time considered Christianity not necessarily their new religious home, but saw its potential for calling white people to task regarding secular as well as spiritual concepts of freedom. The ideological insistence on the human right to freedom would eventually change the course of New World slavery forever. In addition, the spiritual foundation brought by the Moravians, very likely, must also have offered a great deal more of secular empowerment and maturing of a political consciousness not only to the thousands of slaves but also to the missionaries themselves than has been considered so far in scholarship. Their joint acts of "performing freedom" contributed to a widespread atmosphere that allowed an awakening of possibilities in the unfolding eighteenth century of the New as well as Old World on both sides of the Atlantic.

Notes

1. Beckles, "Caribbean Anti-Slavery," 869.
2. Brown, "Social Death," 1248.
3. Ibid., 1245.
4. For further information, see Gagliardo, *Germany, 1600–1790*.
5. Sheehan, *German History, 1770–1866*, 97.
6. Despite their radical theology of equality, at no time in their history were Moravian communities themselves free of the secular constraints of their immediate surroundings. This fact led them to some questionable decisions throughout their history. For example, during their initial contact with slavery, Moravian leaders back in Herrnhut, Saxony struggled with the concept of slavery, but realizing that any protests would endanger their mission, they made it official church doctrine to settle for the division between physical slavery on earth and spiritual slavery in eternity. Throughout the centuries, Moravian leadership has always stressed political neutrality and has encouraged members to be as politically uninvolved as possible in order to not endanger their missionary work – a dangerous and ambivalent attitude that was also observed during the Third Reich and the era of the German Democratic Republic. Concerning their attitudes toward slavery, for example, the World Council of the Moravian Church issued an official apology only as late as 1996 for several problematic attitudes they held during the era of slavery, including buying and owning slaves themselves without subsequently granting them freedom. For a detailed discussion of Moravian initial struggle with slavery, their changing attitudes over time, and changing biblical justifications, see Sensbach, *Rebecca's Revival*; Faull, "Self-Encounters."
7. For detailed information about Bloch's theory of the *not yet*, see Raphael-Hernandez, *Utopian Aesthetics*, 13–32.
8. For a detailed overview of the Moravians' international missionary activities throughout their history, see Beck, *Brüder in vielen Völkern* and Mettele, *Herrnhuter Brüdergemeine*. Unfortunately, both works have not been translated into English.
9. For a short, but solid overview of the Moravian missionary history's first years in the Danish West Indies, see Richards, "Moravian Missions," 55–74.
10. For more details, see Kröger, *Dober*.
11. For a very detailed account of the Moravian missionaries' first years in the Danish West Indies written by one of their contemporaries, see Oldendorp, *Historie*. Oldendorp's original manuscript was published only in 2002, albeit in German, and is now an important source for

scholars of Moravian and of Caribbean history, alongside the other material in the archives. The shortened form of his work was published in 1777, see *Geschichte der Mission der evangelischen Brüder*. For an English translation see *History of the Mission of the Evangelical Brethren*.
12. For a good overview of the Moravian presence in Suriname, see Staehelin, *Brüdergemeine in Suriname*.
13. According to Hoogbergen's research, a total of 300,000 to 325,000 Africans were sold to planters in Suriname between 1667 and 1826; in 1740, the percentage of slaves born in Africa was 90%; by 1760, Suriname listed 591 plantations, about 50,000 Africans, but only 3000 Europeans. See Hoogbergen, "Marronage in Suriname," 167–168. For an account of the exceptional brutality of Suriname's plantation society, see Stedman, *A Five Years Expedition*.
14. Hoogbergen, "Marronage in Suriname," 168. Hoogbergen estimates that a half percent of the entire slave population fled each year.
15. For more details, see Staehelin, *Brüdergemeine in Suriname*.
16. Sensbach, "Slavery, Race, Global Fellowship"; Lampe, *Mission or Submission*; Frey, *Water from the Rock*; Frey and Wood, *Come Shouting to Zion*.
17. Sensbach, "Slavery, Race, Global Fellowship," 225.
18. Raphael-Hernandez, *Utopian Aesthetics*, 29.
19. Ibid., 25.
20. See Sensbach, *Rebecca's Revival*.
21. See material in folders for MissWI 152, MissWI 153, MAB, and MissSur 14, MAB; the two examples are MissWI 153.1, MAB, and MissWI 153.2, MAB.
22. The German original reads: "bitten gar sehr herzlich die Gemeine zu grüßen" (MissWI 160.4, MAB).
23. Br. Ronners Kinder *Diarium* von St. Thomas, 1752–1759: "unsere lieben schwarzen Schwestern auf Peter de Winth Plantage" (MissWI 119.2, MAB).
24. St. Croix, 1755 (MissWI 163.7, MAB); see also Johann Böhner, 3 June 1755 (MissWI 163.4, MA); and Matthäus Kremser, 6 January 1758 (MissWI 163.9, MAB).
25. Raboteau, "Blood," 24.
26. See, for example, UA R.6.A.a.No74.2-5, Unitäts-Archiv, Herrnhut, Germany.
27. The German original reads:

> Ich habe [?] wilden Sclaven nun in seinem 8ten oder 9ten Jahren ordentlich angenommen, ihn in der christlichen Religion gehörig erziehen und unterweisen, auch neben herrschaftlicher Bedienung das Schneider Handwerk erlernen lassen, ingleichen ihn zur heili. Tauffe befördert und überhaupt alles dasjenige 13 Jahre hindurch sowohl allhier als anderwärts an ihm gethan und erweisen lassen, was man nur irgend von Herrschaften, Eltern und Vormündern bey einem Leibeigenen und Pflegebefohlenen erwarten kann. Der Unterhalt und Verpflegung dieses armen Menschen kommt mir in diesen 13 Jahren weit über 1000 f. [?] zu stehen und seine dagegen geleisteten Dienste sind vor nichts zu rechnen. Aus diesem angeführten wenigen ergiebet sich von selbsten, dass ich nebst Gott ohnstreitig das alleinige Recht zu dem Besitz und Gebrauch dieses Menschen habe, auch in der ganzten Welt niemand gefunden worden mag, der außer mir einigen Anspruch an denselben machen kann. (UA R.6.A.a.No74.4, Unitäts-Archiv, Herrnhut, Germany; my translation)

28. See, for example, Oldendorp's reports on the early years, 1732–1736, in Oldendorp, *Historie*.
29. Leonard Dober in a letter to the Countess zu Stolberg-Wernigerode: The German original reads: "freye Taffel auf Jahr und Tag anbot, welches letztere ich mit Danck abschlug, weil mir die worte unendlich im Gemüth lagen: damit man nicht sage der habe Abraham reich gemacht" (UA, R.15.B.a.1.III.2, Unitäts-Archiv, Herrnhut, Germany).
30. Lawatsch's letter to Leonard Dober, August 5, 1765: The German original reads: "Es hat ihm auch unser Gouverneur gesagt, daß sie's wollten allhier beim Hofe anbringen, daß sie ein gewißes vor die Brüder zu ihrem Unterhalt unter den Frey Negern ausmachen möchten, aber wir beide tragen deswegen Bedenken, denn dadurch machten wir uns verbindlich zu thun, wie sie's gerne haben wollten, so bald wir was von ihnen nehmen, es ist uns genug,

wenn wir die Freiheit haben, das Evangelium unter ihnen zu predigen." See Staehelin, *Brüdergemeine in Suriname*, 11.
31. Patterson, *Social Death*, 44.
32. The following excerpt from Dober's *diarium* can serve as example for the claim of rudimentary literacy; the text does not follow any conventional requirements for German spelling rules: The German original reads: "Sankt Thomas den 16. Aprill 1733 Gieng bruder Nitschman an bort. Den 17. Früh gieng das Schief unter Seegel. Zu abent besucht ich die Anna und Aberham" (UA, R.15.B.a.2.b.2, Unitäts-Archiv, Herrnhut, Germany).
33. Richards, "Moravian Missions," 56.
34. Uttendörfer, *Missionsinstruktionen Zinzendorfs*, 9.
35. Douglass, *Narrative*, 40.
36. For a detailed overview of Moravian activities concerning literacy and the enslaved population in the West Indies, see Hall, *Slave Society*.
37. Oldendorp, *Historie*, 166.
38. Ibid., 166, 177, 185, 187, 210.
39. Suriname, *Diarium*, 1 March 1768: The German original reads: "[...] keine Spur von der Arbeit des Geistes Gottes an den Herzen der Neger gewahr werden können [...] Vater brachte seinen Sohn zu mir und bat angelegentlich denselben schreiben und lesen zu lehren." See Staehelin, *Brüdergemeine in Suriname*, 82.
40. Quoted in Hall, *Slave Society*, 112.
41. Oldendorp, *Historie*, 856. Beckles points out an additional use of slave passes. According to his research, it was indeed common for slaves to write their own passes, thus offering an opportunity for escape to run-away slaves who could use these counterfeit passes to travel to neighboring islands. Once there, they could reinvent themselves as freedmen in such port towns as Charlotte Amalie in St. Thomas, which had a large community of free black people; see Beckles, "Persistent Rebels," 1011.
42. MissWI 152.7, MAB.
43. In October of 1738, Zinzendorf wrote a list of 48 instructions to all missionaries; he considered this list necessary because he had observed mistakes and obstacles in the respective mission fields that, according to him, might potentially endanger the success of the heathen missions. It included even such peculiarities as a ban on becoming homesick (instruction #37). For the complete list, see Kröger, *Dober*, 77–82.
44. In regard to the observation that the early, lower class Moravian missionaries encouraged enslaved people to use the legal system as a method to resist, the research by German historian Eckhart Hellmuth allows claiming that a maturing political consciousness with a transatlantic inspiration could indeed have taken place. In his scholarship on eighteenth-century Saxony, Hellmuth specifically focuses on the lower classes' political consciousness which, according to him, was detectable in their growing awareness of a political culture's possibilities such as the use of the legal system. Most importantly for my thesis, he illustrates that while the late eighteenth century was significant for the actual political process, the lower classes of earlier decades were "definitely participating in shaping such consciousness." See Hellmuth, "Eighteenth-Century Germany," 134.
45. Zander, letter, 27 December 1742: The German original reads:

    es ist hier ein gantz besonderer ort mit finsterniß bedecket, u. ist Jammerns würtig. [...] den wir haben die fernsten Näger Plantagen [...] wir besuchen sie itzo fleißig und sehn was unser liebes lamm [...] andere fangen an u. glaubens das wir sie lieb haben den ihr verderben ist hier so groß, dass kein Näger einem weißen menschen traut, sondern immer denkt, wer weiß, waß mir der blanke mensch thun wirt. (MissSur 17.1, MAB)

46. Suriname, *Diarium*, May 1768: The German original reads:

    [Geerke] ist in seinem gemüth auf's reich werden aus und aus der Idee tractirt er auch die Sclaven unmenschlich, um seine Zwecke zu erreichen. Seine neger haben ih´n auch allhier bei der Obrigkeit verklagt und sich auf Br. Forkel berufen, dass er selbst aus

Mitleid vor sie gebeten habe und so hat Br. F. hier vorm Fiscal erscheinen müssen und da fragte ihn dieser, ob er vor sie gebeten habe. F. gab zur Antwort: ja, es thäte ihm ein jeder schlag wehe, wenn die Neger geschlagen würden, den er wäre noch neu im Lande und hätte die Neger lieb, sie wären doch auch Menschen, die den Heiland sein Blut gekostet haben. (see Staehelin, *Brüdergemeine in Suriname*, 58)

47. Lawatsch's letter to Leonard Dober, 17 August 1765, from the mission station of Saron: The German original reads:

    Das miserable Ding, das unter sie gebracht worden, die Wegläufer von Negern zu fangen (vor einen solchen bekommen sie vom Fiscal 40 fl., wenn sie ihn bringen) oder wenn er sich nicht gefangen giebt, tod zu machen, wenn man das könnte abbringen, wäre mir wohl lieb … Man muss sich aber in Acht nehmen, daß es nicht so aussieht, als verböte man es ihnen, denn wenn so was vor unsre Obrigkeit käme, bekämen wir deswegen die größte Ungelegenheit und wo nicht gar das Exilium. (see Staehelin, *Brüdergemeine in Suriname*, 14 (my translation))

48. The German original reads: "Wißt ihrs denn gewiß, ob ihr über die Nacht Versammlungen halten solt? Wird euch nicht alles in die Schuhe gegossen werden, wenn in der That ein Nachtaufstand entstehen sollte?" (MissWI 129.5, MAB; my translation).
49. The German original reads: "Michlers Kinder-Diarium hat mich sehr erfreut. Ich sehe, dass er fleißig ist, und dass die Kinder mit ihm vertraulich sind" (MissWI 129.20, MAB; my translation).
50. MissWI 129.20, MAB; MissWI 129.22, MAB.
51. The German original reads:

    Br. Michler gedenket unter andren Dingen der Klagen der Neger über die Härte ihrer Herrn. Dabei ist grosse Behutsamkeit nöthig, u. Paulus sagt zur Antwort: ihr Knechte seyd gehorsam eurem Herrn, nicht allein den gütigen u. geleiden [?], sondern auch den wunderlichen. (MissWI 129.22, MAB; my translation)

52. MissWI 129.22, MAB.
53. See, for example, Leonard Dober and David Nitschmann, *Diarium*, St. Thomas, Januarius 1733: "wir sagten ihm aber daß die nicht Christo sondern dem Teuffel angehörten." See Kröger, *Dober*, 49. See also Ibid., 53, 55, 56, 59.
54. *Diarium*, St. Thomas, 30 March 1737 (UA R15. Ba10, Unitäts-Archiv Herrnhut, Germany).
55. See, for example, Lamur, "Slave Religion," 714–721.
56. For further details about the Moravian active involvement in slavery, see, for example, Sensbach, *A Separate Canaan*; Lamur, "Slave Religion"; Hüsgen, *Mission und Sklaverei*.

Acknowledgements

Some of the material in this essay has appeared previously in "Black Caribbean Empowerment and Early Eighteenth-Century Moravian Missions Documents." *Slavery & Abolition* 36, no. 2 (June 2015): 319–334.

Disclosure statement

No potential conflict of interest was reported by the author.

Bibliography

Archives
Moravian Archives, Bethlehem, PA, USA (MAB), MissWI (Missions in the West Indies collection).
Moravian Archives, Bethlehem, PA, USA (MAB), MissSur (Missions in Suriname collection) Unitäts-Archiv, Herrnhut, Germany (UA).

Beck, Hartmut. *Brüder in vielen Völkern. 250 Jahre Mission der Brüdergemeine*. Erlangen: Verlag der Ev.-Lutherischen Mission, 1981.
Beckles, Hilary McD. "Caribbean Anti-Slavery: The Self-Liberation Ethos of Enslaved Blacks (1988)." In *Caribbean Slavery in the Atlantic World*, edited by Verene Shepherd and Hilary McD. Beckles, 869–878. Kingston: Ian Randle, 2000.
Beckles, Hilary McD. "Persistent Rebels: Women and Anti-Slavery Activity." In *Caribbean Slavery in the Atlantic World*, edited by Verene Shepherd and Hilary McD. Beckles, 1001–1016. Kingston: Ian Randle, 2000.
Brown, Vincent. "Social Death and Political Life in the Study of Slavery." *American Historical Review* 14, no. 5 (2009): 1231–1249.
Douglass, Frederick. *Narrative of the Life of Frederick Douglass, an American Slave*. Written by Himself. Boston, MA: Anti-Slavery Office, 1845.
Faull, Katherine M. "Self-encounters: Two Eighteenth-Century African Memoirs from Moravian Bethlehem." In *Crosscurrents: African Americans, Africa, and Germany in the Modern World*, edited by David McBride, Leroy Hopkins, and C. Aisha Blackshire-Belay, 29–52. New York: Camden House, 1998.
Frey, Sylvia R. *Water from the Rock: Black Resistance in a Revolutionary Age*. Princeton, NJ: Princeton University Press, 1991.
Frey, Sylvia R., and Betty Wood. *Come Shouting to Zion: African American Protestantism in the American South and British Caribbean to 1830*. Chapel Hill: The University of North Carolina Press, 1998.
Gagliardo, John. *Germany under the Old Regime, 1600–1790*. London: Longman, 1991.
Hall, Neville A.T. *Slave Society in the Danish West Indies*. Baltimore, MD: The Johns Hopkins University Press, 1992.
Hellmuth, Eckhart. "Toward a Comparative Study of Political Culture: The Cases of Late Eighteenth-Century England and Germany." In *The Transformation of Political Culture: England and Germany in the Late Eighteenth Century*, edited by Eckhart Hellmuth, 1–38. London: Oxford University Press, 1990.
Hoogbergen, Wim. "Marronage and Slave Rebellions in Suriname." In *Slavery in the Americas*, edited by Wolfgang Binder, 165–196. Würzburg: Königshausen & Neumann, 1993.
Hüsgen, Jan. *Mission und Sklaverei: Die Herrnhuter Brüdergemeine und die Sklavenemanzipation in Britisch- und Dänisch-Westindien*. Stuttgart: Franz Steiner, 2016.
Kröger, Rüdiger, ed. *Johann Leonard Dober und der Beginn der Herrnhuter Mission*. Herrnhut: Comenius-Buchhandlung, 2006.
Lampe, Armando. *Mission or Submission? Moravian and Catholic Missionaries in the Dutch Caribbean During the Nineteenth Century*. Göttingen: Vandenhoeck & Ruprecht, 2001.
Lamur, Humphrey. "Slave Religion on the Vossenburg Plantation (Suriname) and Missionaries' Reactions." In *Caribbean Slavery in the Atlantic World*, edited by Verene Shepherd and Hilary McD. Beckles, 714–721. Kingston: Ian Randle, 2000.

Mettele, Gisela. *Weltbürgertum oder Gottesreich: Die Herrnhuter Brüdergemeine als Globale Gemeinschaft 1727–1857*. Göttingen: Vandenhoeck & Ruprecht, 2009.

Oldendorp, Christian Georg Andreas. *Geschichte der Mission der evangelischen Brüder auf den caribischen Inseln S. Thomas, S. Croix und S. Jan*. Edited by Johann Jakob Bossard. Barby: Friedrich Christoph Laux, 1777.

Oldendorp, Christian Georg Andreas. *History of the Mission of the Evangelical Brethren on the Caribbean Islands of St. Thomas, St. Croix, and St. John*. Edited by Johann Jakob Bossard (1777). Translated and edited by Arnold R. Highfield and Vladimir Barac. Ann Arbor, MI: Karoma, 1987.

Oldendorp, Christian Georg Andreas. *Historie der caribischen Inseln Sanct Thomas, Sanct Crux und Sanct Jan, insbesondere der dasigen Neger und der Mission der Evangelischen Brüder unter denselben. Zweiter Teil: Die Missionsgeschichte*. Edited by Hartmut Beck, Gudrun Meier, Stephan Palmié, Aart H. van Soest, Peter Stein, and Horst Ulbricht. Berlin: Verlag für Wissenschaft und Bildung, 2002.

Patterson, Orlando. *Slavery and Social Death: A Comparative Study*. Cambridge, MA: Harvard University Press, 1985.

Raboteau, Albert J. "'The Blood of the Martyrs Is the Seed of Faith': Suffering in the Christianity of American Slaves." In *The Courage to Hope. From Black Suffering to Human Redemption*, edited by Quinton Hosford Dixie and Cornel West, 22–39. Boston, MA: Beacon, 1999.

Raphael-Hernandez, Heike. *The Utopian Aesthetics of Three African American Women (Toni Morrison, Gloria Naylor, Julie Dash): The Principle of Hope*. Lewiston, NY: Edwin Mellen, 2008.

Richards, Helen. "Distant Garden: Moravian Missions and the Culture of Slavery in the Danish West Indies, 1732–1848." *Journal of Moravian History* 2 (2007): 55–74.

Sensbach, Jon. *A Separate Canaan: The Making of an Afro-Moravian World in North Carolina, 1763–1840*. Chapel Hill: University of North Carolina Press, 1998.

Sensbach, Jon. *Rebecca's Revival: Creating Black Christianity in the Atlantic World*. Cambridge. MA: Harvard University Press, 2005.

Sensbach, Jon. "Slavery, Race, and the Global Fellowship: Religious Radicals Confront the Modern Age." In *Pious Pursuits: German Moravians in the Atlantic World*, edited by Michele Gillespie and Robert Beachy, 223–238. New York: Berghahn, 2007.

Sheehan, James J. *German History 1770–1866*. Oxford: Clarendon Press, 1989.

Staehelin, Fritz, ed. *Die Mission der Brüdergemeine in Suriname und Berbice im achtzehnten Jahrhundert. Eine Missionsgeschichte hauptsächlich in Auszügen aus Briefen und Originalberichten*. Herrnhut: Verlag von C. Kersten & Co., n.y. [approx. 1913].

Stedman, John Gabriel. *A Narrative of a Five Years Expedition Against the Revolted Negroes, in Surinam, Guiana, on the Wild Coast of South America, from the Year 1772–1777*. Edited by Stanbury Thompson. The Journal of John Gabriel Stedman. London: Mitre, 1962.

Uttendörfer, Otto. *Die wichtigsten Missionsinstruktionen Zinzendorfs*. Herrnhut: Verlag der Missionsbuchhandlung, 1913.

Antislavery discourses in nineteenth-century German American women's fiction

Pia Wiegmink

ABSTRACT
The essay discusses the transatlantic as well as the gendered perspectives on US American slavery in the works of two nineteenth-century German immigrant women writers, Therese Robinson (writing under the pseudonym Talvj, 1797–1870) and Mathilde Franziska Anneke (1817–1884). I will argue that German immigrant women were not only critical observers of the practice of slavery in the USA but they used antislavery discourses to negotiate German women's efforts to assimilate to American culture. In nineteenth-century transatlantic culture, German immigrant women engaged in and commented upon intersecting discourses on antislavery, Americanization, and womanhood. With regard to discussions of gender, race, and slavery in nineteenth-century US American fiction, writings of German immigrant women or literary representations of German immigration to the USA have rarely been considered. This essay thus shows how fiction written by German immigrant women expands the scope of US American antislavery literature. Its discussion of two lesser known German immigrant women authors contributes to the research on German American literary culture and transatlantic women's history.

In maintaining the unity of the human race we also reject the disagreeable assumption of superior and inferior peoples. Some people are more pliable, more highly educated and ennobled by intellectual culture, but there are no races which are more noble than others. All are equally entitled to freedom [...].

Alexander von Humboldt, *Kosmos, Band 1*, 1845[1]

Beyond all question the German has a great work to do in the New World [...]. He must [...] by his native cosmopolitan, universal spirit, boldly and energetically master the Anglo-American nature, appropriate its virtues, and then breathe into it, as far as it may be desirable, the breath of his own spirit and life.

Phillip Schaff, *America: A Sketch of the Political, Social, and Religious Character of the United States*, 1855.[2]

Now that I have – following my innermost conviction – praised American women of higher social status, my German sisters may ask: "Do you honestly believe that [... they] possess

the same virtues which were so highly regarded in our homeland?" My answer must be: no. […] "You knit?" asked me one of my new girlfriends with greatest surprise when she found me knitting a sock. "Oh, yes," I replied with a smile, "I am, you know, a German woman."
['Wenn mich nun, nachdem ich das Lob der Amerikanerinnen der höheren Stände nach meiner innigsten Überzeugung ausgesprochen, meine deutschen Schwestern auf's Gewissen fragen, […] ob man bei ihnen die Tugenden findet, die in unserem Vaterlande so hoch angeschlagen werden? so muss ich darauf mit nein antworten. […] "you knit?" fragte mich eine meiner neuen Freundinnen im Tone der höchsten Verwunderung, als sie mich mit einem Strickstrumpf fand, "oh yes," war meine lächelnd gegebene Antwort. "I am, you know, a german [sic] woman."]

Amalie Schoppe, "Die Amerikanterin," 1853.[3]

Introduction

This essay discusses German women's perspectives on US American slavery in nineteenth-century American antislavery fiction. More precisely, I examine the representation of antislavery discourses in works written by German American women[4] and show how authors use antislavery discourses to negotiate German women's efforts to assimilate to America culture. Germans were neither a major slaveholding colonial power nor did they actively participate in the slave trade. However, as Heike Raphael-Hernandez has recently observed, what has so far remained largely unnoticed in scholarship on the Black Atlantic and global slavery is that as merchants, travelers, poets, and thinkers, Germans had multiple economic and intellectual entanglements with slavery.[5] Discourses of slavery profoundly impacted notions of self and other as well as processes of national and cultural self-fashioning. As scholars like Alison Clark Efford, Mischa Honeck, Hartmut Keil, or Bruce Levine have shown, for German immigrants to the United States, debates over slavery became an important site of negotiating possible pathways of Americanization.[6]

Building on the work of these scholars, my discussion of the fiction of Therese Albertine Louise von Jakob Robinson, writing under the pseudonym "Talvj," and Mathilde Franziska Anneke pursues a twofold aim: First, I argue that German immigrant women were not only critical observers of the practice of slavery, but they used antislavery discourses to negotiate German women's efforts to assimilate to American culture. Second, with regard to discussions of gender, race, and slavery in nineteenth-century US American fiction, the writings of German immigrant women or literary representations of German immigration to the USA have rarely been considered. This essay will show how fiction written by German immigrant women expands the scope of US American antislavery literature.

This essay focuses on two lesser known works by German women writers, Talvj's *The Exiles* (1852) and Mathilde Franziska Anneke's novella *Uhland in Texas* (1866). *The Exiles* chronicles the dramatic events of the emigration of the female protagonist Clotilde Osten, her meticulous observations of the system of slavery in the urban domestic environment of her host family in Charleston, South Carolina, and her subsequent attempts as well as ultimate failure to build a new home, family, and life in America. While Talvj (1797–1870) successfully marketed her novel on both sides of the Atlantic, the novella *Uhland in Texas* by Mathilde Franziska Anneke (1817–1884), a women's rights activist and active participant in the German Revolutions of 1848/1849, was published in German in the *Illinois Staatsanzeiger* and predominantly addressed the German-speaking immigrant community in Chicago. *Uhland in Texas* chronicles the story of a German immigrant family, the Wallensteins, whose members are tossed into the midst of the Civil War in their new home in Texas.

In both works, the critique of slavery is inextricably entwined with a negotiation of German immigrant female identity. Although the outside-perspective of the character of the female immigrant offers critical and, in the case of Anneke's novella, unconventional perspectives on slavery and race relations in the United States, these works have rarely been examined as part of American antislavery fiction. This is even more astounding given what James G. Basker considered "the democratic inclusiveness" and diversity of this genre of literature.[7] In both *The Exiles* and in *Uhland in Texas*, the critique of US slavery is embedded in complex discourses about German processes of Americanization and competing notions of German and American womanhood. In this essay, I will unpack and discuss some of the tensions inherent in the hyphenated identities of the German women authors living in the United States and their female German immigrant protagonists. Both Talvj and Anneke wrote their fiction not just as German immigrant women, but as women living and working in close proximity to Anglo-Americans: Anneke's antislavery fiction is in large parts the product of transcultural cooperation between Anneke and her friend Mary Booth.[8] Talvj was married to an American and left Germany to live with him in the USA.[9] Yet, although both Talvj and Anneke equip their German immigrant women characters with the moral and intellectual acumen to critically reflect upon the political and social life of their new country of residence, ultimately, both authors deny their German female protagonists any future in the New World.

Antislavery, immigration, and German American women writers

From the emergence of the first antislavery societies at the end of the eighteenth-century until the end of slavery after the Civil War, US American advocates of antislavery maintained strong ties with supporters on the other side of the Atlantic. For example, both black and white advocates of immediate abolition participated in a transatlantic dialogue about the moral and political wrongs of slavery. In this dialogue the discussion of what US American supporters of slavery wanted to confine to a domestic affair was often embedded within a global frame of reference and world politics. Complementing the dominant networks of exchange between British and US American antislavery advocates,[10] recent scholarship has demonstrated a (re-)emerging research interest in the broader transatlantic and transnational entanglements of US slavery and abolition, including a focus on slavery in other parts of the Atlantic world, on repressive states and their forms of resistance, or on reform movements in Europe.[11] Among other aspects, scholars have brought to attention that in particular during the peak time of US abolition (1830–1865), the political agitators affiliated with the American Anti-Slavery Society spearheaded by William Lloyd Garrison often maintained close personal ties with and took political interest in revolutionaries like Joseph O'Donnell (Ireland), Joseph Mazzini (Italy), or Louis Kossuth (Hungary) on the other side of the Atlantic. As historian Caleb McDaniel points out:

> Close attention to these [transatlantic abolitionists] networks is crucial not just for mapping the nineteenth-century Atlantic World of reform, but also for understanding the Garrisonians. [...] [F]ocusing on the extent of their transatlantic networks makes clearer why Garrisonians so often described themselves not only as democratic agitators, but also as citizens of the world.[12]

McDaniel draws attention to how American abolitionists saw their cause closely connected to other reform movements and how William Lloyd Garrison in particular was convinced that reform movements, which supported emancipation, democratization, and equality and freedom of human beings, would ultimately benefit the cause of US abolition.

However, despite the noteworthy exception of Mischa Honeck's study, *We are the Revolutionists: German Speaking Immigrants and American Abolitionists after 1848*, reflections on the multifaceted alliances between Germans, German Americans, and Americans in the fight against slavery in the USA are still largely absent in this transatlantic discourse of abolition. This is even more astounding due to the fact that many German political refugees, in particular those fleeing the failed revolutions of the 1830s and 1848/1849 as well as the events leading to these revolutions,[13] became prominent advocates of different facets of antislavery: Charles Follen, for example, who fled Germany because of his involvement in the assassination of August von Kotzebue, became an ardent supporter of Garrison and a Harvard professor of German literature.[14] Carl Schurz, a lieutenant in the revolution of 1848/1849, became a supporter of Lincoln's Republican Party and a major general of the Union army.[15] Adolf Douai, another former participant in the revolution of 1848/1849, edited a radical newspaper in San Antonio and fought for a free-soil Texas.[16]

It is mainly due to the work of German political refugees like Follen or Schurz that African American intellectuals like Frederick Douglass hailed Germans as innately antislavery. Douglass enthusiastically exclaimed,

> many noble and high-minded men, most of whom, swept over by the tide of the revolution of 1848, have become our active allies against oppression and prejudice. [...] A German has only to be a German to be utterly opposed to slavery. In feeling, as well as in conviction and principle, they are anti-slavery.[17]

It is thus not astonishing that the famous German scientist Alexander von Humboldt, whom American travel writer Bayard Taylor referred to as "the world's greatest living man," was recruited by American abolitionists.[18] From the other side of the Atlantic, Humboldt actively supported the Republican candidate John C. Frémont against the pro-slavery Democratic candidate James Buchanan in the presidential elections of 1856. In addition, Humboldt's critique of Daniel Webster's Fugitive Slave Law of 1850 and his outrage over an English translation of his *Essai politique sur l'île de Cuba* (1826), in which his chapter on slavery had been omitted, were frequently reprinted in the American antislavery press.[19] As historian Laura Dassow Walls observes, "Such newspaper notices circulated far more widely than any of Humboldt's books. Many thousands of Americans who knew little of Humboldt's contributions to science thought of him instead as one of the age's great humanitarians."[20] This brief look at the connection between Alexander von Humboldt and American antislavery advocates exemplifies that a vibrant culture of personal and ideological exchange existed across the Atlantic in the antebellum period. American antislavery activists eagerly embraced the ideological support offered not only by the celebrity persona of Humboldt but also by political veterans, social critics, and novelists. However, whereas the contributions to the cause of antislavery by personalities like Charles Follen and Carl Schurz are still present in public memory today, female supporters like, for example, Ottilie Assing, who translated Frederick Douglass' first autobiography into German, remain still largely unacknowledged.[21]

When Alexander von Humboldt exclaimed shortly before his death in front of a reporter of an American newspaper, "I am half American," he did not refer to his ethnic background, but expressed support for American democracy.[22] He continued, "[M]y aspirations are all with you [Americans], but I don't like the present position of your politics. The influence of Slavery is increasing, I fear. So too is the mistaken view of negro inferiority."[23] In contrast to Humboldt's voluntary Americanness, many of his German contemporaries who immigrated to America had to show more commitment in their effort to become American citizens. During the 1850s, more than one million Germans came to the USA, followed by another peak of German immigration in the 1880s.[24] As Kathleen Neils Conzen points out, in the mid-nineteenth century, when a great wave of German immigrants swept the nation, Germans eagerly debated how and on what conditions German immigrants shall become Americans. Between cultural and political isolationism, the idea of establishing German colonies outside the Western confines of the USA and the refusal to learn English, and demands of appropriating Anglo-American culture, German American public figures promoted a "middle way."[25] For the pursuit of this "middle way," the issue of slavery became one major issue with which German immigrants in the 1850s negotiated their process of Americanization, while they simultaneously maintained core traits of what was perceived as a German identity.

German American antislavery fiction seems to be a particularly apt means of tracing how German immigrants publicly negotiated their assimilation into American culture via their participation in antislavery discourse as *Germans*. In nineteenth-century German American literature, the arrival in the New World, challenges of Americanization, and the issue of slavery were in fact prominent issues. However, while the writings by male German American writers like Friedrich Armand Strubberg, Adolf Douai, or Friedrich Gerstäcker[26] put the male immigrant (antislavery) experience center stage, immigrant women writers, who produced antislavery texts, often blended their critique of slavery with negotiations of Old and New World notions of womanhood.

German American women's views about the journey across the Atlantic, their assimilation into American society, and their reflection on this society still largely remain a blank spot in the historiography of German Americans since first-hand accounts of German American women are rare. As Germanist Martha Kaarsberg Wallach observes, "the women who immigrated to North America from the German speaking countries of Europe usually came as the wives, daughters, or other dependent female relatives of immigrant men."[27] She further observes that "what little commentary can be found in German-American history books is usually very laudatory of the skills of the German-American housewife."[28] Concordant to this domesticity ascribed to German immigrant women, historian Christiane Harzig observes that in German immigrant communities, "women became an important indicator of German *Kultur*,"[29] that is, women were considered to be responsible for passing on and preserving German traditions and customs. Despite the general assumption that German immigrant women primarily came to the USA as companions of their male peers and were ascribed the "roles of bearers and maintainers of culture"[30] in the domestic sphere, the biographical background of Talvj and Anneke and their literary works exemplify that women contributed to German American culture in other ways as well: The *Dictionary of Literary Biography* introduces Talvj as "a translator, philologist, folklorist, ethnologist, historian, social critic, and novelist," and argues that she "deserves to be recognized as one of the most significant women intellectuals of the nineteenth century."[31] In a similar vein, soon after her arrival in Milwaukee in 1850, Mathilde Anneke, who had actively participated in the Baden revolution in 1847, not only published the *Deutsche Frauen-Zeitung*, wrote antislavery fiction, and founded an academy for girls (the Milwaukee *Töchterinstitut*) but, as her biographer Susan L. Piepke observes, "Anneke was probably [also] the most noted speaker in her native tongue in America."[32]

Nineteenth-century German American women writers such as Mathilde Franziska Anneke, Therese Albertine Luise von Jakob Robinson, Amalie Struve, Maria Weisselberg, Louise Weil, Clara Berens, Fernande Richter (Edna Fern), and Kathinka Suto-Schücking wrote poems, plays, novels, and essays in which they presented their views of their transatlantic travels and migrations, commented upon German and American women's roles, and discussed American customs, identities, and politics.[33] In addition, many of these writers were also ardent critics of slavery in America. Against this background it is surprising that the works of German American women writers are largely absent not only from the canon of American immigrant literature and women's fiction, but also from the broad genre of American antislavery literature.

The Exiles: German antislavery sentiments and the cult of German womanhood in America

Little is known today about Therese Albertine Luise von Jakob Robinson, also known under her pen name "Talvj."[34] This is surprising, given the fact that before she married the renowned American biblical scholar and Orientalist Edward Robinson in 1828 and immigrated to the USA, Talvj had already become well-known among German intellectuals. Johann Wolfgang Goethe, for example, encouraged her to publish.[35] Her literary work as well as her scholarly work as a folklorist, historian, and translator was published on both sides of the Atlantic. In her scholarly work that was published in the USA in distinguished magazines like the *North Atlantic Review*, the *Atlantic Monthly*, or *Putnam's Monthly Magazine*, Talvj capitalizes on her knowledge of European languages and history.[36] Concordantly, her various publications for the German market aimed at providing German readers with information on the lives and cultures of the New World.[37] Her scholarly work thus specifically introduced American readers to European and German history and culture (and vice versa).

With regard to the thematic focus of this special issue of *Atlantic Studies*, German entanglements with slavery, Talvj's novel is a suitable case study. The novel was published in both English and German by two leading publishers in the United States and Germany, Putnam and Brockhaus, and thus addressed a broad readership on both sides of the Atlantic. The publication history of *The Exiles* indicates that the topic of German immigrants reflecting upon America, and in particular upon slavery, was of cultural merit for both American and German readers.[38]

In *The Exiles*, the reader follows the trials and tribulations of the orphaned, twenty-three year old Clotilde Osten: her departure from Germany, her meticulous observations of the system of slavery in the urban domestic environment of her host family in Charleston, South Carolina, and her subsequent attempts as well as ultimate failure to find a new home and family in Vermont. At the beginning of the novel, Clotilde leaves Germany with her love, Franz Hubert. Hubert, a former student of her father, had been imprisoned for his involvement in revolutionary activities of the German *Vormärz* of the 1830s – a time during which German nationalists and liberals tried to start a revolution – but thanks to Clotilde's wheeling and dealing, he had been prematurely released on the condition that he leave the country at once. On their passage to New Orleans, the couple experiences a shipwreck on the coast of Florida; Clotilde barely survives and assumes that Hubert is dead. In the following months she works as a German teacher for two young women in Charleston, South Carolina until the couple is unexpectedly reunited and moves into a little house in rural Vermont. However, at the end of the novel, Hubert is killed in a duel with his American half-brother and Clotilde dies shortly after.

The Exiles is an apt novel to assess both antislavery discourses and the negotiation of different notions of womanhood in German American women's fiction. Antislavery and womanhood are both inextricably tied to what is presented as a distinct German identity in the novel. After the shipwreck, Clotilde finds herself with other starving survivors of the shipwreck on the coast of Florida. Reminiscent of William Bradford's providential account of the Pilgrims' encounter with the Wampanoag Squanto, who helped the settlers survive the first winter, in *The Exiles*, "God sent the poor sufferers help, by leading in that direction two negroes" (42), who are slaves of the nearby plantation and who share their provisions with the shipwrecked. Clotilde is then nursed back to physical and mental health by the plantation owner Alonzo Castleton, who later turns out to be Hubert's half-brother, and who eventually also gives her a job: after her recovery from the traumatic experience of the shipwreck, Clotilde tutors Sarah and Virginia Castleton, Alonzo Castleton's nieces, in Charleston, South Carolina, and instructs the two girls in German language, literature, and music.

Clotilde clearly functions as the focalizer of the narrative: Through Clotilde's observations of these two late teens and their family, Talvj voices her antislavery sentiment. Clotilde notices, for example, that the house slaves do not get food until after the morning prayer (when they have already worked for several hours), but the Castletons get to have a solid breakfast before that (94). In addition, she observes that the pious Aunt Gardiner from the North comes for a visit to sell the slaves she inherited from her husband most "advantageously" (83). The irreconcilable ideas of Christian compassion and slavery soon turn into a manifest critique of the peculiar institution:

> Clotilde [...] had been in this *land of liberty* long enough to have found that a *foreigner* cannot express *his* abhorrence against the slavery of the Southern States, and *his* disapprobation of the lukewarmness of the Northern, without solely wounding the national feeling of the Americans, and drawing upon *himself* the reproach of arrogantly meddling with their domestic affairs. (121–122, emphases added)

What is particularly striking here is that it is not only a foreigner who criticizes slavery but a foreign *woman*. Through Clotilde's observations, the German woman in exile, Talvj closely examines American *women's* attitudes towards slavery and exposes both the hypocrisy of Sarah's pietism and Virginia's zealous but inconsistent antislavery attitude. In addition, through the character of Aunt Gardiner, she also criticizes white Northern women's complicity in slavery: although Sarah's overt piety motivates her to instruct her father's slaves in Christian principles, she does not question the practice of slavery itself, an attitude that stands in stark contrast to Clotilde's own idea of Christianity (122). Virginia, the Southern Belle, has only very recently become interested in the antislavery cause, an interest sparked by a romantic encounter with a Polish count, who later in the novel turns out to be Clotilde's Hubert, and who has been imprisoned for aiding in the escape of slaves. As Virginia exclaims, "Berghedorf hates slavery and he has taught me to hate it. He hates all oppression" (120). However, rather than presenting the American young woman as a true antislavery advocate, Talvj soon draws attention to the hypocrisy inherent in Virginia's crush on the European freethinker; Clotilde observes, for example,

> that the ideas of liberty and equality of human rights, were yet more familiar to her [Virginia] in theory than in practice. In her daily life, she [Virginia] never thought of looking upon her slaves as anything but the means of her own convenience. (125)

A little later, this observation is vividly affirmed when Virginia's slave Phyllis, who had provoked Virginia with spiteful remarks concerning her beloved Berghedorf, accidentally destroys the bust of Virginia's dead mother and Virginia, forgetting all her recent sympathy for abolitionism, orders Phyllis's whipping (155). While Talvj presents her German protagonist Clotilde as a critical observer of slavery, it should also be noted that the novel's antislavery sentiment is exclusively tied to German humanist ideals; neither the very few African American nor any white American characters are antislavery advocates.

The novel not only clearly distinguishes between US American supporters of slavery and German humanists, but it also contrasts the idealized young German woman, Clotilde, with the American girls Sarah and Virginia. As the single true guardian of ideas of liberty, equality, and humanism, Talvj celebrates Clotilde as a prototypical German woman who is the bearer of German *Hochkultur* and thus inevitably also an opponent of slavery. Both American girls are admirers of German language and art. However, while both are eager to acquire German language and culture, and although both might be inquisitive and open-minded characters, the author denies both of them the stamina to master the German language and the moral fortitude to truly embrace German humanism.[39] Furthermore, Virginia, who functions in the novel as Clotilde's American female counterpart (they both compete for the love of the same man, Berghedorf/Hubert), is presented as a self-confident and rebellious woman, who exploits the good-will of her male admirers for her own benefit but who has no interest in getting married (111). In contrast, when Clotilde and Hubert are finally able to make up for the delayed marriage which was planned prior to their emigration, Clotilde's views of marriage are informed by both piousness and decency (207). Talvj clearly presents Clotilde's views of marriage as preferable to those of Virginia[40] and further emphasizes the contrast between German and American women: although Clotilde was warmly welcomed into the Castleton's house (102), Clotilde perceives her environment as "so foreign to her utmost nature" (127). As German studies scholar Dorothea Stuecher observes, "the idea of Clotilde becoming 'American' would be a contradiction in terms, for Clotilde's raison d'être lay in the perpetuation of an ideal German womanhood."[41]

Talvj manages to successfully contrast the idealized and morally mature Clotilde, who thoroughly analyzes each American character's attitude towards slavery, with the girlish Virginia. However, when it comes to the relationship between Clotilde and Hubert, the previously praised superiority of German womanhood becomes a corset that not only restricts Clotilde's autonomy, but also her ability to critically analyze the social, political, and religious environment she previously dissected so meticulously. With Hubert's release from prison and the couple's marriage, the character of Clotilde undergoes a profound change. Whereas prior to this event Clotilde appeared to be a lonely but self-confident, determined woman, upon their reunion the novel changes in tone and perspective; as soon as the marriage vows are performed in the story, the narrative shifts the focalization from Clotilde to Hubert, and Clotilde becomes a mere interlocutor and listener to his story and his observations.[42] This impression is complemented by Clotilde's retreat to their little house in the woods of New England where, after Hubert's tragic death, Talvj has Clotilde simply die of grief over the loss of her husband. Despite all the obstacles Clotilde overcame on her own in the world, Talvj does not permit her female protagonist to prosper. Given Talvj's status as a writer in the USA who published scholarly work on a wide range of topics, her depiction of Clotilde seems so different from her own life as an independent immigrant woman intellectual.

Furthermore, when Hubert reappears and Clotilde becomes a German wife, the character of Clotilde loses all her critical impetus and suddenly adopts an odd Old World elitist class-consciousness that threatens to undercut the novel's humanist antislavery sentiment. When Clotilde is finally happily married to Hubert and the two settle in their idyllic home near Middlebury, Vermont, she ponders over the absence of class in American society. Talvj writes:

> Clotilde felt how impossible it was for the individual to bring about, in a country where no difference of *rank* exists, where there is legally but *one* class, a general recognition of that distinction in society, without which no scientific culture can be attained, no art can be practised to perfection, without which no grace of manners can exist, no refinement of domestic life can take place – the distinction between master and servant, between those who labor and those who pay. (339)

Talvj has Clotilde sharply denounce the racial bias that almost all American characters fall prey to in the novel, yet her protagonist seems blind towards her own preoccupations concerning class, a distinction that is utterly at odds with ideas of American equality.[43] German womanhood, Talvj seems to imply, is characterized by moral superiority and a dedicated, elite humanism (which, in America, seems to naturally affiliate with antislavery), but it does not transgress the hierarchies of class; rather, the recognition of "distinction in society" is even presented as a defining trait of this notion of womanhood.[44]

It is through the lens of debates on womanhood and slavery that Talvj assesses the conditions of a German identity in America. Clotilde's struggle to come to terms with what she perceives as her German female identity and her successful attempt to release Hubert not only from prison but also from the clutches of Virginia do not reward her with the domestic life she so desires.[45] In contrast, Talvj has Hubert and Clotilde as well as their unborn child, a symbol of their future in America, die at the end of *The Exiles*. Rather than presenting the couple as a perfect fit for American reform movements and the democratic endeavor of American national self-fashioning, in *The Exiles*, German moral superiority can only be lamented but not put to use in America. And rather than presenting her protagonist as an independent German immigrant woman and ardent critic of slavery, Talvj has Clotilde die. Both German idealism and womanhood, the novel seems to conclude, cannot adjust to and survive in the New World.

German American utopian communities: *Uhland in Texas*

While Talvj successfully marketed her novel on both sides of the Atlantic, the novella, *Uhland in Texas*, by 1848er and women's rights activist Mathilde Franziska Anneke was published in the *Illinois Staatsanzeiger* as a serial novel from April to June 1866, and predominantly addressed the German-speaking immigrant community in Chicago.[46] With approximately 160 newspapers in the USA, "German immigrants established more newspapers than did any other immigrant group" in the USA in the nineteenth century.[47] In addition to providing the newcomers with important pragmatic information, such as where new lands and jobs were available, "newspapers," as historian James Bergquist observes, performed the important function of "introduc[ing] newcomers to American society and politics."[48] It was here, in the newspapers, that most German American fiction like Anneke's *Uhland* was first distributed to an immigrant readership.[49] As historian Tobias Brinkmann points out, the *Illinois Staatszeitung* was not only one of the nation's principal German American newspapers edited by former 1848ers, but had a circulation of 25–30% of the popular English-language *Chicago Tribune*.[50] Taking into account that the *Illinois Staatszeitung* was printed in German and thus only addressed a German immigrant readership, this number illustrates the pivotal role German newspapers played in disseminating views of German American politics and culture.

Like Talvj, Anneke's political and literary work in the USA gives evidence of German immigrant women's vital role in German American identity formation in mid-nineteenth century America. More precisely, it sheds light on German immigrants' perspectives on antislavery. In my close reading of the novel, I will show how Anneke's novella decisively expands the repertoire of American antislavery fiction, as it includes aspects that that are rarely found in this body of literature.

Uhland began as a joint venture between Anneke and Mary Booth, the wife of Wisconsin abolitionist Sherman Booth. By the time the novella was published, Mary Booth had died and Anneke published the novel solely under her name.[51] Despite this close collaboration of the author with an Anglo-American woman, in her novella, like Talvj in *The Exiles*, Anneke fails to include her German female immigrant protagonist in US antebellum society. Although this *post*bellum novella celebrates German American interculturality in its personal, political, and cultural variations, the German woman is not part of America's multiracial prospect.

Uhland in Texas chronicles the story of a German immigrant family who arrives in Texas on the eve of the Civil War and whose presence positively influences the befriended Gilmore family. More precisely, the novella begins with the happy reunion of William Gilmore with his German college friend, Carl von Wallenstein from Mainz, and his twin sons Adalbert and Engelbert and their sister Antonie, in Texas.[52] Having sold all his belongings in Germany, Carl's dream has long been to immigrate to "the land of longing and of magnolias" where he could realize his "socialist ideas and utopian desires" (59).

Here, Anneke's protagonist is very much reminiscent of the prototypical German *Adelsverein*-immigrant, a society founded in 1842 to promote German emigration to Texas with the aim of "establish[ing] a new Germany on Texas soil."[53] The German immigrants in *Uhland* honor their German culture by naming their new home after the German revolutionary poet Ludwig Uhland (1787–1862) who, in the novella, is also a college friend of Gilmore and Wallenstein. However, unlike the immigrants affiliated with the *Adelsverein*, who sought to establish insular German immigrant communities, that is, "a new Germany abroad,"[54] the German immigrants in *Uhland* want to become exemplary and dedicated Americans.

Similar to *The Exiles*, in *Uhland* the German immigrants are antislavery advocates. When the Civil War breaks out, they try to defend their newly found German American community, Uhland, against pro-slavery "guerilla gangs" (153), and after their successful defense of their new home, Wallenstein joins the Union army and commands a black regiment.[55] In contrast to *The Exiles*, in which antislavery sentiments were first and foremost raised by the only two German characters Clotilde and Hubert, in *Uhland*, it is the presence of Gilmore's Yankee nephew John, a stern abolitionist who slowly and steadily convinces his company of the moral wrongs of slave-holding. In addition, the novella includes several references to other American abolitionists such as John Brown or Gerrit Smith (118). Like Talvj in *The Exiles*, Anneke presents American abolitionism and German humanism as closely linked. Among many references in the novella, this is best symbolized by the romance between John and Wallenstein's daughter Antonie.[56] Accordingly, the German presence in Texas is perceived as a decisive and positive influence on Gilmore and his two daughters, Indianna and Marianna, and helps to awaken their antislavery sentiment. It is thus no coincidence that the grand opening ceremony of the Wallensteins' new home, Uhland, is initiated by the signing of Marzell's manumission documents, an act which Wallenstein comments on as follows:

> Let us honor the beginning of our new Uhland with this act; an act which befits the principles of men, whose youthful dreams of freedom may now that they are old be realized at last. Soon, I hope, no unfree man, no slave, will enter our premises and wander under the shade of our groves, for which Antonie conjured up the spirit of the eternal German poet and our close friend Uhland in whose memory we gather here today. (128)

> ["So laß uns den Antritt unsers schönen neuen Uhlands ehren mit der Vollbringung einer That," setzte Herr von Wallenstein hinzu, "wie sie den Grundsätzen von Männern geziemt, deren Jugendtraum die Freiheit gewesen und deren reiferes Alter diesen Traum wenigstens verwirklichen helfen soll. Bald, so hoffe ich, wird kein Unfreier, wenigstens kein Sklave mehr, unsere Grunde betreten und unter den Schatten unserer Haine wandern, zu welchen Antonie die Geister eines deutschen Dichters mit seinem unsterblichen Namen beschworen hat, zu welchem wir das Andenken eines Freundes wie Uhland geladen haben."]

By establishing a relation between German culture (symbolized by the German political poet Ludwig Uhland), the German political ideology of the *Vormärz* ("youthful dream"), and the abolition of slavery, Anneke models Wallenstein after the aforementioned prototypical German whom Frederick Douglass hailed as essentially antislavery, and for whom antislavery sentiment was a natural fit to Germanness.

When, soon after the opening ceremony of the Wallensteins' new home, Texas declares its secession from the Union, Uhland is turned into a fortress, a "military fortification" (155), which offers refuge for other German settlers and the Gilmore family, including all of Gilmore's slaves. Soon thereafter, the German men (father Wallenstein, a former 1848er, and his two sons) turn into ardent fighters for the Union. Whereas Talvj's novel presents German idealism, class-consciousness, and in particular German womanhood as incompatible with American society, Anneke's Germans become, as literary historian Dorothea Stuecher observes, "model citizen[s]" and "the possible redeemers of New World social chaos."[57] America is not perceived as foreign soil but a "new fatherland" (188), and the Star-Spangled Banner, which is raised by the former slave Marzell (182), protects the German/Union settlement from their confederate perpetrators. At the end, Uhland symbolizes a space for an American multicultural identity that not only unites white Americans and German immigrants in a marital bond between Gilmore's daughters and Wallenstein's sons but that – albeit in a rather problematic fashion – wants to include both African and Native Americans in this utopian community. Interestingly, in the midst of the fight for Uhland, it is a "horde" (184) of Native Americans who ultimately defend and rescue the diverse group of refugees: the Northern abolitionist John, the Texan supporters of the Union, the German settlers, the new German immigrants, and Gilmore's former African American slaves. Furthermore, it is due to the former slave, Marzell, that the Native American "choir of revenge" (184) appears as *deus ex machina* in the penultimate chapter, saves the surrounded fortress, and hails Wallenstein as a "great patriarch" (174). This happens because earlier in the plot Marzell functioned as an important mediator between Native Americans and Germans as he is fluent in several languages.[58] Despite the flaws in this depiction, it must be observed that with the representation of interracial cooperation that includes both slave and Native American agency, *Uhland in Texas* presents characters and plot twists that are rarely found in American antislavery fiction.

What seems striking is that in this multicultural scenario, Anneke, like Talvj, does not see any future for German womanhood in America. While she allows Adalbert and Engelbert to easily adapt to their new "fatherland" – they not only fight for the Union but also marry Indianna and Marianna – their sister Antonie is presented as an epitome of German culture: she plays the harp, recites German poetry, looks like a blond, blue-eyed angel, and above all falls in love with the abolitionist, John. In contrast, Anneke iconizes both Indianna and Marianna as strong and beautiful young American women. In particular Indianna is introduced as a strong, independent woman who does not shy away from verbal skirmishes with men (53). In the context of these young, vital, and self-confident American women, despite her supposed moral superiority, Antonie appears frail and utterly out of place. When, for example, she finds herself in a carriage, she asks surprised: "Alas, you want me to steer the carriage myself?" – a question which is answered by Indianna with a decisive: "Of course, [...] from this moment on you are an American lady and as such you need to learn to take the reigns" (109). ["Wie, ich soll allein fahren?" "Freilich [...] Du bist von diesem Moment an eine amerikanische Lady und hast als solche zu lernen, die Zügel zu regieren."][59] Antonie, it seems, has difficulties adjusting to this idea of the American new woman: on the one hand, she falls in love with the ardent abolitionist John and lovingly nurtures a black slave boy before he dies. Both actions represent the compatibility of German womanhood with American abolitionism. Yet, Anneke has Antonie wilt slowly but steadily (150). Antonie does not seem to be part of the New World. Like Talvj's Clotilde, she is doomed to die and denied a role in the multicultural utopian community of Uhland. After Antonie's death, "the grave of a German virgin" is planted with white lilies in the valley. In other words, German womanhood is buried and turned into a celestial symbol of purity and hope (153). America, Anneke's character constellation seems to imply, needs new, that is, truly American types of women, who are strong and reliable companions and who lend a hand and help build this new American community. Given the fact that *Uhland* was to a large extent the result of a collaborative writing process of the German immigrant Mathilde Anneke and the American-born Mary Booth, a collaboration Dorothea Stuecher referred to as a "bicultural writing team," it is odd that German women are not granted a future in this community.[60]

Anneke positions several aspects in the plot that emphasize her multiracial vision of America. When, for example, the pro-slavery advocate and Robert Hale, who wants to marry Marianna, hears rumors that Marianna might be of African descent, he breaks off their engagement. When Wallenstein's son Engelbert, who had also fallen in love with Marianna, learned of this rumor, he happily exclaimed: "Blessed be this little drop of blood which frees you from the fiend. Now I am publicly allowed to love you the way I could hitherto do so only in secret" (147). ["Gesegnet sei dies kleine Tröpfchen Blut [...] das Dich frei macht von dem Unhold. Jetzt darf ich dich lieben, offen, ich bisher im Geheimen dich geliebt habe."] Whereas the one-drop-rule scares off the white American slaveholder Robert, who then tries to court Antonie, the German immigrant considers Marianna's supposedly black ancestry (and, according to nineteenth-century US American racial thinking, their improper miscegenation) a blessing.

What is also notable is that the novella not only anticipates an American community under the lead of German humanists, but that it also adapts key American symbols to present its truly multiracial vision. The inauguration ceremony of Uhland, to give just one example, features among other performances the following tableau:

> At the center of the tableau stood an imposing figure that represented the goddess of liberty. She carried in her hands a white banner with opulent embroidery in gold and blue silk. There was an inscription, "Liberty, God and our Country," on the banner, decorated with a wreath of flowers. Our beautiful Negro Josephine, the sister of Marzell and the twins Romulus and Remus, personified the goddess. (121)

> [Eine imposante Gestalt, die Freiheitsgöttin darstellend, bildete den Mittelpunkt der Scene. Sie trug in ihren Händen ein weißes Banner, das [...] sich durch seine reiche Stickerei in Gold und blauer Seide auszeichnete. Es führte die Inschrift, umgeben von einem Blumenkranz: "Liberty, God and our Country." Unsere hübsche Negerin Josephine, die Schwester Marzells und der Zwillinge Romulus und Remus, personifizierte die Gottheit.]

In this tableau, Marzell's slave sister Josephine represents Columbia, the allegorical figure of the United States. Anneke depicts Josephine as the perfect person to embody the nation, her "dark brown countenance [...] is especially suitable to represent the godly liberty" (121–122). ["Ihr dunkelbraunes Antlitz und der Ausdruck desselben eignete sich vortrefflich zur Darstellung der göttlichen Freiheit."] The antislavery message contained in this tableau is further emphasized by the fact that one of the thirty-two little girls accompanying Josephine is dressed in black; she is in chains, kneels in front of the American self-image, and represents the state of Kansas, which, in the aftermath of the Kansas-Nebraska act of 1857, became the scene of violent confrontations over the issue of slavery.[61] Whereas, the bi-racial character of the "tragic mulatta" was a common trope in American antislavery literature that was used as a means to criticize the sexual exploitation of female slaves, white authors seldom used black women characters as heroic personifications of the USA.[62]

The epitome of Anneke's multiracial American community Uhland comes at the very end of the story when it is exposed that Marianna and Indianna are the descendants of John Randolph, the grandson of Pocahontas (190). In *Uhland* German immigrants are envisioned as exemplary Americans. Furthermore, the model community of the immigrants' home is one in which slavery is abolished and African Americans idolized as genuine representatives of the nation. Finally, the female protagonists' Native American ancestry and the peaceful co-existence of Native Americans and Texan settlers further enhance the multiracial vision of the novella. Strikingly, from the angelic German Antonie to black Josephine, and from the supposedly "tainted" Marianna to the sisters' indigenous ancestry, in Anneke's novella, women represent an American multiracial identity in which German immigrants mix with white Anglo-American settlers, African Americans, and indigenous peoples.

Conclusion

This essay illustrated how German women writers contributed to German, transatlantic, and US American debates about slavery; it drew attention to the aesthetic and political range with which German American women engaged in and commented upon the intersecting discourses of antislavery, Americanization, and womanhood in nineteenth-century transatlantic culture. In both *The Exiles* and *Uhland*, the German immigrant experiences, the reflection on prevalent German and American gender norms, and the critique of US slavery are inextricably entwined. More precisely, my analysis of *The Exiles* and *Uhland* illustrated how German American women writers expand the repertoire of US American antislavery literature by strategically using the perspective of the immigrant's insider-outsider perspective to provide an ethnically distinct yet effective critique of slavery for a US American audience.

The female German immigrants in Talvj's and Anneke's fiction actively participate in their new socio-political environment. Both Talvj and Anneke have their characters' Germanness naturally translate into antislavery sentiment. In both novels, German immigrant women do not occupy the position of "dependent female relatives of immigrant men," a role that, as Germanist Martha Kaarsberg Wallach has pointed out, was often ascribed to nineteenth-century immigrant women in German American history books.[63] In a similar vein, both novels chronicle how German immigrants used debates about slavery as an important discourse to negotiate and envision their Americanization. In both novels, the reader encounters female characters who are active participants in the antislavery cause, who attentively observe, reflect upon, and compare the New World with their native country, and who thus appear as social commentators on and critics of both slavery and America.

It is, nevertheless, striking that the female German immigrants ultimately do not survive their cultural uprootedness on the other side of the Atlantic. Both novels are characterized by the absence of idealized German women in post-bellum US America. This absence becomes even more striking in light of the authors' biographies. While Talvj left Germany for an American man, had a child in America, and spent several decades of her life in the USA, the end of her novel nevertheless emphatically confirms Clotilde's vision of uprootedness. This is obvious at the beginning of the novel when departing for America, Clotilde feels "she must [...] with unsparing hand, cut off the stem of her existence at the root" (24), a process that proves to be a lethal endeavor. In turn, Anneke, who, with her husband Fritz, participated in a fight for liberty and equality in the Baden Revolution (1848/1849), denies the German female characters of her novella any agency in the Civil War. Antonie, the incarnation of German womanhood, is a relic from the old World who is solemnly remembered but who has no place in the emerging German American community. Both Talvj and Anneke use the image of a plant that does not survive its transplantation. However, while Talvj laments the extinction of German womanhood in the new world, Anneke celebrates her disappearance and enthusiastically replaces her with a more active, genuinely American type of woman.

Notes

1. Translated in Foner, *Humboldt on Slavery*, 24.
2. Quoted in Neils Conzen, "Invention of Ethnicity," 140.
3. Reprinted in Wagner, *Was die Deutschen*, 22. All translations from German into English are mine.
4. I define German American women writers as women of German descent, who published literature in and about the United States, and who lived in the United States for an extended period of time.
5. Raphael-Hernandez, "Deutsche Verwicklungen," 35.
6. Efford, *German Immigrants*; Honeck, *Revolutionists*; Keil, "German Immigrants"; Levine, *The Spirit of 1848*.
7. US American antislavery literature is often used as an umbrella term for a broad variety of literature that criticizes the practice of slavery. As James G. Basker observes in his introduction to the Library of America's *American Anti-slavery Literature: Colonial Beginnings to Emancipation*:

    > The authors themselves are strikingly diverse: white and black, male and female, southern and northern, wealthy and poor, educated city dwellers and rural autodidacts, amateurs as well as professional writers. It is the democratic inclusiveness of this literature, almost as much as its revolutionary content, that marks it as so surprising and worthy of our attention. (Basker, xxx)

    Despite the fact that Basker emphasizes the diversity and the "democratic inclusiveness" of this genre, immigrant authors are, to a great extent, absent from his anthology.
8. Honeck, *Revolutionists*, 104–136.
9. Wallach, "Talvj," 284.
10. See, for instance, Blackett, *Antislavery Wall*; Taylor, *British and American Abolitionists*; Meer, *Uncle Tom Mania*; Sweeney, *Frederick Douglass*.
11. Studies on this topic are, for instance, McDaniel, *Problem of Democracy*; Dal Lago, *American Slavery, Atlantic Slavery*; Gemme, *Domesticating Foreign Struggles*.
12. McDaniel, *Democracy*, 13.
13. In this essay, I will refer to this period as the German *Vormärz*. Although historians disagree about the exact beginning of this period, it is consensus that the *Vormärz* was a period during which German intellectuals lobbied for German nationalism and liberalism, which resulted in a series of several attempts to ignite a revolution, such as the political mass demonstration known as the Hambacher Fest in 1832, the attack of the Frankfurt police quarters in 1833, known as the Frankfurter Wachensturm, and finally the Märzrevolution (March Revolution) of 1848/1849, which aimed at achieving German unification. See, Sieber, "Vormärz," 1284–1285. Many of the political agitators of these revolutions fled to the United States. For more information on the impact of German 1848ers in the USA, see, for instance, Honeck, *We are the Revolutionists*; Levine, *The Spirit of 1848*.
14. Mehring, Frank. "Karl (Charles) Follen," 59–62.
15. Hochbruck, "Schurz, Carl," 953.
16. Honeck, *Revolutionists*, 42–70.
17. Douglass, "Adopted Citizens," also quoted in Keil, "German Immigrants," 157.
18. Quoted in Foner, *Humboldt on Slavery*, 10.
19. In 1856, the American supporter of slavery, John S. Thrasher, published a translation of Humboldt's *Essai politique sur l'île de Cuba* but omitted chapter seven, in which Humboldt harshly attacks Cuban slavery. As Foner observes, "the major reason why Thrasher translated Humboldt's work into English was to furnish information about an island which pro-slavery forces in the United States were plotting to annex." See Foner, *Humboldt on Slavery*, 18–19. Humboldt not only opposed the annexation of Cuba as another slave state but also harshly criticized Thrasher's translation. The exchange between Thrasher and Humboldt was printed in *The New York Times* and, as Laura Dassow Walls observes, "Thrasher's act of silencing actually helped Humboldt's view ring loud and clear across the United States, and from then

on he was honored by antislavery activists as their ally and sympathizer." See Walls, *Passage to Cosmos*, 206.
20. Ibid., 208; see also Parker, "Tribute to Humboldt," 110–111.
21. Although the German Americanist Maria Diedrich gives evidence of Assing's pivotal contributions to US American antislavery discourses and chronicles Assing's personal and professional relationship with Frederick Douglass, Assing's work is largely absent from US scholarship on American antislavery. See, Diedrich, *Love*.
22. Humboldt, quoted in Sachs, *Humboldt Current*, 6.
23. Ibid.
24. Rippley, "German Americans."
25. Conzen, "Invention of Ethnicity," 138.
26. See, for instance, Armand Strubberg's *Schwarzes Blut oder Sklaverei in den Vereinigten Staaten*, 1862; Adolf Douai's *Fata Morgana*, 1858, or Friedrich Gerstäcker's *In America: A Picture of American Life in Recent Times*, 1872.
27. Wallach, "German Immigrant Women," 100.
28. Ibid.
29. Harzig, "Gender, Transatlantic Space," 168.
30. Ibid.
31. Haeussler, "Therese Robinson," 292.
32. Piepke, *Mathilde Franziska Anneke*, 8.
33. For an extended list (that, however, does not include Clara Berens, Louise Weil, and Marie Anna Weisselberg), see the Appendix II in Stuecher, *Twice Removed*, 211–212. For a very recent discussion of German-speaking women authors who wrote about the Americas in the eighteenth, nineteenth, twentieth, and twenty-first centuries, see also McFarland and James, eds. *Sophie Discovers Amerika*. In addition to Talvj and Anneke of the above-mentioned authors, Clara Berens, Louise Weil, and Maria Weisselberg voiced strong antislavery sentiments in their literary works. See, for example, Clara Berens's novel: *Aus vergangenen Tagen: Eine Erzählung aus der Sklavenzeit* (1906); Louise Weil's short story "Der deutsche Sklavenhalter" (1865), or Marie Anna Weisselberg's poems (published in Vines, "Pioneer Poet"). Although not a writer of fiction, Ottilie Assing should be mentioned in this context as well. Not only did the journalist publish numerous articles that attacked slavery but she also translated Frederick Douglass' *Narrative of the Live of Frederick Douglass, An American Slave* (1845) into German.
34. American scholar of German literature, Martha Kaarsberg Wallach, is among the few scholars who are familiar with Talvj's work and who published several articles on her work. Jeffrey Sammons has a brief (10-page) 'excursus' on *The Exiles* in his *Ideology, Mimesis, Fantasy*. Along with Mathilde Anneke's fiction and the work of Kathinka Sutro-Schücking, Talvj's novels are also discussed in Dorothea Stuecher, *Twice Removed*. For a biographical reference, see Haeussler, "Therese Robinson."
35. Wallach, "Talvj," 284.
36. Nikola R. Pribić provides a detailed overview of Talvj's publications in the USA and in Germany: From the 1830s onwards until her death in 1870, Talvj published essays on Slavic Languages, Teutonic, Slavic, French, and Spanish poetry and songs as well as articles on Russian serfdom (which she compared to American slavery), and essays on the legend of Doctor Faustus and Charles the Great (Pribić, "Talvj in America," 599–605).
37. Among these works are a 700-page *Geschichte der Colonisation von New England* (Brockhaus, 1847), a translation of an essay on Native American languages, an essay on the Shakers, and a travel report on Virginia appeared in German serial magazines such as *Westermann's Monatshefte* (Pribić, "Talvj in America," 603–605).
38. The author, Talvj, occupies a mediating position here. For each edition, Talvj complemented her texts with footnotes, explaining important habits or events for respective audiences. In the German edition of her novel, she explains, for example, the patterns of formal address in America (Talvj, *Auswanderer*, vol. 1, 128), idiomatic American expressions such as "Uncle Sam" (180), the "domestic institution of Slavery" (180), or comments on the popularity of

39. Clotilde's antislavery sentiment is, however, at times, contrasted with rather problematic and at times, even racist depictions of African Americans. Upon her rescue on the coast of Florida, one of the African American slaves who helps the shipwrecked is described in a distorted, stereotypical way that emphasized thick lips and white teeth (43) and when Clotilde watches the passersby in the streets of New York, she notices "an African face" which she describes as "belong[ing] to the monkey tribe rather than to the human race" (304). Yet, in another instance, Clotilde perceives the sight of a black mother, who is described as a "tall, noble figure," and her four children "with deep compassion" and as a "heart-rending group" (173).
40. To give just one example, chapter 21, entitled "Domestic Scenes," begins with the following observation: "And so the goal was reached, and our lovers had once more a home. Hubert was for the first time master of a house – Clotilde again at the head of a household" (330).
41. Stuecher, *Twice Removed*, 68.
42. This is particularly prevalent in chapters 15–18 in which Franz Hubert recounts his story, presents his views of American gender relations, and introduces Clotilde to the life story of his father.
43. One aspect that I have thus far neglected in my analysis is that of interracial cooperation. Despite the fact that Talvj presents Clotilde as an ardent critic of slavery, the author does not attribute her German protagonist any interest in African Americans. In addition, Talvj denies African American characters any agency. The few African American characters that appear in the novel are stock characters who are presented in a stereotypical and racist manner (43–44, 304) and Virginia's slave Phyllis, who is at least equipped with wit and individual character traits, cares more about her mistress's red dress than freedom (158). The novel's explicit antislavery sentiment functions first and foremost to emphasize German moral superiority and is presented as an issue that is only discussed among white characters.
44. This impression is furthered by another scene in which, as literary scholar Jeffrey Sammons observes, "Talvj has absorbed American prejudices." See Sammons, *Mimesis*, 206. In the novel, Clotilde watches "[f]rom the windows of the palatial Astor House," observes the crowd in the streets, and makes several nativists remarks. Rather than expressing solidarity with other immigrants, Clotilde denounces the Irish as "wild-looking, bandit like fellow saunters" (304), looks down upon the newly arrived German immigrants in their "provincial costumes" (304), and comments upon the "insolent beggar children of all nations" (305).
45. Dorothea Stuecher comments on Franz Hubert's attraction to Virginia as follows: "In the case of Hubert's erotic cum cultural temptation with Virginia Castleton, the author played on the standard immigrant polarization of German and American women to cast the young woman [Virginia] as the incarnation of the seductions of the New World" (*Twice Removed*, 66). Talvj heightens this dangerous lure of the exotic woman even more as Franz Hubert is actually on the verge of repeating the sin of his father: Hubert's father had cheated on this German wife with an American woman, lived with her, and fathered children with her until he regretted his unfaithfulness and returned to his German wife. In a letter to his son, Hubert, he confessed: "I felt like a sinner who kneels before the image of saint" (Talvj, *The Exiles*, 268). However, in the end, Hubert is killed in a duel by his half brother, Alonzo (the son his father had with the American woman); Clotilde has a miscarriage and, not able to live without her beloved Hubert, dies. As Stuecher concludes, "The New World has exacted its dues from those who had dared to trifle with its attractions, and Clotilde's dream of maintaining a cultural island in the midst was revealed as impotent and illusory" (*Twice Removed*, 67).
46. Wagner, "German-American Press," 12.
47. Bergquist, *Daily Life*, 159–160.
48. Ibid., 160.
49. Merrill, "Serial Novel," 16. Like Merrill and Wagner, Patricia Herminghouse and Brent Peterson, and more recently Lorie A. Vanchena emphasize the importance to re-assess German

American serial literature. Patricia Herminghouse, for example, draws attention to the fact that most German American novels only appeared in book form after they had been serialized in the German American newspapers ("Radicalism," 306). Aspects like its serial character, its language other than English, and the often ascribed low-brow character of this genre of literature contributed to the fact that today, many works of German American fiction are buried in the archives. Peterson, "How and Why," 91. See also Vanchena, "Taking Stock."

50. Brinkmann, "Illinois Staatsanzeiger," 541.
51. Dorothea Stuecher labeled the collaboration between Anneke and Mary Booth a "unique cooperative effort" [...]. As they shared in the financial and child care-responsibilities of their mutual household, they also collaborated in their literary activities [...]. See Stuecher, *Twice Removed*, 141. See also Mischa Honeck's detailed discussion of this relationship, Honeck, *Revolutionists*, 104–136.
52. In a recent discussion of this novella, Denise M. Della Rossa writes that the Gilmores and the Wallensteins are "two German immigrant families" ("Anneke's Novella," 83). This is a profound misinterpretation of the novella. The basic character constellation is one of a (re)evolving bond between the *American* Gilmore and the *German* immigrant Wallenstein which will be continued by the marriage between Gilmore's daughters and Wallenstein's sons and explicitly identifies Gilmore as an American from South Carolina who studied in Tübingen, Germany, before he returned to the United States (Anneke, *Uhland*, 60). Subsequent references to the novella will appear in textual parentheses.
53. Brister, "Adelsverein."
54. Struve, *Germans & Texans*, 47.
55. Anneke situates her fictional account of the German plantation Uhland within the historical events of the Civil War. Here, she turns Wallenstein into a Union colonel who commanded the First Louisiana Native Guard, a colored regiment that was – except for some notable exceptions – headed by white men.
56. Anneke often refers to the shared moral values of abolition and humanism in the novella. For example, in chapter 19, there is a dialogue between several pro-slavery Southerners who make fun of Wallenstein: "'He stands on the platform of German Humanism.' 'Well, this might be even better than the abolitionist platform' replied the chivalrous Southerner. 'Alas, much, much worse!'" (148). ["'Der steht auf der Plattform der deutschen Humanität.' 'Nun, die ist womöglich noch schöner, wie die Abolitionisten-Plattform.' 'Hoho, viel, viel schlimmer!'"]
57. Stuecher, *Twice Removed*, 74, 72.
58. What is, nevertheless, disturbing in this scene is that Anneke refers to the Native American characters as a "horde" (185), their respective identity and tribal affiliation is not further explored as they are merely referred to as "Indianer" ("Native Americans"); they are not allowed to engage in direct speech in the novella and as stereotypical depictions of Noble Savages; they are in sync with nature; and they do not enter or interfere with the domestic sphere of the Uhland house but retreat back into the wilderness (185). However, in contrast the stereotypical representation of Native American characters, most of Gilmore's slaves are depicted as highly educated persons. Not only can they read and write but they are also able to speak several languages (first and foremost German) and, like their master, they are fond of German culture (see, for example 58).
59. See also Stuecher's discussion of this scene (*Twice Removed*, 78).
60. Stuecher, *Twice Romoved*, 141.
61. The Kansas-Nebraska Act allowed the newly formed states Kansas and Nebraska to decide whether they want to join the United States as slave states or free states. As a result, Kansas became contested territory and the scene of violent confrontations. Abolitionists encouraged antislavery advocates to settle in Kansas and pro-slavery Southerners sought to support the spread of slavery in the state.
62. A good example of a "tragic mulatta"-character in American antislavery literature is Lydia Maria Child's short story "The Octoroon" (1842), for a further discussion of the character of the "tragic mulatta," see Sollors, *Neither Black Nor White*, 220–246.
63. Wallach, "German Immigrant Women," 100.

Acknowledgements

I want to thank Heike Raphael-Hernandez, Mita Banerjee, Matthias Oppermann, and the peer-reviewers for their valuable comments on previous versions of this essay.

Disclosure statement

No potential conflict of interest was reported by the author.

Bibliography

Anneke, Mathilde Fransziska. "Uhland in Texas." 1866. In *Die gebrochenen Ketten: Erzählungen, Reportagen und Reden (1861–1873)*, edited by Maria M. Wagner, 49–190. Stuttgart: Heinz, 1983.
Basker, James G., ed. *American Antislavery Writings: Colonial Beginnings Cto Emancipation*. New York: Library of America, 2012.
Berens, Clara. *Aus Vergangenen Tagen: Eine Erzählung aus der Sklavenzeit*. St. Louis: Eden Press, 1906.
Bergquist, James. *Daily Life in Immigrant America, 1820–1870*. Westport: Greenwood Press, 2008.
Blackett, Richard. *Building an Antislavery Wall: Black Americans in the Atlantic Abolitionist Movement, 1830–1860*. Baton Rouge: Louisiana State University Press, 1983.
Brinkmann, Tobias. "Illinois Staatsanzeiger." In *Germany and the Americas: Culture, Politics, History*, edited by Thomas Adam, Vol. 2, 540–542. Santa Barbara: ABC-Clio, 2005.
Brister, Louis E. "Adelsverein." In *Handbook of Texas Online*. Texas State Historical Association, 9 June 2010. https://tshaonline.org/handbook/online/articles/ufa01.
Child, Lydia Maria. "The Quadroons." In *The Liberty Bell*, edited by Friends of Freedom, 115–141. Boston: Massachusetts Anti-Slavery Fair, 1842.
Conzen, Kathleen Neils. "German Americans and the Invention of Ethnicity." In *America and the Germans: An Assessment of a Three-hundred-year History*, edited by Frank Trommler and Joseph McVeigh, Vol. 1, 131–147. Philadelphia: University of Pennsylvania Press, 1985.
Dal Lago, Enrico. *American Slavery, Atlantic Slavery, and Beyond: The U.S. "Peculiar Institution" in International Perspective*. Boulder: Paradigm, 2012.
Della Rossa, Denise. "Mathilde Fransziska Anneke's Anti-Slavery Novella Uhland in Texas (1866)." In *Sophie Discovers Amerika: German-Speaking Women Write the New World*, edited by Rob McFarland and Michelle Stott James, 81–90. Rochester: Camden House, 2014.
Diedrich, Maria. *Love Across Color Lines: Ottilie Assing and Frederick Douglass*. New York: Hill and Wang, 1999.
Douai, Adolf. *Fata Morgana. Deutsch-amerikanische Preis-Novelle*. St. Louis, MO: Verlag des Anzeiger des Westens, 1858.
Douglass, Frederick. "Adopted Citizens and Slavery." *Douglass Monthly* (August 1859): 116.
Efford, Alison Clark. *German Immigrants, Race, and Citizenship in the Civil War Era*. New York: Cambridge University Press, 2013.

Foner, Philip S., ed. *Alexander von Humboldt on Slavery in the United States*. Berlin: Humboldt-Universität zu Berlin, 1984.

Gemme, Paola. *Domesticating Foreign Struggles. The Italian Risorgimento and Antebellum American Identity*. Athens: University of Georgia Press, 2011.

Gerstäcker, Friedrich. "From *In America: A Picture of American Life in Recent Times* [1872]." In *Gerstäcker's Louisiana: Fiction and Travel Sketches from Antebellum Times through Reconstruction*, edited and translated by Irene S. Di Maio, 263–276. Baton Rouge: Louisiana State University Press, 2006.

Haeussler, Thomas. "Therese Robinson (Talvj or Talvi)." In *American Literary Critics and Scholars, 1800–1850. Dictionary of Literary Biography*, edited by John W. Rathbun and Monica M. Grecu, Vol. 59, 292–296. Detroit: Gale, 1987.

Harzig, Christiane. "Gender, Transatlantic Space, and the Presence of German-Speaking People in North America." In *Traveling Between Worlds: German-American Encounters*, edited by Thomas Adam, 146–182. College Station: Texas A & M University Press, 2006.

Herminghouse, Patricia. "Radicalism and the 'Great Cause': The German-American Serial Novel in the Antebellum Era." In *America and the Germans: An Assessment of a Three-hundred-year History*, edited by Frank Trommler and Joseph McVeigh, Vol. 1, 306–320. Philadelphia: University of Pennsylvania Press, 1985.

Hochbruck, Wolfgang. "Schurz, Carl." In *Germany and the Americas: Culture, Politics, History*, edited by Thomas Adam, Vol. 3, 953–954. Santa Barbara: ABC-Clio, 2005.

Honeck, Mischa. *We are the Revolutionists: German-Speaking Immigrants and American Abolitionists after 1848*. Athens: University of Georgia Press, 2011.

Keil, Hartmut. "German Immigrants and African-Americans in Mid-Nineteenth Century America." In *Enemy Images in American History*, edited by Ragnhild Fiebig-von Hase and Ursula Lehmkuhl, 137–157. Providence: Berghahn, 1997.

Levine, Bruce. *The Spirit of 1848: German Immigrants, Labor Conflict, and the Coming of the Civil War*. Urbana: University of Illinois Press, 1992.

McDaniel, Caleb. *The Problem of Democracy in the Age of Slavery: Garrisonian Abolitionists and Transatlantic Reform*. Baton Rouge: Louisiana State University Press, 2013.

McFarland, Rob, and Michelle Stott James, eds. *Sophie Discovers Amerika: German-Speaking Women Write the New World*. Rochester, NY: Camden House, 2014.

Meer, Sarah. *Uncle Tom Mania: Slavery, Minstrelsy and Transatlantic Culture in the 1850s*. Athens: University of Georgia Press, 2005.

Mehring, Frank. "Karl (Charles) Follen: Zwischen radikalem Revolutionär und demokratischem Reformer." *Gießener Universitätsblätter* 47 (2014): 49–63.

Merrill, Peter. "The Serial Novel in the German American Press of the 19th Century." *Journal of German-American Studies* 13, no. 1 (1978): 16–23.

Parker, Theodore. "Tribute to Baron von Humboldt." *The Liberator* 9 July 1858, 110–111.

Peterson, Brent. "How (and Why) to Read German-American Literature." In *The German-American Encounter: Conflict and Cooperation between Two Cultures, 1800–2000*, edited by Frank Trommler and Elliott Shore, 88–102. New York: Berghahn Books, 2001.

Piepke, Susan. *Mathilde Franziska Anneke: The Works and Life of a German-American Activists*. New York: Peter Lang, 2006.

Pribic, Nicola. "Talvj in America." In *Serta Slavica in Memoriam Aloisii Schmaus*, edited by Wolfgang Gesemann and Johannes Holthusen, 589–606. München: Dr. Rudolf Trofenik Verlag, 1971.

Raphael-Hernandez, Heike. "Deutsche Verwicklungen in den transatlantischen Sklavenhandel." *Aus Politik und Zeitgeschichte* 50/51 (2015): 35–40.

Rippley, La Vern. "German Americans." In *Encyclopedia of American Studies*, edited by Simon J. Bronner. Baltimore: Johns Hopkins University Press, 2015. http://eas-ref.press.jhu.edu/view?aid=421.

Sachs, Aaron. *The Humboldt Current: Nineteenth-Century Exploration and the Roots of American Environmentalism*. New York: Penguin, 2007.

Sammons, Jeffrey L. *Ideology, Mimesis, Fantasy: Charles Sealsfield, Friedrich Gerstäcker, Karl May, and Other German Novelists of America*. Chapel Hill: University of North Carolina Press, 1998.

Sieber, Eberhard. "Vormärz." In *Lexikon der deutschen Geschichte: Personen, Ereignisse, Institutionen; von der Zeitwende bis zum Ausgang des 2. Weltkriegs*, edited by Gerhard Taddy, 1284–1285. Stuttgart: Alfred Kröner, 1983.

Sollors, Werner. *Neither Black Nor White Yet Both: Thematic Explorations of Interracial Literature.* Cambridge, MA: Harvard University Press, 1999.

Strubberg, Frederic Armand. *Sklaverei in Amerika, oder Schwarzes Blut*. Hannover: Karl Rümpler, 1862.

Struve, Walter. *Germans & Texans: Commerce, Migration and Culture in the Days of the Lone Star Republic*. Austin: University Press of Texas, 1996.

Stuecher, Dorothea Diver. *Twice Removed: The Experience of German-American Women Writers in the 19th Century*. New York: Peter Lang, 1990.

Sweeney, Fionnghuala. *Frederick Douglass and the Atlantic World*. Liverpool: Liverpool University Press, 2007.

Talvj. *Die Auswanderer: Eine Erzählung*, Vol. 1 and 2. Leipzig: Brockhaus, 1852.

Talvj. *The Exiles: A Tale*. New York: Putnam, 1853.

Taylor, Clare. *British and American Abolitionists: An Episode in Understanding*. Edinburgh: Edinburgh University Press, 1974.

Vanchena, Lorie. "Taking Stock: The Disappearance of German-American Literature?" In *Paths Crossing: Essays in German-American Studies*, edited by Cora Lee Kluge, 101–114. Oxford: Peter Lang, 2011.

Vines, Mary Jo. "Pioneer Poet of Texas." *The American-German Review* 14, no. 5 (1948): 28–30.

Wagner, Maria. "Mathilde Anneke's Stories of Slavery in the German-American Press." *MELUS* 6, no. 4 (1979): 9–16.

Wagner, Maria. *Was die Deutschen aus Amerika berichteten, 1828–1865*. Stuttgart: Akademischer Verlag, 1985.

Wallach, Martha Kaarsberg. "German American Women." *Journal of German-American Studies* 15, no. 4 (1978): 99–106.

Wallach, Martha Kaarsberg. "Talvj (Therese Albertine Luise von Jakob Robinson)." In *Nineteenth-century German Writers to 1840. Dictionary of Literary Biography*, edited by James Hardin and Siegfried Mews, Vol. 133, 280–288. Detroit: Gale, 1993.

Walls, Laura Dassow. *The Passage to Cosmos: Alexander von Humboldt and the Shaping of America*. Chicago: University of Chicago Press, 2009.

Weil, Louise. "Der deutsche Sklavenhalter." In *Amerikanische Lebensbilder oder Erlebnisse Deutscher Auswanderer in Amerika*, 1–61. Stuttgart: Frank'sche Verlagshandlung, 1865.

Strategic tangles: Slavery, colonial policy, and religion in German East Africa, 1885–1918

Jörg Haustein

ABSTRACT
When Germany occupied Tanganyika in 1889, the mobilising rhetoric was built around ending slavery, which in turn was framed religiously, as a "Muslim" institution to be ended by "Christian civilisation." However, while the German colonisers subsequently suppressed slave-raiding and the large-scale slave trade, they never abolished slavery itself or the private sale of slaves. Moreover, the political utility of framing slavery as an "Islamic" practice quickly faded as the German government rested its political rule on the established Omani and Swahili Muslim elites and their economic networks. Settlers and planters, in turn, were soon discussing how to solve the problem of labour shortage by coercive means. Only missionaries had an interest to continue framing slavery as a Muslim practice in order to raise support for their Christianising endeavours. This led to an extended conflict about German colonial policy, in which settlers invoked Islam as an ally for "civilising" Africans for modern labour regimes, while missionaries continued to highlight slavery as an aspect of the "Islamic danger" in the colony. The essay traces the German debate of slavery in East Africa with a special interest in how it was connected to perceptions of Christianity and Islam. It demonstrates that the vicissitudes of the debate about slavery were not so much governed by the issue of slavery itself as by entangled strategic interests in the colonial nexus of politics, economy, and religion.

Introduction

Slavery and the slave trade in East Africa were quite distinct from their West African and transatlantic counterparts. In East Africa, the translocal slave trade did not emerge until the late eighteenth century and grew throughout the nineteenth century, fuelled by the expansion of ivory hunting and the caravan economy into the hinterland, as well as by the labour demands of Zanzibar's booming clove plantations. When the clove market declined in the 1870s and the British forced the Zanzibari sultan to end slave exports in 1873, the slave trade in Tanganyika did not decrease, but was now driven by the demand from coconut and sugar plantations along the coast as well as the acquisitions by wealthy households along the caravan routes.[1] In the 1860s, European missionaries began to discover East African slavery as a rallying cause, most notably the Universities'

Mission to Central Africa and the Spiritan Fathers, followed by the White Fathers and the Church Missionary Society in the following decade.[2]

By the end of the nineteenth century, slavery in East Africa was a fairly complex and multi-dimensional industry, a fact which was often lost in the fairly monochromatic descriptions of anti-slavery societies.[3] There were different classes of slaves and slave occupations, from plantation serfdom and concubinage to house servants, tax collectors, and skilled merchants, who managed to retain part of their profits and build up some property. Social hierarchies between slaves depended on their origin, their occupation, degree of autonomy, and their acquired possessions. On the coast, manumission was a regular occurrence; it was seen as a pious act and often coincided with the owner's death. Slaves were also able to buy their freedom through their acquired trade profits. In some instances, this led to considerable social mobility, for example, in the case of Sheikh Ramiya of Bagamoyo. Captured as a child in the eastern Congo, he was sold to a household in Bagamoyo, the most important trading hub of the Tanganyikan coast. Over time, he was not only able to ransom himself, but rose to become the town's wealthiest and most respected political and religious authority, building a significant clientele through his leadership of the local *Qādirīya* brotherhood.[4]

Given the relevance of slavery to the East African economy and to colonial conquest narratives in general, slavery and the slave trade quickly became prominent issues when Germany began its colonial acquisitions in East Africa during the 1880s. However, the newly founded Empire had no previous experience with anti-slavery measures nor possessed relevant policies in this regard. Even the German missions had no previous presence in the region, but followed on the heels of colonial expansion, and the emergence of anti-slavery societies was directly linked to the German conquest. Given this lack of experience, the German approach to slavery and the slave trade in East Africa was quite haphazard and volatile. It was marked by political circumstances and competing interests, and discussions of the matter were entwined with debates about religion, race, contractual labour, and economic strategy. The outcome was accordingly inconsistent: Enslaving and slave-raiding were suppressed early on, while the sale of existing slaves was bureaucratised. Emancipation was encouraged, but unlike in the adjoining British territories, the institution of slavery was never banned. Instead, it remained a controversial and politically charged issue until the end of German rule, while the institution itself declined significantly due to the changing economic structures.[5]

This essay studies how colonial discourses on religion played into the German debate about slavery in East Africa, especially with regard to Islam. During the German conquest, a politically engineered anti-slavery platform bridged divides by proclaiming a "civilising mission" against "Arabdom," Islam and slavery. However, this coalition quickly broke apart with the establishment of the colonial government in East Africa. Gubernatorial pragmatism prevented an effective anti-slavery policy as long as scandals could be avoided, while settlers and missionaries were increasingly coming into conflict with each other over the issue of indigenous labour. By the end of the German rule, the debate had inverted: Islam was now seen by the government as a mobilising power on behalf of Germany in the First World War, while settlers heralded the religion as a necessary force for disciplining indigenous labour, simultaneously critiquing the Christian "civilising" efforts.

Tracing the various political turns, the essay highlights how the invocation of slavery served as a strategic or tactical instrument for achieving other political aims. Moreover, it examines the role religion played in these debates, from the activation of certain stereotypes about Islam, to inter-confessional politics and the role of Christianity in the "civilising mission." These utilitarian and ideological debates will show that the volatility of German slavery policy must be attributed most of all to the entanglement of competing colonial visions, which also prevented a proper recognition of the institution of slavery itself.

Acquisition and conquest: ending the slave trade as colonial cause against Muslim "Arabs"

Initially, slavery and the slave trade were of no concern to the German colonial acquisitions. Carl Peters, the infamous pioneer of German acquisitions in East Africa, and his German East Africa Company sought to lay the economic and political foundations for their nationalist expansionist ideology, and had no interest in the humanitarian rhetoric of their abolitionist contemporaries. Instead, the Company pondered various measures of how to "raise the Negro to plantation work," and its schemes for labour coercion soon provoked the criticism that the Company was itself practising a form of slavery.[6] Likewise, on the side of Imperial politics, there was no incentive to get involved in the fight against slavery and the slave trade. Bismarck's charter policy only allowed for political interference as far as German trade interests were concerned and did not make room for larger geopolitical narratives of "civilisation." When in 1885 the German consul in Zanzibar, Gerhard Rohlfs, suggested to use the German corvette "Gneisenau" for disrupting the slave trade as a way of bolstering German authority in the region, Bismarck famously replied: "[...] the slaves are none of your business. You are to strive for friendship and transit."[7] Similarly, a judicial expertise by the Foreign Office concluded a few months later that subjects in the territories of the German East Africa Company could not be seen as German citizens and thereby could not claim a constitutional right of freedom from slavery.[8]

All of this drastically changed in 1888, when the Sultan of Zanzibar leased the coastal strip of Tanganyika to the German East Africa Company, whose assertive attempts to enforce their treaty with the Sultan led to an uprising that the Company was not able to control. Dubbed the "Arab Revolt" by the Germans, this uprising was not "Arab" at its core, but a simultaneous rejection of German and Omani authority by various elements along the coast, from Swahili patricians and merchants to porters and plebeians who were defending their respective interests in the changing caravan economy.[9] However, despite this considerable heterogeneity of the coastal opposition, the term "Arab Revolt" made political sense. In this rhetoric, "Arabs" were designated as Muslims, slave hunters, slave traders, and a non-indigenous power – all good reasons to assert "Christian civilisation" in the region.

Colonial interest groups had already prepared the way to this conquest narrative, most importantly the Deutsche Kolonialgesellschaft (German Colonial Society), formed in early 1888 as a conglomerate of previous colonial associations.[10] Its media outlet, the *Deutsche Kolonialzeitung*, had already run a series of anti-"Arab" articles by the time the uprising began. These articles were compounds of racist stereotypes ("dirty" and "degraded" Arabs vs. "clean" but yet "uncivilised" "Negroes"), denunciations of Islam, and exhortations to end the slave trade.[11] The conflation of religious and "civilising" aspects also helped to integrate both Catholic and Protestant missionaries. Unlike the conquests of other colonial powers in Africa, German missions did not precede the advances of their Empire, but more or less followed in their wake. On the Catholic side, the Benedictines sought to form a German counter-weight to the earlier and ultimately more influential French societies (Spiritan Fathers and White Fathers), who were instrumentally engaged in anti-slavery causes. On the Protestant side, two of the Berlin societies were especially significant early on: the Evangelical Mission Society for German East Africa in Berlin (Berlin III), founded in 1886 as a nationalist missionary counterpart to Carl Peters' colonial efforts, and the more established Berlin Missionary Society (Berlin I), which commenced its work in Tanganyika in 1891.

The latter engaged in the anti-slavery cause right away through its Inspector Alexander Merensky, who was to lead the Mission's first expedition into the Tanganyikan hinterland. In April 1888, Merensky published his first article in the *Deutsche Kolonialzeitung*, claiming that the "domineering and violent Mohammedanism" was the "actual enemy of Christian culture in Africa."[12] In the summer of 1888, the *Deutsche Kolonialzeitung* began to echo Catholic missionary efforts against slavery by closely following Cardinal Charles Lavigerie's "crusade" proposition, in which the White Fathers' founder pursued ending slavery in Africa through the creation of a religiously inspired, international band of mercenaries, tasked to enforce an arms embargo against "Arabs." Non-missionary articles largely agreed with these religious overtones, diagnosing a critical religio-political juncture. Already in February 1888, the paper's editor, Gustav Meinecke had echoed racist sentiments in an editorial, contending that it was now time for the "Japhetites" to rule the African "Hamites," which would require replacing the "Semite" rule of the "Arabs," whose Islam was the biggest obstacle to "Christian civilisation."[13] Other articles conflated various incidents, like slave traders' attacks on Livingstonia missionaries in Nyasaland, and the Mahdi Uprising almost 2000 miles north, into a pan-Islamic resistance against European civilisation. When mobilising for a German "Emin Pasha Expedition," which was to compete with the earlier British efforts to rescue the German-born governor of the Egyptian Equatoria province (led by Henry Morton Stanley), Hermann von Wissmann painted a particularly dire (und unrealistic) geopolitical drama: If the "Arabs of the South and the Mahdists join hands," he argued, the continent would be sealed off to Europeans by a strong religious alliance, all ivory and arms trade would be siphoned off via Egypt, and slave-raiding would depopulate the continent.[14] In some ways, this was a departure from Wissmann's earlier rhetoric about "Arabs." His memoir of his 1883 Africa crossing, published only months before these remarks, was similarly full of disdain for "Arabs" and detected a rising anti-European sentiment among them, but here Wissmann also asserted that this sentiment was based on "racial hatred" and had nothing to do with religion, in contrast to the assertions above.[15]

Therefore, the newspaper's geopolitical clamour about "Arabs" and Islam reflected the rise of colonial activism,[16] as well as the realisation that the German endeavours in East Africa would require a powerful narrative for replacing the current rulers there. However, this did little to sway Bismarck's opinion, who even after the East African uprising was opposed to military aid for the German East Africa Company.[17] This is where the issue of slavery rose to ultimate prominence. In early October 1888, Friedrich Fabri, the former Lead Inspector of the Rhenish Missionary Society and prime architect of the German colonial movement, suggested to Bismarck that he utilise the anti-slavery movement for foreign and domestic politics alike. This would not only provide international legitimacy to German intervention, but could also serve as a cause to bridge the confessional divides of the *Kulturkampf*, which ran right through parliament via the strong Centre Party, which formed the Catholic opposition to Prussian rule.[18] Bismarck, who had only months before reacted with disdain to a petition by Lavigerie, began to turn-around, especially in light of these domestic considerations.[19] A few weeks later, Fabri organised a large anti-slave trade assembly in Cologne, which saw the participation of clergy, politicians, military officers, industrialists, merchants, workers, and tradesmen alike. It was attended by a Catholic bishop and a Protestant superintendent, and its unanimously adopted resolution demanding German interference against slavery was echoed widely by similar conventions in other German towns during the following weeks.[20] This was just the broad and politically useful anti-slave trade platform Fabri had promised, gaining momentum still with the foundation of the Africa Society of German Catholics in December 1888, which listed the suppression of the slave trade and slavery as its first goal.

Fabri's efforts were flanked by a number of articles in the *Deutsche Kolonialzeitung*, continuing the already established narrative about "Arabdom." They now began to foreground slavery rather than religious conflict. In the newspaper's first editorial about the uprising in East Africa, Gustav Meinecke opined, despite his earlier assertions about Islam, that the uprising had been caused by the economic interests of Arabs, who were "lukewarm Ibadis or Shafi'is" and would refrain from religious proselytisation because a "population turned Mohammedan no longer provides slaves."[21] Wissmann also changed his tune again. He now denied that religious sentiments played a role in the East African uprising but attributed it to protecting the economic interests of the slave trade, while asserting that the Arabs of East Africa were "lax" in their religion.[22]

The same pivot from religious to economic causality can also be observed in the government's rhetoric. As Bismarck began to move, he sought to win British support for a naval blockade of the East African coast in order to quench the uprising without direct intervention. However, this support was not immediately forthcoming, especially since the British believed that the uprising was a German problem, sparked by the inappropriate behaviour of the German East Africa Company's representatives toward local rulers and religious sentiment.[23] In pushing back against the British view, Bismarck's first instinct was to play up the pan-Islamic dimension, invoking a number of unrelated events as indicators of a larger movement: the Mahdi Uprising, the hostile behaviour of the Arab ivory and slave trader Tippu Tip against Stanley, attacks against English mission stations in Uganda, and raids against merchants on Lake Nyasa.[24] However, the meetings between the German ambassador in London and Prime Minister Lord Salisbury made it clear that the British were unimpressed by this religious narrative and wary of exacerbating the crisis, while viewing the issue of slavery as the "deeper and real cause" of the uprising.[25] The German government, therefore, changed its tactics, now going as far as attributing the rise of "Muhammadan fanaticism" to the British efforts of abolishing the more than "1000 year custom" of slavery. Thus, they called on the British to support the naval blockade as part of the anti-slavery cause and even threatened to publicly isolate and shame England by going alone in seeking public support from anti-slavery societies and Cardinal Lavigerie.[26] At the time this response was drafted, England had already agreed to participate in the blockade for *realpolitik* reasons,[27] but the response was sent out nevertheless to keep up the pressure for the technical negotiations. Salisbury later mimicked the German turn to anti-slavery measures, when he had to answer an interpellation in the

House of Lords, which asked why England was risking its reputation in helping the Germans, when the uprising had been caused by their tactlessness.[28] Interestingly, this interpellation was supported by UMCA missionaries, who feared that military measures might be injurious to their work, which reportedly flourished under Muslim rulers.[29]

After successfully utilising the anti-slavery movement in foreign affairs, Bismarck turned to domestic politics. Via Fabri he skilfully moved Ludwig Windthorst, the Speaker of the Centre Party, toward introducing a resolution calling on the government to fight slavery and pledging full parliamentary support. The Windthorst Resolution was passed with a large majority on 14 December 1888.[30] It not only enabled Bismarck to delegate the responsibility for his strategic pivot from charter politics to colonial intervention to the Reichstag, it was also a master piece of confessional politics. The Centre Party was not only the main representation of Catholics in the Reichstag, it had also formed a consistent opposition to colonialism alongside the Social Democrats. Injecting the resolution from this wing of Parliament had only been possible via the Christian anti-slavery coalition Fabri had built and through his work behind the scenes.[31] The government's first white paper on the uprising in East Africa also flanked these efforts, being devoted mostly to anti-slavery measures.[32]

On 26 January 1889 the government introduced a bill requesting two million German Reichsmark for "measures to repress the slave trade and to protect the German interests in East Africa," explicitly invoking the Windthorst Resolution.[33] The bill foresaw the installation of an Imperial Commissioner to lead these efforts, and Hermann von Wissmann, the chosen candidate, introduced his plan of a coastal occupation to the parliament. This move to open colonialism was not uncontroversial. Windthorst himself critiqued the considerable expansion of the original remit of his resolution. However, the law cleared the parliamentary readings within three days and was passed on 29 January 1889. Wissmann immediately began his mission to suppress the uprising and occupy the coast, a process which culminated in 1890 with Germany taking over the German East Africa Company's possession, negotiating borders with Britain, and establishing the German East African colony.

Colonial governance: diverging interests

Fabri's anti-slave-trading platform of government, colonial advocates and missionaries barely lived to see the day of the German take-over. Especially the colonial advocacy groups moved on quite quickly, looking for ways to channel the public humanitarian interest into enthusiasm for the colonies themselves, in order to build up support for substantial investments and to recast the colonies as a nation-building project. Once again, Fabri was to lead the way. Already in April 1889, he delivered a summary assessment of the anti-slavery movement in his book *Fünf Jahre deutscher Kolonialpolitik: Rück-und Ausblicke* (*Five Years of German Colonial Policy: Retrospects and Prospects*).[34] Apparently eager to harvest the colonial-political fruits of his endeavours, he contended that the movement had been ebbing down for three months and began to unravel the coalition he had crafted only months before. He now argued that Cardinal Lavigerie's anti-slavery efforts were "noble aims," but misguided since he underestimated the scale of Arab power in Africa and overlooked the fact that slavery was an "African, customary institution," which could only be overcome gradually by introducing a "higher civilisation."[35] Moreover, he revealed

Bismarck's political motivation for adopting the anti-slavery movement for domestic politics, and asserted that the Centre Party would from now on be supportive of further necessary measures.[36] Echoing David Livingstone, the famous Scottish missionary, explorer and anti-slavery campaigner, Fabri asserted that the fight against slavery necessitated a different trade economy and infrastructure. He proposed to construct a railway from the coast to the great lakes – pioneering the call for the most controversial and protracted colonial projects in German East Africa, only completed in 1914. Summarising the achievements of the anti-slavery movement as having aroused public interest for colonialism, united the confessions, and furthered the cause of missions, *Fünf Jahre deutscher Kolonialpolitik* was all but an implicit obituary for the movement. Fabri repeated his views in front of the second Anti-Slavery Congress in Cologne later in 1889, which ended with remarkably placid resolutions: the Congress thanked the government, proclaimed its trust in the further extension of German endeavours, and called for international treaties on slavery between colonial powers paired with a mutual recognition of spheres of interest.[37]

With few exceptions, the *Deutsche Kolonialzeitung* followed in this change of pursuit. Whereas in early 1889, a critical commentary on the idea of utilising Arabs and Islam for "civilising" Africa chided that "only the French" would form a coalition with human traffickers,[38] the paper soon adopted a different tone. An editorial from March 1890 commented that it had been a mistake to not properly consider the economic and cultural interests of the Arabs. Rather, it would be necessary to integrate them via an extensive knowledge of their legal and religious customs.[39] The article also called for a utilisation of Emin Pasha in the German colonial service, given his knowledge of the Islamic world, and later that year, the paper agreed with Emin's assessment that one could very well build a political alliance with Arabs if refraining from "hasty" measures against slavery and small-scale slave trade.[40] Likewise, an 1893 article about a government memorandum on "East Africa and the Arabs" bemoaned the lack of consideration for Islam and its legal precepts, the codification of which could be an instrument for controlling Arabs and Suaheli alike.[41] Two years later, a critical commentary on the British push to abolish slavery in Zanzibar via a Sultan's decree contended that the Sultan was breaking Islamic law, which only allowed manumission as an act of free will.[42] Later articles offered similar critical sentiments on British abolition from religious and economic vantage points.[43] Interestingly, this reappraisal of slavery as an Arab custom and religious sentiment came alongside debates about the colonial utility of Islam (rather than Christianity). It was now portrayed as the politically more useful religion of "fatalism"[44] or as the economically more suitable alternative for "civilising" and disciplining Africans.[45] Overall, the quick and complete turn-around in this central colonial advocacy paper was quite remarkable.

The political system was slower to manoeuvre, but soon made a similar volte-face, determined by the practical demands of governance and political pragmatics. Whatever Wissmann and Fabri may have fantasised about exiling all Arabs from the mainland in 1888,[46] it had quickly become obvious that the local colonial governance needed to rely on established power structures and "Arab" collaborators. From the adoption of Swahili as administrative language (at first in Arabic script) and the retention of liwalis as local government representatives, to the establishment of "secular" government schools for the education of the children of Muslim notables, German colonial policy was built on the erstwhile elites of the caravan economy. With the exception of suppressing slave-raiding and large-scale slave trade, such a policy would not lend itself to drastic measures against existing slavery or the local slave trade.

In September of 1890, English newspapers began to claim that the Germans had officially sanctioned the slave trade in Bagamoyo in an attempt to siphon off the business from Zanzibar and British East Africa, where prohibition was more strictly enforced. The German press reacted vividly, with colonial-critical papers demanding an explanation and conservative outlets insisting that slave-raiding had been banned, but that slave ownership and sales had to be phased out gradually.[47] The German executive denied the claims and ordered an investigation, while the British government insisted that the accusations were accurate, even handing over a copy of the alleged decree to the German consul in Zanzibar.[48] The decree stated that in order to re-encourage agricultural activity, all land owners in the wider area of Bagamoyo were allowed to "recover and retain their slaves" and sell them "to the people of Bagamoyo," while it was forbidden to ship them by sea. Germany could not deny the existence of the text itself, but the investigation claimed that it had only been a draft – created by their most important Omani collaborator, Soliman bin Nasr, yet not officially sanctioned by the district officer.[49] Soliman's intervention reflected the local agency of Omani planters, who were pushing for legal clarity for repossessing their slaves and protecting their share in the plantation economy and the corollary forced labour market, while acquiescing to the fact that the translocal slave trade was no longer allowed.

The German "clarification" of the origin and draft nature of the decree put the affair to rest, but ironically the document accurately described the established German practice, which was to turn a blind eye to slavery and the local slave trade within the colony while suppressing slave-raiding and the export of slaves. Slowly, this became official policy as well. When attempting to ratify the anti-slavery measures of the 1890 Brussels Conference Act, the government presented a bill to the Reichstag containing the respective provisions, but made it clear in the parliamentary debate that private slave trading and slavery were not targeted by these provisions.[50] Defending (especially domestic) slavery as a customary, benign and necessary institution for the social and economic well-being in the German colonies in Africa, the government representative indicated that its abolition could only be envisioned in a long term process of "civilising." The Centre Party opposed this stance, though not so much on principal grounds, but because of the lack of a clear time-line for abolition. It is important to note, that due to the fundamental legal constitution of German colonialism, any legislation only applied to "non-natives,"[51] whereas matters concerning "natives," a category comprising all "coloured" inhabitants like Arabs and Indians, were regulated by executive diction only. This meant that the parliamentary bill only legislated against Europeans capturing and trading slaves, something which was not known to occur.[52] The bill was therefore unnecessary and controversial, and died in committee.

In 1894, the Reichstag brought up the matter again, demanding a revised draft of the anti-slave-trade bill, which finally reached parliament in January of 1895 and was debated in May.[53] As before, this bill was largely symbolic since it would not apply to Africans or any other "coloured" inhabitants. The debate, therefore, quickly turned on the institution of slavery itself. While conservative parties were supportive of the draft and voiced their trust in the government for finding adequate measures to end slavery, the Social Democrats demanded full abolition. The Centre Party again took a pragmatic middle position. It sided with the government in insisting that it would be an impossible if not brutal imposition to abolish slavery right away, invoking its ties with polygamy and religious views.[54] However, it also insisted that further steps must be taken to prepare abolition, even if this required the "transitional measure" of regulating the rights and duties of slaves and slave owners. In the end, parliament passed the bill as well as a Centre Party resolution requiring the government to take further measures to prepare the abolition of domestic slavery and debt bondage.[55]

Any regulation of slavery, however, would have amounted to an official recognition of the institution. Therefore, the government did not move on this matter until prompted by another Reichstag debate in 1901. By then, respective regulations had emerged in the colonies. In 1897 the governor of East Africa had drafted a decree, which provided some guidelines for district officers on how to adjudicate slavery matters, for example, in dealing with fugitive slaves.[56] Circumventing the Brussels Conference Act, the governor redefined slavery as "serfdom" and regulated the rights and obligations of serfs and their masters, including measures of punishment. Berlin approved the guidelines in March 1899 under the condition that they would not be made public in any manner. In response to the 1901 parliamentary debate, the Chancellor now issued rules based on the East African guidelines, which remained in place until the end of German colonial rule. The only major amendment came in 1904, when the Chancellor declared that all children born to slaves after 31 December 1905 were to be regarded as free.

While the political interest in abolishing the institution of slavery rapidly waned with the suppression of slave-raiding and of the translocal slave trade, missionaries retained the old abolitionist narrative for years to come, even though they now ran counter to the mainstream. Anti-slavery efforts wielded a great potential for mobilising support, and therefore remained a part of the missionary portfolio regardless of changing circumstances. While the former naval blockade had yielded a steady stream of liberated slaves for the missions, the post-conquest policy of repressing the large-scale slave trade whilst ignoring the private market meant that the supply of freed slaves soon dried up. Already in 1894, when the newly formed Evangelical Africa Society (a belated Protestant counterpart to the anti-slavery efforts of the Africa Society of German Catholics) submitted plans to found a station for freed slaves in Usambara, the colonial government argued that there was no need for such a work.[57] In 1898, the East African government sent out a circular stating that neglected street children should from now on be seized and assigned to mission stations, a decree which was motivated by missionary complaints about a lack of referred slave children.[58] Missionaries continued to report about the slave trade and slave raids in remote regions, but the veracity of these reports was often doubted by the government, arguing that it was the missions' "business to complain about the atrocities of the slave trade."[59]

However, despite this evidently shrinking "business," the missionary anti-slavery rhetoric remained unchanged for a different reason: They sought to capitalise on the issue for mobilising Christian efforts against Islam. Already in 1889, Alexander Merensky published an article about slavery in the Qur'ān, seeking to theologically document the alleged connection between the two, which before had only been made rather externally via "Arabdom" and Muslim geopolitics.[60] The last two articles heralding the anti-slavery cause in the *Deutsche Kolonialzeitung* were published in 1891 and made a similarly strong connection between slavery and the missionary efforts against Islam.[61] With the

Deutsche Kolonialzeitung then fully pivoting in the direction outlined above, such inputs by missionaries disappeared from the paper, but they continued to make the case against Islam on account of slavery elsewhere. This was especially the case, as they felt increasingly threatened by gubernatorial policy in East Africa with regard to language policy, the recruitment of native government workers and soldiers, and the opening of government schools for Muslim children without the normally compulsory Christian education.

A clear example of the continued conflation of Islam with slavery in missionary rhetoric can be seen in the first Colonial Congress of 1902. This was an assembly of over 1300 representatives from 70 organisations, convened by the President of the German Colonial Society, Duke Johann Albrecht of Mecklenburg.[62] During this first Colonial Congress, the only paper on slavery was delivered in the section "Religious and Cultural Conditions" by Pater Amandus Acker, a former Spiritan missionary in Zanzibar and head of the Spiritan convent and mission school in Knechtstedten. He contended that slavery was so closely interwoven with Islam in religious, moral, and economic aspects that it is possible to conclude that "wherever there are Mohammedans, slavery rules, and as long as there are Mohammedans, there will be slavery."[63] Acker even laboured to distinguish "Mohammedan" slavery from African forms, contending that in the latter case, slaves were still seen as humans and would find release, whereas Muslims viewed slaves as their property, similar to a donkey or horse. Acker reasoned that the government first needed to stop patronising Islam through its pro-Islamic policies, before other measures would successfully end slavery.[64] This kind of rhetoric would only increase in the coming years and formed a major line of conflict between missionaries and various other colonial interest groups.

Overall, it is clear that Fabri's anti-slavery coalition had little chance of surviving the rhetoric of the German colonial conquest. As various stakeholders sought to guide colonial policy, their aims, methods, and views became increasingly irreconcilable. Slavery, accordingly, became a subject of political debate, as settlers and colonial interest groups put economic profitability in the forefront of their concerns, while missionaries sought to employ slavery as a cause against the perceived "Islam-friendly" policies of the government. The government, in turn, mostly sought to avoid scandal and to administer the colony with a thin layer of personnel.

Colonial conflict: labour shortage, "Islamic danger" and slavery

In the years to come, slavery and Islam became major battlegrounds in the clash between missionaries and other colonial interest groups. A first fault line for this conflict had already emerged when in June 1890 the *Münchener Allgemeine Zeitung* published an interview with Wissmann, who praised Catholic missions as introducing "Christian influence, culture and morality," whereas Protestant missions hindered his work through political intrigue.[65] This prompted strong Protestant reactions, most notably by the Berlin Mission inspector Alexander Merensky and the doyen of German missiology, Gustav Warneck. They not only refuted the alleged political intrigue and pointed to Protestant mission successes, but attacked Catholic missions as a violent, but hollow imposition of Christian values and practices which would not produce lasting results. Especially the Spiritan Fathers' work in Bagamoyo was characterised as a continuation of slavery. In ransoming ("buying") children, benefitting from their labour and retaining power over them, Merensky contended that the priests in Bagamoyo were no different from slave traders and owners.[66] Wissmann countered that the Catholic discipline and the "outwardness" of its cult was the key to its success because one could not expect nations on such a "low level of civilisation" to understand "the Christian religion of love." He, therefore, saw the "labora et ora" of the Catholic missions as the right approach to raise the "savage" to higher culture, as against the "ora et labora" of Protestant missionaries.[67] The dispute escalated into an exchange of open letters between Warneck and Wissmann, in which both espoused similar racist sentiments toward Africans and a commitment to the European civilising mission, but Warneck advocated that a true conversion to Christianity would lead to higher culture, earnestness, and discipline, whereas Wissmann made the connection the other way around.[68] Wissmann, a Prussian Protestant, had no personal reason to defend Catholic missions, but seemed to evaluate the missionary input solely from his rather militant understanding of effective colonial rule. Warneck, in turn, had been a vociferous critic of the anti-slavery "euphoria" all along, mostly from a narrow confessional standpoint of fearing an "ultramontane" take-over of German missions, but also from a deep-seated aversion against making missions subservient to the colonial project.[69] The implicit heart of the matter was the question of native labour: was the creation of disciplined labourers a missionary task (and indeed a prerequisite to instilling Christianity as Wissmann had implied), or was the missionary merely to provide "morally raised" individuals whom the colonial economy then might turn into diligent labourers compliant with a modern capitalist regime?

As the German colonial hold increased, the so-called "labour question" became one of the most pressing economic issues. With large infrastructure projects and the rise of sisal, rubber, and coffee production, settlers and the government were in constant need to coerce the Tanganyikan population from a subsistence economy into wage-labour relations. A number of debates and measures to address this question formed an eerie echo of slavery and the slave trade. The treatment of labourers on plantations was hardly preferable to slavery. Already in 1891, the fairly liberal East African governor Julius von Soden had remarked that one of the main obstacles to abolition was that slaves would rather remain in their current state than become "free labourers" on a plantation, where they had to work harder and were punished more severely.[70] However, he did little to curtail these practices and when Wissmann returned to the colony as governor, he legalised the right of employers to chastise labourers. In consequence, brutality was rife and undoubtedly exacerbated the recruitment problem in addition to the often dire living conditions on plantations.[71] The legal right to chastise labourers was not curtailed until the Rechenberg years (1906–1912), and while the measures he took contributed to his ongoing conflict with settler interests, they seemed to do little to improve plantation recruitment.[72] All other measures to address the labour shortage were coercive ones. Various tax regimes were introduced with the aim of monetising the economy and pressing people into some form of regular wage dependence. Whoever could not pay the tax, was forced to pay off his debt by working for the local district office in infrastructure projects and similar measures. Some districts introduced a mandatory labour card scheme, requiring male inhabitants to work for European employers for a certain part of their time. "Breaking of contract" was made a criminal offence, typically punished by chained imprisonment, with the ubiquitous neck chains forming a cynical echo of the slave trade the Germans had vowed to end. Another such parallel was the conduct of recruitment agents, who hired labourers with false promises, bribes and force, and after moving them toward the plantations on the coast, offered their labour in bulk to plantation owners. A free labour market never emerged in such conditions, nor was this deemed achievable, since the prevalence of racist attitudes caused settlers and colonial officers to attribute the labour shortage to the "indolence" and "laziness" of Africans.[73]

In this atmosphere, the missionary critique of colonial policy as aiding the spread of Islam, was increasingly misplaced and encountered strong resistance among settlers, who accused the missions of disseminating a potentially dangerous propaganda, while not addressing the "civilising" issues at hand. The *Deutsch-Ostafrikanische Zeitung* in Dar es Salaam was the first to voice these sentiments. Reacting to a German newspaper article about the "Islamic Danger," an editorial titled "Spectres" dismissed the rhetoric of "danger" as an "un-Christian" attempt to repress another religion and pointed out that the government's primary task was not to spread "Christian mores," but to "raise useful citizens out of the native element."[74] To reach this goal, the article advocated a spread of government schools all over the colony in order to complement the missionary shortcomings. When the Benedictine bishop Cassian Spieß submitted a critical response to the article, the paper replied by calling into question the economic usefulness of mission protégés overall.[75] In the following years, attacks against missions became a regular feature of the paper, often in connection with labour issues and the alleged failure of missionaries to properly discipline Africans.[76]

In Germany the same dynamic unfolded after the second Colonial Congress in 1905. At the Congress, missionaries had once again bemoaned the spread of Islam and asserted the importance of Christianity to the colonial project. The Protestant theologian Julius Richter forecast a Muslim uprising and a return of the slave trade as a result of German policy, while affirming the patriotic outlook of German missions.[77] The Superior of the White Fathers, Joseph Froberger, contended that the "cultural value" of Islam was overrated and that far from advancing civilisation it would promote "moral decay."[78] The Apostolic Prefect of German South-West Africa, August Nachtwey, also asserted that missions were an important part of the colonial project and reckoned that the instilling of work ethics was one of the "civilising" tasks of missions. This in turn sparked the critical remark from the Protestant side that "personal freedom" was an equally important Christian value, which was necessary to prevent the "slave-like dependence" of workers in "Manchesterdom."[79] In the end, the missions managed to get two important resolutions passed by the Congress, one recommending the creation of a "strong German-Christian culture" as counter-weight to the spread of Islam, and the other calling for the "full moral support" of mission work.

The colonial papers reacted with ire to these resolutions. The most vociferous among them was the *Koloniale Zeitschrift*, founded in 1900 as a nationalistic and economy-centred rival to the *Deutsche Kolonialzeitung*. Having fought with missionaries about their criticism of the brutal exploitation of Africans before,[80] the paper now argued that missionaries only focused on Islam to cover up their own failures. It also printed a counter-resolution by its trustees, titled "Against the New Crusade,"[81] which contended that the genetic disposition of Africans made them much more susceptible to the "realistic teachings of Islam" than to the "transcendental" mores of Christianity.[82] Moreover, it argued that Richter's arguments regarding slavery were invalid, since the slave trade was carried out by "half-blooded Negroes" with a "doubtful religion" rather than by Arabs. The latter had "merely made the Negroes subservient and forced them to work" as the colonisers had also attempted to do "more or less – unfortunately rather less [than more]." The *Deutsche Kolonialzeitung* began to exhibit a similar tendency to downplay the institution of slavery. A number of articles argued that slavery in the Orient and East Africa was nothing like its counterpart in antiquity or in America, but more like a mild paternalistic arrangement, providing housing and welfare to dependent labourers. As slavery was increasingly characterised as a benign social institution, the scale and even existence of the pre-conquest slave raids was also cast in doubt.[83]

Despite this strong resistance from colonial advocacy groups, missionaries gradually gained some ground with their rhetoric of "Islamic danger." The criticisms in the colonial newspapers began to subside, and when a similar resolution against Islam was passed by the Colonial Congress of 1910, it received no such echo.[84] This change in public perception can be attributed to a number of causes. By 1910 the rise of Islam in the German colony was much more evident than only five years before, making it plausible to consider its rising political potential. This perception was aided by the so-called "Mecca letter affair" of 1908, when letters were discovered all over the colony, containing an alleged admonition by the Sharif of Mecca to all Muslims not to collaborate with unbelievers. While the letters did not directly incite uprisings and had little political consequences, their content and sudden emergence was used to argue that one should not underestimate the political potentiality of Islam. Finally, leading scholars of Islam, such as Carl Heinrich Becker, now joined the conversation about how to best govern Islam and how to deal with its less favourable potentialities. While the scholars had different intentions and different opinions on this matter, their participation in the missionary debates helped to raise the issue to prominence, which ultimately forced the German government to some concessions.

However, this new rhetoric of "Islamic danger" was no longer fully connected to the issue of slavery nor did it allow a re-emergence of the erstwhile anti-slavery coalition between political and missionary interests, as can be seen in subsequent parliamentary debates. In 1912, Matthias Erzberger, a leading representative of the Centre Party, inserted a resolution into the budget debate, urging the Chancellor to prepare for full abolition in East Africa by 1920. During the debate, Erzberger profiled his resolution specifically against the more principled Social Democratic criticism of colonial and missionary imperialism, arguing that the "civilising project" had yielded a measurable success and that in order to further "uplift the natives," Germany now had to "crown a great German civilising work" by the abolition of slavery.[85] His strategy was successful at first. Social Democrats could hardly be against the proposal itself and the government's representatives could not argue against its "civilising" principle, but only asked for a more flexible time frame. The resolution passed with support from all parties.

Erzberger followed up in the next budget debate in March 1913, asking the director of the Colonial Office, Wilhelm Solf, what had been done in response to the resolution. The exchange of arguments closely resembled that between missionaries and colonial advocates years before. Erzberger attempted to connected the issue of slavery to Islam, the "main enemy of natives in East Africa," alleging that this religion was spread through government policy and advocated a stronger support of missions.[86] Solf, in turn, deflected the question of religion by insisting government neutrality and attributing the spread of Islam to missionary failures in countering Muslim "propaganda." With regard to the issues of labour and slavery, he repeated the established racist sentiments about the necessity of keeping the "natives" subservient to "white intelligence" by teaching them how to work, and it became clear that he had done nothing more on the issue of slavery than to demand a report from East Africa.[87] The Social Democrats, forming the largest party in parliament at this time, sided with Erzberger in insisting on the 1920 deadline, but otherwise strongly criticised his comments about Islam, making clear that this was hardly a helpful argument in forming a political coalition against slavery.[88]

The East African governor's report reached parliament in early 1914. It insisted that the still existing form of slavery, or "serfdom," was a mild arrangement with mutual benefits, stating moreover that to enforce abolition would have severe economic consequences. It would be better to let the institution die out in due course, relying on manumission and a decreased supply as everyone born after 1905 had been declared free.[89] The Social Democrats and the Centre Party reacted with strong criticism of these sentiments and the continued presence of forced labour. The former likened the government's approach to that of the confederate states in the American Civil War, while Erzberger bemoaned that the governor did not even consider some of the practical propositions the parliament had made, but had simply declared abolition an economic impossibility.[90] However, while the Social Democrat Wilhelm Dittmann led a more foundational attack and argued that plantation capitalism had produced an unprecedented form of slavery, Erzberger sought to distance himself from this critique by affirming that economic interests should be part of an "ora et labora" form of colonialism. He continued to argue for mission support, but did not return to the "Islamic danger"-argument he had brought up rather unsuccessfully the year before. Some liberals joined in with the criticism of the opposition, and it became clear that any attempt by the government to stretch the deadline for abolition would be rejected by the majority. The debate consumed over four days, and in the end the budget was passed with a new resolution, calling on the Chancellor to report by 1915 on concrete measures taken toward abolition.[91]

This resolution is the closest Germany ever came to abolition, since the First World War prevented parliament from following up on its implicit budget threat. The war also shifted the political calculations with regard to religion yet again, away from whatever gains missionaries made in convincing the public and the government of a potential "Islamic danger." Now the Reich sought to capitalise on the Ottoman alliance by inciting Muslims into a "Holy War" against the Entente. On 15 November 1914 the Shaykh al-Islām in Istanbul proclaimed his well-known jihād fatwā, which mandated all Sunni Muslims (or those respecting the Ottoman caliphate) to enter the war against England, France, and Russia.[92] While the Ottoman Empire certainly had its own intentions and political calculations in this proclamation, the proclamation was prepared and flanked by German diplomacy and propaganda.[93] Among its many uses in German publications and prison camps, the fatwā was also translated into Swahili and distributed in the East African colony.[94] The actual impact of this measure is disputable, but it certainly affected the outlook toward Islam in the colonial press, as can be seen in an article in the *Koloniale Zeitschrift* from 1915. It contended that the "Holy War" declaration had aroused Muslim enthusiasm for the war in a way that "Christian missions cannot have, and perhaps should not have in accordance with their character."[95] The article called for an end to all criticism of Islam-friendly German policies, and returning to the issue of labour, the author made the following peculiar remarks:

Christianity and Islam will operate in our colonies in equal measure. Of course, we do not think of a reintroduction of slavery. We could do without the passages about the treatment of slaves in the Koran. But the absence of any compulsion to work would mean to leave idle the enormous economic values which our colonies hold. Thus we hope and wish that in practical economic life there will be a compromise between the Islamitic and Christian world view, which introduces labour compulsion in such a measure and form that it guarantees the reproduction and increase of the natives, as well as their economic and cultural uplift [...][96]

In many ways, this quote can be seen as the cynical antithesis to where the colonial propaganda on East Africa had begun during the years of conquest. Then, slavery had been invoked as an issue compelling the German nation to interfere, before a strategic Muslim alliance would forever impose the institution onto the African continent and seal it from Christian "civilisation." Now, some sort of strategic alliance with Islam was invoked in order to balance out Christian influence and bring about "cultural uplift" via labour compulsion. The short-lived anti-slavery coalition had fully inverted.

Conclusion

The vicissitudes of the German slavery debate certainly point to the volatility of early colonial politics. As multiple actors and interest groups attempted to influence the public, the issue of slavery was defined and discussed as it suited their respective purposes, which changed over time.

However, in many ways it is also possible to argue that the conversation did not change at all, because its fundamental premises remained the same. Firstly, slavery was characterised throughout as an "Arab" or Muslim issue of geopolitical significance. For as long as the strategic vectors of colonialism and mission coincided, their narratives on slavery and Islam matched, but when they pivoted toward economic and religious empire building, respectively, they clashed precisely on the discursively linked topics of slavery and Islam. Moreover, this geopolitical utilisation of Islam was remarkably distant from actual Muslim practices and discussions on the coast. As Jan-Georg Deutsch has pointed out, Islamic teachings and piety were a major motivator for manumission, which played an important role in the decline of slavery along the coast,[97] but this aspect is not reflected in any of the German debates about Islam and slavery. Secondly, the racist paternalism of the "civilising mission" continued to govern the debate as Wissmann's 1890 altercation with Protestants was replayed time and again: in the settler-missionary conflicts, the parliamentary debates about ending slavery, and even in the 1915 colonial press musings about post-war East Africa. While Wissmann heralded Catholic missions over Protestants as the role model for disciplining the African labour force, later discussions centred on whether Islam or Christianity was the preferable religious force to achieve the same. While not necessarily agreeing on their sequence, all sides of the debate envisioned a connection between "ora" and "labora," between the religious capability and the labour capacity of their African subjects. Finally, the moral discourse connected to slavery retained an enormous utility throughout the German colonial period. Fabri and Bismarck adopted the cause in order to move toward an interventionist colonialism, missionaries built their resources and legitimacy around fighting slavery and the parliamentary opposition used the moral discourse on slavery to pressure the government on colonial policies. Whoever was on the other side of these arguments, needed to deflate the moral narrative about slavery – be it Warneck's accusation of Catholic missions harbouring ulterior motives (ultramontanism), the East African government's tactical refusal to recognise and regulate the institution, or the colonial advocates' re-definition of slavery as mild serfdom with welfare benefits.

Given that these three fundamental premises remained constant and yet sufficiently explain the various developments in the German discourse and policies on slavery, one may suspect that the debate was at its core all about strategic gains in colonial politics rather than the institution of slavery itself.

Notes

1. For the East African slave economy, see especially Iliffe, *A Modern History of Tanganyika*, 40–87; Sheriff, *Slaves, Spices and Ivory in Zanzibar*; Deutsch, *Emancipation Without Abolition*, 17–52.
2. See Anderson-Morshead, *The History of the Universities' Mission*; Stoner-Eby, "African Leaders Engage Mission Christianity"; Kollman, *Evangelization*; Henschel, *Argwöhnisch beobachtet*; Kilaini, *The Catholic Evangelization of Kagera in North-West Tanzania*; Stock, *The History of the Church Missionary Society*.
3. For a detailed social history of slavery in nineteenth-century Tanganyika, see especially Deutsch, *Emancipation Without Abolition*, 53–96; Glassman, *Feasts and Riot*, 79–114. For a contemporary account of both, see Swann, *Fighting the Slave Hunters in Central Africa*.
4. See Nimtz, *Islam and Politics*, 119–123.
5. For a detailed analysis of these contradictions, see Deutsch, *Emancipation Without Abolition*.
6. See Bückendorf, *Schwarz-weiß-rot über Ostafrika!*, 294–295.
7. See Schneppen, *Sansibar und die Deutschen*, 94. Klaus Bade pointed out the irony, that this statement came only three weeks after the conclusion of the Berlin Conference, whose (not yet ratified) General Act mandated the signatory powers to suppress slave trade by all means, see Bade, "Antisklavereibewegung," 40.
8. See Kolonialakten, Bundesarchiv Lichterfelde (hereafter BArch) BArch R 1001/1002, 3–13.
9. For the plebeian dynamics of the uprising, see Glassman, *Feasts and Riot*; for the others, see especially Iliffe, *A Modern History of Tanganyika*, 92–98.
10. For this process, see Bade, *Friedrich Fabri*, 471–503.
11. See, for example, Toeppen, "Aus Sansibar"; Hellgrewe, "Bilder aus Sansibar"; Meinecke, "Wandlungen."
12. Merensky, "Der mohammedanische Gegenstoß."
13. Meinecke, "Wandlungen."
14. Wissmann, "Die Bedeutung der Emin Pascha-Expedition."
15. Wissmann, *Unter deutscher Flagge*, 197, 282, 299.
16. The print run of the *Deutsche Kolonialzeitung* had reached 18,500 in 1890. It probably closely followed the Colonial Society's membership, which was roughly 16,000 in 1888. See Bade, *Friedrich Fabri*, 498.
17. See Bückendorf, *Schwarz-weiß-rot über Ostafrika!*, 353–355.
18. See Bade, "Antisklavereibewegung," 44–45. Fabri had successfully advised Bismarck on colonial politics before, see Bade, *Friedrich Fabri*, 513–547.
19. Bade perhaps overstates Fabri's influence in turning Bismarck around, since the Chancellor had already instructed the Foreign Office on 30 September to contact Cardinal Lavigerie, see Schneppen, *Sansibar und die Deutschen*, 246. However, the political utility of the anti-slavery societies for domestic purposes almost certainly was Fabri's injection.
20. See Bade, *Friedrich Fabri*, 534–538.
21. Meinecke, "Die Lage in Ostafrika und die Araber," 317.
22. "Die Araberfrage und der Sklavenhandel." Wissmann had been a speaker at Fabri's anti-slavery assembly in Cologne and was likely oriented about his political moves.

23. One of the main complaints against the Germans in Pangani was the desecration of a mosque, for details, see Glassman, *Feasts and Riot*, 215–218. For the early British view, see Leyden to Bismarck, 9 October 1888, BArch R 1001/706, 51–57.
24. See drafts of a position paper for the German consul in London, BArch R 1001/706, 89–101.
25. Hatzfeld to Bismarck, 19 October 1888, BArch R 1001/706, 104–112.
26. Bismarck to Hatzfeld, 22 October 1888; and 23 October 1888, BArch R 1001/707, 4–9; 24–29.
27. See Schneppen, *Sansibar und die Deutschen*, 244.
28. See Hatzfeld to Bismarck, 7 November 1888. BArch R 1001/709, 12–22.
29. See articles in the *Times* from 25 October, 1 November, and 7 November 1888, kept in the German records: BArch R 1001/691, 52; BArch R 1001/692, 76; 89–90.
30. See *Stenographische Berichte* 105, 303–321; Anlage 27, *Stenographische Berichte* 108, 182. For the political background to this, see Klaus Bade's meticulous documentation in *Friedrich Fabri*, 537–542.
31. Ibid., 539–541.
32. Anlage 42, *Stenographische Berichte* 108, 389–417.
33. Anlage 71, *Stenographische Berichte* 108, 491–493; *Stenographische Berichte* 105, 603.
34. See Fabri, *Fünf Jahre deutscher Kolonialpolitik*, especially, 49–57. Compare Bade, *Friedrich Fabri*, 542–544.
35. Fabri, *Fünf Jahre deutscher Kolonialpolitik*, 51.
36. Ibid., 52–53.
37. "Gegen den Sklavenhandel," 354.
38. "Die Araber in Mittelafrika."
39. "Die Araberfrage und Emin Pascha."
40. "Korrespondenzen," 29 November 1890; "Aufruf zur Unterstützung der Vorschläge Emin Paschas."
41. "Die Denkschrift über Ostafrika und die Araber."
42. "Die Sklaverei auf Sansibar und Pemba."
43. "Die Aufhebung der Sklaverei in Sansibar," 17 April 1897; "Die Aufhebung der Sklaverei in Sansibar," 4 August 1898.
44. "Ein Schreiben von Prof. Dr. Schweinfurth"; Hirsch, "Arabische Weltanschauung."
45. "Mission oder Islam?"; Passarge, "Mission oder Islam?"
46. See Bade, "Antisklavereibewegung," 54; Bade, *Friedrich Fabri*, 542.
47. The various press clippings collected on this matter in September 1890 fill more than 100 pages of the corresponding Foreign Office file, see BArch R 1001/1002.
48. Charles Euan-Smith to Gustav Michahelles, 13 September 1890, BArch R 1001/1003, 23–25.
49. See BArch R 1001/1003, 16–22, 47–48.
50. Anlage 501, *Stenographische Berichte* 124, 2800–2803; *Stenographische Berichte* 118, 2891–2895.
51. This was acknowledged in the explanatory statement for the bill, see ibid., 2801. The fundamental colonial law was the Protectorates' Act, for its genesis and legal implications, see especially Grohmann, *Exotische Verfassung*.
52. See Deutsch, *Emancipation Without Abolition*, 107–109. See also Soden to Caprivi 25 November 1892, BArch R 1001/1003, 121–124.
53. Anlage 138, *Stenographische Berichte* 141, 683–700; *Stenographische Berichte* 140, 2339–2358.
54. See Deutsch, *Emancipation Without Abolition*, 113. Incidentally policy makers and legal commentators frequently invoked polygamy and slavery as reasons for the incompatibility of Muslim and German law and the resulting need for the category of the "native" – the circle was complete.
55. *Stenographische Berichte* 140, 2416–2420.
56. For this and the following, see Deutsch, *Emancipation Without Abolition*, 145–151.
57. See Tanzania National Archives (hereafter TNA), German collection G 9/34. In the end, this work turned into an orphanage and later into a sanatorium for Europeans.

58. See TNA G 9/1, 135. For the decree, see Kaiserliches Gouvernement von Deutsch-Ostafrika, *Die Landes-Gesetzgebung des Deutsch-Ostafrikanischen Schutzgebiets, Teil II*, 308.
59. Bismarck to Hohenlohe-Schillingsfürst, 17 December 1895. BArch R1001/1004, 21. For reports see, for example, the roughly 100 pages about Ruanda in TNA G 9/18.
60. Merensky, "Was sagt der Koran über Sklavenjagden und Sklaverei?"
61. "Korrespondenzen," 20 May 1891; v. C., "Was thun wir Deutsche gegen den Sklavenhandel?"
62. See *Verhandlungen des Deutschen Kolonialkongresses 1902*.
63. Acker, "Über einige Mittel zur Abschaffung der Sklaverei," 453.
64. Ibid., 456.
65. "Deutsches Reich."
66. Merensky, "Das Urtheil des Reichskommissars Wißmann über römische und evangelische Missionserfolge in Afrika."
67. "Deutsches Reich." See also Katharina Stornig's essay in this volume, "Catholic missionary associations and the saving of African child slaves in nineteenth-century Germany."
68. Warneck, "Zur Abwehr und Verständigung"; Wissmann, *Antwort auf den offenen Brief des Herrn Dr. Warneck*. The German government stayed neutral: they reminded Wissmann of regulations regarding publications in the press, but did not comment on the debate in any way, see BArch R 1001/836.
69. This was not true of all German missions and in part explains Warneck's harsh assessment of the new Evangelical Mission Society for German East Africa (Berlin III), which explicitly allied with colonial causes.
70. "Bericht des Lieutenants Sigl über den Sklavenhandel," 511.
71. See Schröder, *Prügelstrafe und Züchtigungsrecht*, 112–117.
72. See Iliffe, *Tanganyika under German Rule*, 106–107.
73. See Deutsch, *Emancipation Without Abolition*, 218–227; Iliffe, *Tanganyika under German Rule*, 64–68, 133–138.
74. "Schreckgespenster."
75. "Verschiedene Stimmen aus unserem Leserkreise."
76. "Unsere Schwarzen"; "Eingesandt"; "Regulirung und Verschärfung der Prügelstrafe"; "Der Aufstand und der Einfluß der Missionen."
77. Richter, "Der Islam eine Gefahr für unsere afrikanischen Kolonien."
78. Froberger, "Welches ist der Kulturwert des Islam für koloniale Entwickelung?"
79. See Nachtwey, "Die Mission als Förderin der Kultur und Wissenschaft," 557, 561.
80. "Koloniale Umschau"; "Mission und wirtschaftliche Kolonialpolitik"; Elpons, "Der Missionsanwalt."
81. See in particular, "Übersicht der Presse"; Der Vorstand des Deutschen Kolonialbundes, "Gegen den neuen Kreuzzug"; the ensuing debate stretched over more articles later that year.
82. See also the longer defense of this same argument in Zache, "Koloniale Eingeborenenpolitik (Fortsetzung)."
83. Bongard, "Die Studienreise des Staatsekretärs Dernburg nach Deutsch-Ostafrika (Fortsetzung)"; Leue, "Vor dem Sturm"; Leue, "Tipputip"; see also Leue, "Die Sklaverei in Deutsch-Ostafrika."
84. For the debate and resolution, see Redaktionsausschuss des deutschen Kolonialkongresses, *Verhandlungen des Deutschen Kolonialkongresses 1910*, 662–673.
85. *Stenographische Berichte* 284, 1529. On the resolution and its further development, see also Deutsch, *Emancipation Without Abolition*, 118–122.
86. *Stenographische Berichte* 288, 4309–4310.
87. Ibid., 4334–4337
88. Ibid., 4350, 4354–4355.
89. Anlage 1395, *Stenographische Berichte* 303, 2885–2891.
90. *Stenographische Berichte* 294, 7903–7906, 7912–7914.
91. Ibid., 8106.
92. Tschudi, "Die Fetwa des Schejch-ül-Islâm."
93. Schwanitz, "Djihad 'Made in Germany'."

94. Pesek, *Das Ende eines Kolonialreiches*, 282–295.
95. Förster, "Die christliche Mission und der Islam in den deutschen Kolonien," 2.
96. Ibid.
97. Deutsch, "The 'Freeing' of Slaves in German East Africa."

Acknowledgements

I would like to thank Heike Raphael-Hernandez and Pia Wiegmink for their invitation to contribute to this volume as well as their patience and their careful editorial comments to my drafts of this essay. I would also like to thank the anonymous peer reviewers and Salvatory Nyanto for their encouraging and insightful comments.

Disclosure statement

No potential conflict of interest was reported by the author.

ORCID

Jörg Haustein http://orcid.org/0000-0001-5792-5205

Bibliography

Acker, Amandus. "Über einige Mittel zur Abschaffung der Sklaverei." In *Verhandlungen des Deutschen Kolonialkongresses 1902 zu Berlin am 10. und 11. Oktober 1902*, 452–459. Berlin: Dietrich Reimer, 1903.
Anderson-Morshead, Anne Elizabeth Mary. *The History of the Universities' Mission to Central Africa 1859–1909*. New and revised. London: Office of the Universities' Mission to Central Africa, 1909.
"Aufruf zur Unterstützung der Vorschläge Emin Paschas." *Deutsche Kolonialzeitung*, 13 December 1890.
Bade, Klaus J. "Antisklavereibewegung in Deutschland und Kolonialkrieg in Deutsch-Ostafrika 1888–1890: Bismarck und Friedrich Fabri." *Geschichte und Gesellschaft* 3 (1977): 31–58.
Bade, Klaus J. *Friedrich Fabri und der Imperialismus in der Bismarckzeit: Revolution – Depression – Expansion*. 2nd, Internet edition ed. Osnabrück, 2005. www.imis.uni-osnabrueck.de/BadeFabri.pdf.
"Bericht des Lieutenants Sigl über den Sklavenhandel." *Deutsches Kolonialblatt*, 1 December 1891.
Bongard, Oscar. "Die Studienreise des Staatsekretärs Dernburg nach Deutsch-Ostafrika (Fortsetzung)." *Deutsche Kolonialzeitung*, 30 November 1907.
Bückendorf, Jutta. *"Schwarz-weiß-rot über Ostafrika!" Deutsche Kolonialpläne und afrikanische Realität*. Europa – Übersee; 5. Münster: Lit, 1997.
"Der Aufstand und der Einfluß der Missionen." *Deutsch-Ostafrikanische Zeitung*, 21 October 1905.
Der Vorstand des Deutschen Kolonialbundes. "Gegen den neuen Kreuzzug." *Koloniale Zeitschrift*, 7 December 1905.
Deutsch, Jan-Georg. "The 'Freeing' of Slaves in German East Africa: The Statistical Record 1890–1914." In *Slavery and Colonial Rule in Africa*, edited by Suzanne Miers and Martin A. Klein, 109–132. London: Frank Cass, 1999.

Deutsch, Jan-Georg. *Emancipation Without Abolition in German East Africa c.1884–1914*. Oxford: James Currey, 2004.

"Deutsches Reich." *Münchener Allgemeine Zeitung*, 26 June 1890, morning edition.

"Die Araber in Mittelafrika." *Deutsche Kolonialzeitung*, 16 February 1889.

"Die Araberfrage und der Sklavenhandel." *Deutsche Kolonialzeitung*, 3 November 1888.

"Die Araberfrage und Emin Pascha." *Deutsche Kolonialzeitung*, 15 March 1890.

"Die Aufhebung der Sklaverei in Sansibar." *Deutsche Kolonialzeitung*, 17 April 1897.

"Die Aufhebung der Sklaverei in Sansibar." *Deutsche Kolonialzeitung*, 4 August 1898.

"Die Denkschrift über Ostafrika und die Araber." *Deutsche Kolonialzeitung*, 7 January 1893.

"Die Sklaverei auf Sansibar und Pemba." *Deutsche Kolonialzeitung*, 18 May 1895.

"Eingesandt." *Deutsch-Ostafrikanische Zeitung*, 2 July 1904.

"Ein Schreiben von Prof. Dr. Schweinfurth." *Deutsche Kolonialzeitung*, February 1, 1890.

Elpons, Georg von. "Der Missionsanwalt." *Koloniale Zeitschrift*, 29 May 1902.

Fabri, Friedrich. *Fünf Jahre deutscher Kolonialpolitik: Rück- und Ausblicke*. Gotha: Friedrich Andreas Perthes, 1889.

Förster, Wilhelm. "Die christliche Mission und der Islam in den deutschen Kolonien." *Koloniale Zeitschrift*, 11 August 1915.

Froberger, Joseph. "Welches ist der Kulturwert des Islam für koloniale Entwickelung?" In *Verhandlungen des Deutschen Kolonialkongresses 1905 zu Berlin am 5., 6. und 7. Oktober 1905*, edited by Redaktionsausschuss des deutschen Kolonialkongresses, 527–531. Berlin: Dietrich Reimer, 1906.

"Gegen den Sklavenhandel." *Deutsche Kolonialzeitung*, 7 December 1889.

Glassman, Jonathon. *Feasts and Riot: Revelry, Rebellion, and Popular Consciousness on the Swahili Coast, 1856–1888*. Portsmouth, NH: Heinemann, 1995.

Grohmann, Marc. *Exotische Verfassung: Die Kompetenzen des Reichstags für die deutschen Kolonien in Gesetzgebung und Staatsrechtswissenschaft des Kaiserreichs (1884–1914)*. Beiträge zur Rechtsgeschichte des 20. Jahrhunderts; 30. Tübingen: Mohr Siebeck, 2001.

Hellgrewe, Rudolf. "Bilder aus Sansibar: II." *Deutsche Kolonialzeitung*, 18 February 1888.

Henschel, Johannes. *Argwöhnisch beobachtet: Das gespannte Verhältnis zwischen deutschen Kolonialbeamten und katholischen Missionaren in Bagamoyo/Ostafrika*. Berlin: trafo Wissenschaftsverlag, 2013.

Hirsch, Leo. "Arabische Weltanschauung." *Deutsche Kolonialzeitung*, 1 March 1890.

Iliffe, John. *Tanganyika under German Rule 1905–1912*. Cambridge: Cambridge University Press, 1969.

Iliffe, John. *A Modern History of Tanganyika*. African Studies Series; 25. Cambridge: Cambridge University Press, 1979.

Kaiserliches Gouvernement von Deutsch-Ostafrika, ed. *Die Landes-Gesetzgebung des Deutsch-Ostafrikanischen Schutzgebiets. Teil II: Systematische Zusammenstellung der den Behörden zugegangenen Dienstanweisungen, Runderlasse usw., abgeschlossen am 30. November 1911*. 2nd ed. Tanga/Daressalam, 1911.

Kilaini, Method M. P. *The Catholic Evangelization of Kagera in North-West Tanzania: The Pioneer Period 1892–1912*. Rome: Pontificia Universitate Gregoriana, 1990.

Kollman, Paul V. *The Evangelization of Slaves and Catholic Origins in Eastern Africa*. Maryknoll, NY: Orbis Books, 2005.

Kolonialakten (R1001), Bundesarchiv Lichterfelde (BArch), Berlin.

"Koloniale Umschau: Die Missionskonferenz." *Koloniale Zeitschrift*, 20 April 1902.

"Korrespondenzen." *Deutsche Kolonialzeitung*, 29 November 1890.

"Korrespondenzen." *Deutsche Kolonialzeitung*, 20 May 1891.

Leue, August. "Die Sklaverei in Deutsch-Ostafrika." *Beiträge zur Kolonialpolitik und Kolonialwirtschaft* 2, no. 19–20 (1900/1901): 606–608, 617–625.

Leue, August. "Tipputip." *Deutsche Kolonialzeitung*, 22 July 1905.

Leue, August. "Vor dem Sturm." *Deutsche Kolonialzeitung*, 20 October 1906.

Meinecke, Gustav. "Die Lage in Ostafrika und die Araber." *Deutsche Kolonialzeitung*, 6 October 1888.

Meinecke, Gustav. "Wandlungen." *Deutsche Kolonialzeitung*, 18 February 1888.

Merensky, Alexander. "Der mohammedanische Gegenstoß gegen christliche Einflüsse in Zentral-Afrika." *Deutsche Kolonialzeitung*, 28 April 1888.

Merensky, Alexander. "Was sagt der Koran über Sklavenjagden und Sklaverei?" *Deutsche Kolonialzeitung*, 27 April 1889.

Merensky, Alexander. "Das Urtheil des Reichskommissars Wißmann über römische und evangelische Missionserfolge in Afrika." *Neue Preußische Zeitung*, 5 July 1890.

"Mission oder Islam?" *Deutsche Kolonialzeitung*, 9 November 1895.

"Mission und wirtschaftliche Kolonialpolitik." *Koloniale Zeitschrift*, 1 May 1902.

Nachtwey, August. "Die Mission als Förderin der Kultur und Wissenschaft." In *Verhandlungen des Deutschen Kolonialkongresses 1905 zu Berlin am 5., 6. und 7. Oktober 1905*, edited by Redaktionsausschuss des deutschen Kolonialkongresses, 553–563. Berlin: Dietrich Reimer, 1906.

Nimtz, August H. *Islam and Politics in East Africa: The Sufi Order in Tanzania*. Minneapolis: University of Minnesota Press, 1980.

Passarge, Siegfried. "Mission oder Islam?" *Deutsche Kolonialzeitung*, 14 December 1895.

Pesek, Michael. *Das Ende eines Kolonialreiches: Ostafrika im Ersten Weltkrieg*. Frankfurt am Main: Campus Verlag, 2010.

Redaktionsausschuss des deutschen Kolonialkongresses, ed. *Verhandlungen des Deutschen Kolonialkongresses 1910 zu Berlin am 6., 7. und 8. Oktober 1910*. Berlin: Dietrich Reimer, 1910.

"Regulirung und Verschärfung der Prügelstrafe." *Deutsch-Ostafrikanische Zeitung*, 8 July 1905.

Richter, Julius. "Der Islam eine Gefahr für unsere afrikanischen Kolonien." In *Verhandlungen des Deutschen Kolonialkongresses 1905 zu Berlin am 5., 6. und 7. Oktober 1905*, edited by Redaktionsausschuss des deutschen Kolonialkongresses, 510–527. Berlin: Dietrich Reimer, 1906.

Schneppen, Heinz. *Sansibar und die Deutschen: Ein besonderes Verhältnis 1844–1966*. Europa - Übersee: Historische Studien; 11. Münster: LIT Verlag, 2006.

"Schreckgespenster." *Deutsch-Ostafrikanische Zeitung*, 7 March 1903.

Schröder, Martin. *Prügelstrafe und Züchtigungsrecht in den deutschen Schutzgebieten Schwarzafrikas*. Europa-Übersee; 6. Münster: LIT Verlag, 1997.

Schwanitz, Wolfgang. "Djihad 'Made in Germany': Der Streit um den heiligen Krieg 1914–1915." *Sozial.Geschichte* 18 (2003): 7–34.

Sheriff, Abdul. *Slaves, Spices and Ivory in Zanzibar: Integration of an East African Commercial Empire into the World Economy, 1770–1873*. London: James Currey, 1997.

Stenographische Berichte der Verhandlungen des Reichstags (Stenographic Reports of the Debates of the Reichstag). http://www.reichstagsprotokolle.de/rtbiiauf.html.

Stock, Eugene. *The History of the Church Missionary Society, Its Environment, Its Men and Its Work*. London: Christian Missionary Society, 1899.

Stoner-Eby, Anne Marie. "African Leaders Engage Mission Christianity: Anglicans in Tanzania, 1876–1926." PhD diss., University of Pennsylvania, 2003.

Swann, Alfred J. *Fighting the Slave Hunters in Central Africa: A Record of Twenty-six Years of Travel and Adventure Round the Great Lakes and of the Overthrow of Tip-Pu-Tib, Rumaliza and Other Great Slave Traders*. London: Seeley, 1910.

Toeppen, Curt. "Aus Sansibar." *Deutsche Kolonialzeitung*, 18 September 1887.

Tschudi, Rudolf. "Die Fetwa des Schejch-ül-Islâm über die Erklärung des heiligen Krieges, nach dem Tanîn, Nummer 2119 vom 15. November 1914." *Islam* 5 (1914): 391–393.

"Übersicht der Presse." *Koloniale Zeitschrift*, 26 October 1905.

"Unsere Schwarzen." *Deutsch-Ostafrikanische Zeitung*, 28 May 1904.

v. C. "Was thun wir Deutsche gegen den Sklavenhandel? Eine Frage an das Gewissen des deutschen Volks." *Deutsche Kolonialzeitung*, 27 June 1891.

Verhandlungen des Deutschen Kolonialkongresses 1902 zu Berlin am 10. und 11. Oktober 1902. Berlin: Dietrich Reimer, 1903.

"Verschiedene Stimmen aus unserem Leserkreise." *Deutsch-Ostafrikanische Zeitung*, 21 March 1903.

Warneck, Gustav. "Zur Abwehr und Verständigung. Ein Wort der Erwiderung auf die Urteile des Herrn Majors von Wißmann über die evangelischen und katholischen Missionen." *Allgemeine Missionszeitschrift* 17 (1890): 337–362.

Wissmann, Hermann von. "Die Bedeutung der Emin Pascha-Expedition für die Erschließung von Afrika." *Deutsche Kolonialzeitung*, 29 September 1888.

Wissmann, Hermann von. *Unter deutscher Flagge quer durch Afrika von West nach Ost. Von 1880 bis 1883 ausgeführt von Paul Pogge und Hermann Wissmann*. Berlin: Verlag von Walther and Apolant, 1888.

Wissmann, Hermann von. *Antwort auf den offenen Brief des Herrn Dr. Warneck über die Thätigkeit der Missionen beider christlichen Confessionen*. Berlin: Verlag von Walther and Apolant, 1890.

Zache, Hans. "Koloniale Eingeborenenpolitik (Fortsetzung)." *Koloniale Zeitschrift*, 20 July 1905.

Catholic missionary associations and the saving of African child slaves in nineteenth-century Germany

Katharina Stornig

ABSTRACT

In the second half of the nineteenth century, German-speaking Europe saw the foundation of some Catholic associations, which campaigned against slavery and the slave trade in parts of North and East Africa and promoted the "saving" of slaves and particularly child slaves by, for instance, ransoming boys and girls, baptizing them, and placing them at Catholic institutions and missionary stations. Examining confession-based antislavery activism in its discursive and practical dimensions, the essay argues that the successful foundation and expansion of these associations was due to both transnational structures and church networks of charity, on the one hand, and the activation and exchange of a particular set of ideas on slavery, abolitionism, Christian superiority, gender, childhood, vulnerability, and innocence, on the other. The essay suggests reexamining the relationship between German Catholicism and slavery by pointing to the various ways in which the movement of people and the circulation of information, ideas, and visions about slaves and/or slavery in parts of Africa motivated charitable acts of praying and giving, thus entering the everyday life-worlds of many Catholics in Germany.

Introduction

Scholars have argued that Germans had only limited contact with slavery throughout the last centuries. As historian Jürgen Osterhammel has explained, although news about slaves and reports about slavery and the slave trade in America, Africa, and the Caribbean were familiar to many people in Germany since the early modern period, for the majority of them "slavery existed elsewhere," and only few Germans were actively involved in the slave trade.[1] Yet the issues of slavery and the slave trade nonetheless concerned some writers and publishers in Germany, who followed abolitionist debates in England, France, and the USA, or German emigrants and missionaries in America, who participated in antislavery campaigns.[2] Focusing on Catholic circles in Germany, this essay introduces another group of Germans that became increasingly involved with (anti)slavery in the second half of the nineteenth century. Contrary to the Protestant abolitionist movement, which had formed in Britain since the late eighteenth century and mainly campaigned against the Atlantic slave trade, Catholic antislavery activism emerged only in the mid-nineteenth century and focused mainly on slavery in Africa. As we will see, Catholic antislavery activism was closely linked to the endeavors of the Church to expand missionary activity on the African continent.

This essay discusses the roles of Catholic missionary associations in nineteenth-century Germany and explores the growing impact of African slavery and antislavery propaganda on the day-to-day lives of German Catholics since the 1850s. It pays particular attention to the ways in which the lower clergy and laypeople in Germany, many of them women, got involved in the issue of slavery and started to mobilize support for slaves in geographically distant Africa. As will be shown, during the second half of the nineteenth century, growing numbers of Catholics not only came to face the topics of slavery and the slave trade in their everyday lives but it also caused them to think and act in specific ways. Mobilized by priests, laypeople and/or associations, many Catholic parishioners became active on the behalf of African slaves on a regular basis, for instance, by making donations or praying for their rescue. While the histories of slavery and abolitionism have received broad scholarly attention in the last decades, most studies have tended to focus on the activities of white men and a few white women in eighteenth- and early nineteenth-century Britain and America. Even though the scope of research has recently been broadened with regard to both the geographies and actors of antislavery campaigns, this field of study is still marked by disproportionate attention paid to the activities of secular and Protestant groups in Atlantic contexts. It has only been very recently that historians have taken an interest in nineteenth-century campaigns against slavery in Africa (and particularly East Africa), which were not only driven by missionary endeavors but also by colonial aspirations and what historian Amalia Ribi Forclaz, pointing to the intricate entanglement of imperial and humanitarian concerns in this movement, has aptly termed "humanitarian imperialism."[3]

This essay aims to contribute to this historiography by studying the case of German Catholics. It argues that the expansion of Catholic antislavery activism was basically inspired by both transnational Church networks spanning from Germany to Southern Europe and parts of Africa on the one hand and the transfer of a set of ideas and narratives on slavery and abolitionism from North America on the other. Catholic antislavery activism in Germany cannot be studied within a national framework of analysis, for it relied on connections, traditions, exchanges, transfers, and circulations that well transcended national and continental borders. In other words, the essay shows that Catholic antislavery activism was in fact constructed between movements and transfers in various sites in different regions.[4] As we will see, it relied heavily on references to abolitionist ideas, writings and narratives as they had emerged in Atlantic contexts and with reference to slavery in North America. Although the Catholic movement against slavery in fact focused mostly on Africa, its proponents referred to American abolitionist literature and promoted gendered forms of well-proven activism in Britain and the USA. Besides, the German campaigns formed in a geographical space that transcended both the nation-state and the empire after 1871 and 1884, respectively. Catholic networks of advocacy spanned from Germany to Southern Europe (i.e., Italy) and encompassed missionary infrastructures in several parts of Africa.

Nineteenth-century Catholic antislavery activism not only referenced transatlantic abolitionism but also connected to a long-standing tradition of dealing with slavery in the encounter between Christians and Muslims in the Mediterranean. While some early publications by Catholic activists still contained occasional critiques of Christian slavery in America,[5] such positions largely disappeared after 1865, and authors increasingly located slavery in Africa and deliberately turned it into an "Arab" and/or "Muslim" institution. Scholars have shown that the nineteenth century not only saw abolitionism but also the consolidation of a powerful narrative according to which "civilized" Christians battled slavery among "barbarian" Muslims.[6] This line of thought is part of a European discourse on "barbarianism" and "civilization," which tended to neglect both the history of Christian slavery and the activities of non-Christian antislavery activists. The associations studied in this essay contributed to the European perception of a so-called civilizing mission.[7] They (re)produced depictions of slavery that frequently entailed generalizing and racializing references to Muslims as "lascivious" and "fanatic confessors of the Koran" who, in their capacity as the largest slaveholders in Africa, also used their position of power to impose their faith on their slaves.[8]

Catholic activists deliberately looked to older Christian ways of dealing with slavery in the Mediterranean world, by for instance reviving the old practice of ransoming. In early modern times, both Christians and Muslims had built institutions in order to fund and organize the buyback of enslaved members of their own communities.[9] In the nineteenth century, Catholic activists revived this practice and extended it to non-Christian Africans and particularly to African children, whom they strove to free and raise in Catholic institutions. Even though many secular abolitionists rejected ransoming and considered it a continuation or even promotion of the slave trade,[10] the practice was greatly expanded in nineteenth-century missionary contexts.[11] Rather than engaging in political campaigns, Catholic activists focused on liberating slave children and on what they considered improving their lives. Needless to say, their activities were highly paternalistic, for the freed slaves were not asked about their own plans after liberation. Rather, they entered new forms of social dependency in Catholic institutions, where they were subjected to missionary authority and expected to become pious Catholics. German Catholics promoted Christianization as the only way to achieve abolition, and they conceived of freed slave children as the most promising starting point for that. According to this logic, it was the former slaves, who, raised by missionaries and in a Christian spirit, would eventually abolish slavery on the African continent.[12]

Yet given that, for most Germans, slavery happened in distant lands and affected people who did not belong to their religious, social, or ethnic group, we may still ask why many of them were not only increasingly concerned with the issue but also willing to actively support slaves. This essay also highlights the mobilizing power of slave narratives (many of which came from North America) as well as the great importance of the figure of the innocent, helpless, and suffering child slave in Catholic antislavery discourse and practice, which was constructed as a main object of compassion and gained emotional power along with a set of values that had emerged around nineteenth-century ideals of (gendered) parenting and the family.[13] In that sense, the essay aims to demonstrate the significance that distant slavery acquired for the everyday lives of many Catholics in Germany as well as the ways in which it influenced German society at large. It is divided into three parts. First, I examine the formation of Catholic antislavery activism and highlight the importance of transnational church networks spanning from Germany to Italy, and eventually to East Africa, facilitating the flow of ideas, information, and money across national and continental borders. Second, I ask for the ways in which constructions of gender featured in (anti)slavery writing and I explore how German-speaking authors used references to American abolitionism as well as to specific ideas on family, parenting, and childhood in their discussion of what they termed "African slavery." Third, I examine the quotidian involvement of German Catholics with slavery on a practical level by considering the ways in which they aimed at providing relief to enslaved children in geographically distant Africa. As I will point out, the Catholic recourse to ransoming and its success in fundraising campaigns produced an increasing focus on the individual child, which then became an important feature of methods of humanitarian fundraising in the twentieth century.

The formation of Catholic antislavery activism in Germany

In the nineteenth century, it was not uncommon for missionaries, merchants, or diplomats to buy young boys and/or girls on the slave markets in Northeast Africa and send some of them to Europe, where the children were placed either in religious institutions or in private households.[14] Osterhammel discusses the story of one child named Djalo, who, born, raised, and enslaved in Southern Sudan, became the possession of the Bavarian King at the age of about 12 in 1838.[15] At that time, the presence of African children at German courts or in religious institutions was no exception.[16] Several former slave children had arrived through semi-organized channels and in the company of Catholic priests, who sought to save them both spiritually and physically. Between 1847 and 1864, the Genovese priest Nicolò Olivieri (1792–1864) ransomed about 800 girls on the slave markets of Ottoman Egypt and brought them to Europe, where he distributed the children across more than 100 different convents in Italy, France, Austria, and Germany.[17]

While many of the former slave girls soon died due to the strains of traveling, poor nutrition, disease, and problems when trying to adapt to the European climate, the surviving girls were to some extent also visible in the German public. The few existing studies on the experiences of former slave girls in German-speaking Europe suggest that the local populations were curious about the girls' arrival and some people actively participated in their education.[18] Some residents contributed to the girls' maintenance by giving alms and presents.[19] The reports published by Olivieri claimed that, along the travel routes, inhabitants not only came to see the former slaves but also took great interest in their appearance and well-being. To give but one example, in 1857 he stated that, making his way with some ransomed girls to Munich through Northern Italy and Tyrol, the "poor Negresses" were treated with "compassion" and "attitudes of charity" everywhere.[20] Accordingly, the traveling group not only received food, clothes, and money from the resident Catholics but was also locally accommodated free of charge.

In the second half of the nineteenth century, growing numbers of Germans took interest in former slave children, and some even contributed to the funding of redemptions, travels, and maintenance. In Cologne, the activities of Italian priests like Olivieri even inspired the foundation of a specific organization destined to the saving of child slaves in 1852. Significantly, it was the explicit task of the *Hilfsverein zur Unterstützung der armen Negerkinder* (Aid Organization for the Support of Poor Negro Children) to raise funds for the ransoming of slave children in Ottoman Egypt and Sudan as well as their subsequent upbringing and maintenance in Catholic institutions (i.e., women's convents) in Europe and North Africa.[21] According to the vision promoted, the rescued slaves, once they reached adulthood, should return to their native lands and become key agents in the aspired-to Christianization of Africa.[22] The *Hilfsverein*, just like many other Catholic associations at that time, massively resorted to the religious press as well as to the distribution of leaflets and pamphlets with the goal of raising awareness and mobilizing support for freeing child slaves in Africa.[23] It translated the writings of the Italian priests mentioned, published and distributed fundraising appeals, and issued annual reports, which contained addresses to readers, letters from Africa-based missionaries, short biographical notes of the children saved and lists of donations. While it was precisely through these publications that slavery in Africa became an issue in German parishes since the 1850s, the very existence of the *Hilfsverein* and its connection to Italy-based child savers and Africa-based missionaries enabled German Catholics to actually do something against what they increasingly rejected as the cruel and immoral treatment of human beings and particularly children in distant Africa. More and more Germans contributed, and increasing funds went to Italy and parts of Africa on a regular basis. Already in 1856, the board of the *Hilfsverein* claimed that "all Germany" participated in the association.[24] According to the annual report published in 1863, the *Hilfsverein* had collected about 3000 thalers among Catholics in the dioceses of Cologne, Breslau, Chur, Culm, Eichstätt, Warmia, Freiburg, Litoměřice, Limburg, Lüttich, Mainz, Münster, Olomouc, Osnabrück, Paderborn, Roermond, Rottenburg, Saxony, Sankt Pölten, and Trier, and forwarded the money to Italian priests serving in Africa.[25] In 1917, President Baum stated that by then the Hilfsverein had send more than 750,000 marks to Africa.[26]

The founding of the *Hilfsverein* cannot be separated from both the Catholic endeavors to missionize in Africa and the spread of abolitionist ideas and practices. Given that the Vatican had created the vast Vicariate Apostolic *Africa Centrale* in 1846, Catholic missionaries strove to extend missionary work from Upper Egypt southwards. Protected by the Habsburg monarchy, generations of priests, who came from a range of places in today's Slovenia, Poland, Austria, Italy, Canada, and Germany, took up missionary work in the territories of what was then Egyptian Sudan.[27] Abolitionism constituted a point of reference from the beginning, because already the first missionaries named both the "evangelization of the Negroes" and their "liberation from the horrors of slavery" as major goals.[28] Branding slavery and the slave trade as a "stain on humanity," the proponents of the *Hilfsverein* also deliberately set out to deconstruct long-standing Christian legitimations of the enslavement of Africans, such as, for instance, certain interpretations of Noah's Curse in the Old Testament (Genesis 9:25–26).[29] In Ottoman Egypt, slavery was legally practiced until the late nineteenth century.[30] In combination with the drive to reach what missionaries called the spiritual liberation of Africans, the ongoing existence of slavery led to stronger activism on the part of Catholic actors, for whom slavery paradoxically presented both an immoral institution to be abolished and a useful link allowing them to legitimize broad interventions in local religious, social, and political relations.[31] Significantly, by the mid-nineteenth century, most missionaries particularly focused on the saving of child slaves, a strategy that was inspired by the practical need to fill missionary classrooms as well as their perception of children as the most helpless, needy, and malleable group of enslaved Africans.[32] By ransoming slave children, the missionaries and their supporters in Germany also hoped to achieve the education of a first generation of native missionaries, who would contribute to both the proselytization of the continent and the abolition of slavery.

As indicated, during the 1850s, the *Hilfsverein* mainly supported the activities of Italian priests, who ransomed slave children and moved them to convents in today's Italy, France, Austria, and Germany. Besides, it raised funds for the education of freed children in the so-called *Collegi dei moretti* (Colleges of the little Negros) established in Naples and Verona. Since the mid-1860s, the *Hilfsverein* mostly promoted and funded the activities of Daniele Comboni (1831–1881), another well-known Italian priest and missionary.[33] Unlike Olivieri, Comboni had first-hand experience of Central Africa and spoke not only Arabic but also some African languages.[34] As a much-traveled man, he had actually participated in expeditions and missionary work in Egypt and the Sudan, where he was to become bishop in Khartoum in 1877. Comboni was a prominent expert on the region as well as a fierce critic of slavery and the slave trade. He propagated the Christianization of Africans as the most effective means against what he referred to as "African" slavery. The *Hilfsverein* not only corresponded with Comboni but also translated and distributed his writings to German audiences.

In 1864, Daniele Comboni presented his *Piano per la rigenerazione dell'Africa* (Plan for the regeneration of Africa).[35] He did so in view of the experience of repeated setbacks that had marked missionary work in Central Africa so far: Due to the upheavals as well as the frequent sickness and death of many missionaries, the mission had almost died down. Comboni thus claimed that Africa was to be converted by native missionaries. Contrary to Olivieri who had moved the ransomed children to Europe, Comboni promoted their education in Catholic centers to be established in North Africa. He particularly aimed at establishing Catholic homes for the freed boys and girls of his vast Vicariate in Egypt, where all children should receive religious instruction and gender-specific training. According to individual talent and inclination, the boys were expected to become "able catechists," "teachers," or "artists." In turn, the girls were to be instructed in domestic duties and to receive an education which would help them to become Catholic mothers and "virtuous women," who could then work in girls' welfare and education.[36]

Comboni promoted his ideas internationally. He presented the *Piano* not only to high clergymen in Italy but also to the proponents of the *Hilfsverein* in Cologne. Acknowledging the *Hilfsverein* as an important source of funding, he visited the city several times in order to discuss his ideas in person. In 1867, the proponents of the *Hilfsverein*, who had already celebrated Comboni as a highly educated and cosmopolitan figure during earlier visits,[37] approved of his *Piano* and committed themselves to subsidizing its enactment with an annual sum of 5000 francs. Besides, they provided Comboni with a broad promotional platform by regularly translating, printing, and distributing his texts and reports, many of which not only treated the issue of slavery but also presented Catholic measures against it to a German readership.[38]

However, the activities of the *Hilfsverein* were only the beginning of organized Catholic antislavery activism in Germany. As scholars have pointed out, it was mainly due to the mobilizing campaign launched by Cardinal Lavigerie (1825–1892), the French archbishop of Carthage and Algiers and founder of the *Missionnaires d'Afrique*, that international antislavery activism experienced a revival and shifted its attention toward East Africa since the late 1880s.[39] After organizing the public pilgrimage of French missionaries and ransomed slaves to Rome in 1888, Lavigerie not only appealed to Pope Leo XIII but also addressed the European public in general. His campaign affected German Catholics in mainly two respects: First, the pope issued the encyclical *In Plurimis* and in doing so set both the abolition of slavery and the organization of relief for slaves on the agenda of the Church worldwide.[40] Leo XIII put the issue of antislavery in charge of the Roman Sacred Congregation for the Propagation of the Faith, the Catholic ministry responsible for missionary work, and requested all Africa-based missionaries to engage in ransoming.[41] The pope moreover decreed that all churches worldwide should hold an annual collection in the name of antislavery on the feast of Epiphany. Slavery thus became a regular topic in many churches worldwide and the sources clearly demonstrate that the German dioceses contributed much to these collections.[42] Interestingly, while, according to the Papal decree, the money was to be sent to the Roman Congregation that was to distribute it centrally, the dioceses of Bavaria received special permission to directly hand the sizable antislavery-donations over to the Ottilien Congregation, a Bavarian missionary order.[43] Founded in 1884, the Ottilien Congregation was the first Catholic mission-sending order established on the territory of the *Kaiserreich*.[44] In 1887, it took up missionary work in what had become German East Africa in 1884 and thus in a region that many Europeans had come to consider central to the African slave trade because of its proximity to the infamous slave market in Zanzibar as well as widespread fears of Islamization.[45] For Bavarian Catholics, donating money for African slaves had thus become embedded in a national framework, for their funds were handed over to a local institution, whose activities concentrated on a German colony.

Second, Lavigerie's campaign fueled antislavery activism more generally, for the cardinal visited several European capitals, where he spoke at congresses, lectured in churches, organized donations, and raised awareness through extensive publishing. Given that he was not able to travel to Germany, he addressed the president of the *Deutscher Katholikentag* (German Catholic Congress), which held a session in Freiburg in 1888. Lavigerie's requests were heard in German-speaking Europe: His campaign inspired the foundation of some hundreds of initiatives,[46] among them the *Afrika-Verein deutscher Katholiken* (Africa Association of German Catholics) in Cologne and the St. Petrus Claver-Sodality in Salzburg. While the former operated in an imperial framework and enjoyed some success throughout Germany,[47] the latter developed into an internationally successful fundraising venture.

In contrast to the nationally oriented *Afrika-Verein*,[48] the St. Petrus Claver Sodality insisted on the supranational character of Catholic antislavery.[49] Established by the Austrian-born aristocrat Maria Theresia Ledóchowska (1863–1922) in the late 1880s, the Sodality was composed of nuns and lay members who regularly worked and/or donated money for the association's goals. Ledóchowska, who took religious vows herself, opened a printing press near Salzburg and started to build a huge publishing enterprise, which edited books, periodicals, and leaflets not only for promotional campaigns in Europe but also for missionary use in Africa. Establishing branches in Austria, Italy, Switzerland, Germany, and France, the Sodality issued literature in several languages, used modern technologies (e.g., halftone printing, photography) and distributed periodicals in high circulation, promoting antislavery activism and missionary activity to different target audiences (e.g., women or children). In its principle periodical entitled *Echo aus Afrika* (*Echo from Africa*), Ledóchowska reported on antislavery politics and activities all over Europe and emphasized the importance of the voluntary commitment and contribution of many.[50] She invited her readers to fund ransoms, and printed emotional accounts of lives in slavery and the rescue of slaves. Distributing the *Echo* on a monthly basis, the Sodality used the periodical to communicate with donors and to keep them posted about recent developments and achievements. Containing both supposed eyewitness reports from several parts of Africa as well as letters from readers in Europe, it created the impression of an open platform of transnational communication between donors, Catholic institutions, missionaries, and rescued slaves.

The St. Petrus Claver Sodality was considered a highly successful undertaking, for it raised considerable funds and distributed them internationally.[51] It was particularly foundress Ledóchowska herself who advanced her ideas and visions through extensive traveling and publishing. She wrote and published vast quantities of texts (plays, stories, periodicals, leaflets, pamphlets, literature for children, illustrated postcards, sermons, etc.) and gave speeches in Austria-Hungary, Germany, Switzerland, and Italy. The Sodality published accounts of Ledóchowska's extensive promotional tours, which, to give the example of the year 1907, led her to Venice, Trieste, Klagenfurt, Linz, Munich, Berlin, Hildesheim, Muenster, Hamm, Cologne, Aachen, Luxembourg City, Trier, Metz, Strasbourg, Freiburg, and Basel.[52] The Sodality set up slide shows and (traveling) exhibitions in many places, and established small museums displaying objects from all parts of Africa.[53] In 1900, Ledóchowska co-organized an anti-slavery congress in Vienna, which was attended by approximately 2000–3000 persons, most of them members of Catholic orders and organizations.[54] In the speech she gave at the congress, Ledóchowska introduced the "Catholic missions" as the "true liberators" of "the unhappy Negro slaves,"[55] and left no doubts about the confessional base of this enterprise: Given that "the whole antislavery movement is necessarily connected to the missions," Ledóchowska stated, there "can be no interconfessionality."[56] The Catholic foundation of the St. Petrus Claver Sodality was, moreover, reinforced by its close connection to Rome and its subordination to the Congregation for the Propagation of the Faith. Ledóchowska, who soon relocated to Rome and had family connections to the high clergy,[57] communicated on a regular basis not only with the Congregation but also with donors all over Europe and many missionaries in all parts of Africa.[58] She used large parts of this correspondence to the end of fundraising, inasmuch as she printed many of the letters in her periodicals. Taken together, the Sodality indeed reached a transnational Catholic public that was obviously perceptive to Ledóchowska's vision of religious antislavery activism. In Europe, her writings and her activism were received widely and appreciated also by some male activists, who took her and others as examples to celebrate what they perceived as the natural nurturing qualities of women.[59]

Gender in Catholic antislavery discourse and practice

Constructions of gender obviously mattered to Ledóchowska's early activities. Interestingly, while she had published her first works under the male pseudonym of Alexander Halka, she soon began to write under her own name. Ledóchowska also explained her activism in gendered terms: Despite her initial lack of interest in the issue of (anti)slavery, she was "deeply moved" when, in a brochure by Cardinal Lavigerie, she read about "the atrocities of slavery" and "the physical and moral agony of the poor Negroes in Africa."[60] In this text, Lavigerie had explicitly addressed women, inviting them to participate in the movement and reminding female readers "that it had been the book by a woman – Uncle Tom's Cabin – that had given cause for the abolition of slavery in America."[61] Ledóchowska later claimed that reading these words had been a key experience, for she took them as an encouragement to move to action. As she would recall during a speech in 1900: "I decided to dedicate my pen to the liberation of the poor Negros in Africa from the double chains of slavery."[62] This sentence highlights Ledóchowska's religious approach to slavery, which aimed at both the spiritual liberation of Africans from what she perceived as the chains of "heathendom" and their freeing from worldly bondage. The sentence also refers to the deep impact that Lavigerie's message had left on her. As a consequence, Ledóchowska indeed left her position as a court lady in Salzburg and dedicated her life to what she perceived as the saving of Africa and Africans. What comes as no surprise is that much of her subsequent writing addressed women in general and women writers in particular. Following the example of its founder, the St. Petrus Claver Sodality generally promoted women's participation in antislavery activism in gendered terms.

Ledóchowska promoted writing as a prime means by which women could actively contribute to the Catholic cause in Africa. While her texts promoted charity as a major (and traditional) female missionary activity,[63] they also stressed the importance of writing and publishing as key promotional activities in order to advance Catholic antislavery efforts and to drum up spiritual and material support for slaves and missionaries in Africa. To this end, Ledóchowska particularly invited educated women to join her Sodality. Given that the Sodality published books and periodicals in several languages, she indeed needed both talented writers and members with foreign language skills. The main periodicals of the Sodality, the *Echo aus Africa* and *Das Negerkind*, appeared in monthly intervals not only in German but also in Italian, French, Polish, Hungarian, Czech, Slovakian, and English.[64] Skilled writers were thus greatly needed. Given that the core of the Sodality consisted of a branch of nuns, Ledóchowska was able to place her organization in a long-standing Catholic tradition of female intellectual work as it was cultivated in women's convents over centuries. In a promotional booklet addressed to women readers and potential candidates, Ledóchowska announced the maxim: "[B]etter a strong spirit and a weak body than a weak spirit and a strong body."[65]

Pointing to the often stressful workflow at the Sodality that authored, edited and printed large quantities of text on a regular basis, Ledóchowska described the major tasks performed by the members as "intellectual and mechanical works."[66] While the founder stressed that the Sodality needed all types of diligent and talented women, those working as authors were still the most wanted candidates, because, for advertising purposes, "literary works" continued to define the professed core activity of members.[67] According to Ledóchowska's understanding, she and her co-workers, engaging in promotional activities and fundraising at home, were important "assistants" to the male missionaries in the African field.[68] This gendered conception of activism was widespread in Catholic missionary circles at that time. To give but one example, on the occasion of the foundation of a women's association for the mission in Central Africa in Düsseldorf in 1893, the supporting letter by a noblewoman from Breslau envisioned women's possibilities for engagement in benevolent work as follows: "I am not rich in money and property myself, but I have a heart, a tongue and a pen [...]."[69] Prevailing gender norms also impacted the ways in which priests referred to Ledóchowska's engagement in antislavery, for they repeatedly referred to her as the "mother of the Negroes" or the "mother of the missionaries."[70]

Constructions of gender and appeals to motherhood or motherly attitudes formed an important feature in Leodóchwska's writing more generally. This was, for instance, the case when she addressed women directly as mothers or when she invited them to contribute to the mission cause by sewing and donating clothes for freed slaves.[71] She thus resumed an earlier discourse of aid and assistance that had marked antislavery writing since the mid-nineteenth century more generally. This was also the case for earlier Catholic associations, which likewise made use of highly sentimental notions of childhood and family.[72] In this discourse of filial neediness and adult (i.e., parental) support, the figure of the helpless and lonely child slave played a vital role, for it was used in order to trigger parental (and particularly maternal) sentiments in readers, which would eventually produce an active response.[73] Some promotional texts ended in a direct appeal to readers, who were primarily addressed as parents and especially as mothers. For instance, in 1891, Ledóchowska published in the *Echo aus Africa* a highly emotional serial story entitled "Das Scapulier des Sclaven" ("The Slave's Scapular") about a boy christened Paulus, who has been enslaved and resold by an Arab slave trader together with his mother and several others.[74] At some point, a Catholic priest approaches the caravan of slaves, for he, deeply affected by this "heartbreaking view," seeks to ransom as many slaves as possible. The story reaches a first climax when the priest realizes that he has only enough money left to ransom the mother but not the son. Although Paulus, as a good son and pious Catholic, is glad to know his mother will be safe, the woman is desperate when she sees her son being sold off into slavery. Her "mother's heart was broken" in view of the separation from her son and his desolate future in the hands of cruel slave traders.[75] At that point, Ledóchowska points to the ruptures of family life and mother–child relationships caused by slavery and explicitly addresses her female readers as mothers:

> Oh, you mothers of the civilized world, as you already think to withstand pain of separation when the doors of a reformatory close behind your child for some months, you, who want to despair when God takes one of your beloved to his angels, think of the mother of Paulus and don't be distressed in view of the small gifts that you give to the association for Africa! God will reward your own children for what you did for the unhappy Negroes![76]

In this passage, the author appealed to Catholic mothers by drawing on a supposedly universal feeling of maternal pain when experiencing the separation from or loss of children. In the story, she neither approaches slavery in terms of rights nor does she elaborate on slavery as a fundamental moral wrong. Instead, similar to several abolitionist authors in the USA,[77] she introduces the issue through the story of a mother–son relationship, which is disrupted by the institution of slavery and its agents, and thereby appeals to motherhood and motherly love as key values. That way, she appeals to the identification and compassion of readers, by urging them to see how the brutal reality of slavery renders loving mother–child relationships impossible.

Comparable to many other stories printed in the *Echo aus Africa*, "Das Scapulier des Sclaven" presents the Catholic practice of ransoming individual slaves as a means to re-establish some type of family or, more frequently, to create social relationships that replaced parental care and supervision through the establishment of Catholic orphanages or children's homes. In this type of narrative, priests often emerge as some type of fatherly figure, who take on responsibility for the education and well-being of the children they have ransomed. Sentimental notions of family and parent–child relationships constituted key features in nineteenth-century Catholic antislavery writing. Already the *Hilfsverein* had described the saving of child slaves in terms of parenthood. This can be observed in the fact that its authors consistently used the notion of fatherhood in order to label the actions of priests like Olivieri and Comboni. In 1863, the annual report of the *Hilfsverein* described their ransoming activities and praised them as "relentless fathers of the Negroes."[78] Here, fatherhood referred to both male custody and authority over children, who had come into filial positions through an economic transaction. Although missionary zeal constituted a crucial drive behind the activities of priests, in popular writing, antislavery activism was often advocated in a language of loving and caring attitudes toward children.

The *Hilfsverein* presented itself as an institution providing "care and love for the children of the heathens."[79] A promotional article in the Würzburg-based *Katholische Wochenschrift* (1856) claimed that "the care of Christian love" was the best cure for "the wounds that rough slavery had inflicted on these children."[80] Considering sociologist Viviane Zelizer's well-known argument that, in the nineteenth century, Western societies invested children with great symbolic value and emotional charge, we understand that this new ideology of childhood also entered Catholic antislavery discourse.[81] The *Hilfsverein* drew on contemporary ideals of childhood and emphasized the growing importance of the happiness of children: "[…] we don't claim too much when we state that these children are as happy in their new situations as they were miserable and abandoned earlier."[82]

According to this logic, slave children in Africa especially needed the protection and care provided by Catholic adults and institutions from Europe and specifically Germany. Several texts, whether explicitly or not, suggested that African adults (including parents) and institutions were unable or unwilling to protect African children from being captured in slave raids. Authors often drew on sentimental language as it had also been used in the genre of female slave narratives in North America. Kidnapped by cruel slave raiders at an early age and separated from their families, the *Hilfsverein* referred to the slave children as "most unhappy human beings."[83] Some texts provided emotional narratives of child slaves who had entered into a life marked by the "certainty of never meeting the affectionate gaze of the mother again, never sharing domestic joys again, and of going forever without spending time with the beloved siblings."[84] Other texts stressed the total abandonment of child slaves and their need of missionary support by claiming that, in some cases, cruel parents had actively sold their sons or daughters into servitude.[85] In both narrative strands, the *Hilfsverein* explicitly appealed to Catholics in Germany to imagine themselves as substitute parents of slave children, "who are particularly in need of fatherly and motherly love."[86] Writers thus appealed to a set of values and emotions with which Western notions of family and parent–child relationships had become closely associated in the nineteenth century.[87] At the same time, the *Hilfsverein* suggested that the enslavement of children occurred in parts of Africa due to the general lack of adult protection. Some authors stressed that enslavement could happen to anybody, by addressing their readers directly and inviting them to identify with slave children: "Oh reader, how would that be, if you […] had been snatched away from the arms of your parents, abducted into sordid slavery […]?"[88]

It thus does not seem surprising that due to its emphasis on family values and parenting, the *Hilfsverein* received considerable funding and support from women. The association's 1859 annual report stated that it was "particularly women who had shown charity towards the ransomed" children.[89] In the same vein, a report from 1866 celebrated the support for slave children provided by female members.[90] In addition, the *Hilfsverein* not only referred to Harriet Beecher Stowe's famous and widely read novel but also drew on its gender-specific reception: Claiming that female readers of *Uncle Tom's Cabin* had "shed streams of tears,"[91] the *Hilfsverein* assessed its impact on readers in Germany in 1859 (seven years after the appearance of the first German edition[92]) as follows:

> Just a few years ago, the horrible descriptions of an American writer caused great sensation in the civilized world and just compassion for the slaves in free America. How many tears have been shed in the boudoirs of sensitive ladies on whose reading tables the famous book *Uncle Tom's Cabin* was to be found […]![93]

While the passage shows once more how antislavery activism relied on female writers and readers, it also suggests that women, due to what nineteenth-century discourses of femininity constructed as women's supposedly natural role as caretaker, were especially compassionate with suffering slaves in general and child slaves in particular. Scholars have pointed to the ways in which social constructions of gender and historical debates on natural order and gender relations led to the association of masculinity and femininity with different attitudes and sets of emotions. Nineteenth-century scientists naturalized gender differences and declared male and female social roles and standards of behavior natural propensities.[94] Most prominently, historian Karin Hausen has explored the formation of polarized characterizations of the sexes in European thought.[95] Accordingly, for many thinkers of the nineteenth century, women's sphere of activity became located in the home due to what was considered their highly emotional, responsive, and passive nature. This is significant, because such a historical understanding of the "nature" of women turned them into main target audiences of Catholic writers, who expected female readers to actively respond to highly emotional reports about the suffering of child slaves.

Tackling at one point explicitly the issue of slavery in Christian America, the *Hilfsverein* also approached female readers as domestic consumers: A report in 1859 stated that many products imported from the New World, such as, for instance, rice, coffee, sugar, and cotton, "were plastered with the blood, sweat, and tears of this long-suffering human race."[96] In this passage, the *Hilfsverein* addressed women not only as particularly compassionate human beings but also as persons in charge of domestic spaces and thus economically powerful consumers. It thus connected to discourses and practices of consumer activism that were by then well established in the antislavery movement in Britain and the USA. Already since the 1790s, Quaker women in Britain had used their transatlantic networks and family ties to organize and advertise first consumer boycotts of slave-produced goods (e.g., sugar and cotton). Like male activists, they contributed to a gendered discourse that connected women's domestic choices to the suffering of their enslaved counterparts.[97] As sociologist Mimi Sheller has argued, during the late eighteenth and early nineteenth centuries, antislavery activists in Britain and the USA paved the way for the emergence of "a new culture of ethical consumption," which was obviously not unknown to the proponents of the *Hilfsverein*, who drew on a very similar imagery, such as, for instance, the powerful and widely circulated image of slave-produced commodities soaked with blood.[98]

Taken together, constructions of gender and gendered mores featured very prominently in the ways in which Catholic associations criticized slavery in Muslim societies in

Africa more generally. In this context, several authors (re)produced racialized stereotypes of Arab men and expressed essentialist statements about gender relations in Islam. They described girls and women as the victims of oversexualized men and some reports referenced the warning example of the harem, where slave girls would become "the unfortunate instrument of sin [of] the shameful excesses of the Mussulmen."[99] Such reports contributed to the construction of essentialist stereotypes in which sexual mores, gender relations, and racialized notions of Muslims featured as key issues.

Modes of generating support for African slaves and aid practices

As stated earlier, Catholic associations drew not only on narratives but also on familiar practices of aid and assistance in order to mobilize the German public. Generally speaking, they added much to the idea of a European-Christian civilizing mission in Africa, for they distributed several types of paradigmatic texts explaining the phenomenon and current state of slavery and printed numerous (eye witness) reports penned by missionaries based in Africa. As such, missionaries not only advised church leaders in Rome on antislavery activism and politics but also published corresponding texts, fictive narratives, and interventionist appeals in popular genres and for large audiences. Both the *Hilfsverein* and the St. Petrus Claver Sodality constructed Arabs and/or Muslim men as cruel, greedy, and barbarian slavers, whereby religious, social, and racial attributions intersected. To give but one example, in a fictitious "historical" account published in 1902, the *Echo aus Africa* explained that, in East Africa, "the Arab" had failed to acknowledge Africans as fellow human beings, because firstly the Koran allowed him to enslave others and secondly he was "too lazy and idle to work the land" himself.[100]

These types of texts often not merely neglected the history of Christian slavery but rather warned of the expansion of Islam and presented Christianity as the only effective means to advance abolition in Africa. The perceived expansion of Islam, particularly in colonies such as German East Africa, fueled Islamophobia in many missionary circles in Germany and elsewhere.[101] During the last decades of the nineteenth century, the religious and moral language of Christian (and particularly Catholic) antislavery activism also contributed to a language of imperial responsibilities and colonial conquest. This trend gained momentum from the activities of Cardinal Lavigerie, who not only provided arguments to colonialists[102] but also openly promoted abolition and Christianization "with [both] the cross and the sword."[103] The St. Petrus Claver Sodality distributed similar arguments to large numbers of Catholic readers. In addition, the Sodality, just like other Christian associations at that time, promoted the well-known practice of ransoming with which Catholic actors had dealt with Muslim slavery for a long time.

The history of ransoming goes back to the taking of slaves in piracy, wars, and raids in the Mediterranean world since the Middle Ages. Institutionally, it was based on the organized practice of buying fellow Christians off the hands of Muslims and vice versa. In early modern Europe, ransoming was organized according to the captives' origin, because most communities engaged in the Mediterranean trade developed special institutions which organized financial and logistic support for enslaved compatriots. In Southern Europe, special orders, such as the Trinitarians or the Gonfalons, existed for this purpose.[104] In Northern Europe, trading communities like the Hanse towns set up institutions designed to purchase the freedom of captured fellow citizens.[105] At any rate, ransoming institutions collected money at home in order to arrange the manumission of fellow people in distant countries. In the Christian context, the idea of ransoming had biblical connotations and, as the Latin etymology of the word indicates, alluded to the religious promise of salvation.[106] Ransoming had taken on a high symbolic value; it was a familiar practice to many Europeans and found wide expression in church paintings, literature, and art.[107] It thus seems not surprising that nineteenth-century Catholic activists revitalized ransoming with the goal of drumming up support.

As has been shown, the *Hilfsverein* particularly focused on raising financial, spiritual, and logistic support for the manumission of child slaves. The association relied on ransoming for several reasons. Firstly, it appealed to the sense of Christian solidarity inherent in the tradition of ransoming because it expected that all ransomed individuals would be baptized and subsequently be raised as Catholics. This idea was reinforced by the long-term plan to educate the former slave children and turn them into future missionaries in Africa. Apparently, religion held ground as a basis of transnational support, even though the *Hilfsverein* did not free fellow Christians but, as they put it, "the children of the heathens."[108] Secondly, the *Hilfsverein* revitalized well-established institutions in the field of ransoming and, in doing so, suggested historical continuities. It was the Pope himself who decreed in 1855 that the Trinitarians should support the new Catholic anti-slavery activism. This is indeed significant because the Trinitarian Order had been founded in twelfth-century France for the purpose of ransoming Christian slaves from Turkish bondage. Given that, since the French conquest of Algiers in 1830, its original aim was definitely outdated, Pius IX determined that the order should now support the new ransoming enterprise founded by Olivieri and others.[109] The Pope also transferred the indulgences granted to the supporters of the Trinitarians to all Catholics backing the ransoming of child slaves. Consequently, by circulating this papal advice and by introducing the Trinitarian order and its history to larger audiences, the *Hilfsverein* deliberately suggested long historical continuities with regard to Catholic commitment to (anti)slavery. In 1863, it printed an article according to which already in the twelfth and thirteenth centuries "no Christian heart could remain indifferent in view of the sad destiny of so many Christians who were imprisoned by the savage Saracens."[110] Apart from distinguishing between "Muslim" cruelty and "Christian" sentiments of ransoming, the article explicitly propagated institutional cooperation between the *Hilfsverein* and the Trinitarian order and emphasized their "spiritual connection."[111] Thirdly, by focusing on ransoming, the associations relied on well-established Catholic modes of fundraising. Toward the end of the nineteenth century, the St. Petrus Claver Sodality not only relied on ransoming but also further modernized the practice, by, for instance, publishing stories about ransomed slaves which often gained cogency by the fact that they included both eyewitness reports by Africa-based missionaries and photographic evidence (i.e., portraits of the rescued children).

By informing support groups in Germany about the prices of individual slaves in various parts of Africa, the associations turned aid into a quantifiable good.[112] Slave children and their liberation respectively were presented as commodities, which also acquired spiritual value. According to Catholic doctrine, charitable giving was firmly embedded in a spiritual economy. By funding the ransoming of others, Catholics could become part of a charitable network, which not only connected donors and recipients but also entailed an (imagined) exchange of gratitude, support, indulgences, spiritual rewards, and saving power. Some promotional texts made this explicit, by, for instance, assuring that the ransomed children would certainly pray for their benefactors.[113] In one case, the *Hilfsverein* quoted a missionary who had allegedly stated that "it is a touching sight when these poor children commemorate their benefactors with raised hands and truly heartfelt prayers."[114] The published reports drew on a highly sentimental language, and assured that the ransomed children would obtain spiritual merits for benefactors not only during but also after their lives on earth as intercessors in heaven. However, Catholics in Germany also prayed for children in Africa. The *Hilfsverein* invited its supporters not only to regularly donate money but also to say a Hail Mary every day for the benefit of the "Negro children."[115] Hence, intercession for African children became part of the day-to-day lives of some Catholics in Germany. In an attempt to reinforce a sense of connection between individual donors and the children ransomed with his or her money, the associations entitled the former to choose the baptismal names of the latter. This procedure encouraged the donors to assume some type of transnational sponsorship for the children ransomed and to act as their symbolic godparents.

According to the lists of donations printed by the *Hilfsverein*, many people added names to the donors' roll. In fact, in the 1890s, the sum necessary for the ransoming of an individual slave became a distinct unit in fundraising. The archives of the Roman Congregation show that ordinary Catholics posted exact amounts of money to Rome for the purpose of ransoming a slave.[116] Catholic associations in Germany not only informed their supporters about the prices for boys and girls on African slave markets but also printed and distributed biographical accounts about the lives of ransomed children. This was also the case for some Protestant missions such as the *Norddeutsche Missionsgesellschaft*, which, despite approaching ransoming more critically, participated in this practice well into the 1870s.[117] Interestingly, most institutions promoting ransoming pointed to its great potential for fundraising.[118] The St. Petrus Claver Sodality even posted baptismal certificates and published letters from African children to "godparents" in Europe and thus furthered the idea of individual ties and exchange between the benefactor and the child.[119] Besides, it provided donors with the possibility to finance the education or theological studies of former slaves. This trend is significant, for it shows that Catholic activism increasingly focused on the individual child. It thus initiated what would become a crucial feature of modern humanitarian fundraising in the twentieth century. Indeed, it were Catholic associations who, operating in a more or less formal transnational network between Germany, Italy, and Africa, developed and distributed certain practices of aid, such as transnational child sponsorship, that would vastly expand in the twentieth century and conquer donor markets in many Western countries.

Conclusion

In Germany, Catholic antislavery activism developed under the condition of interaction and exchange between local Catholics, Italian (and French) priests, and Africa-based missionaries of various nationalities. Its formation was shaped by geographically distant events and people as well as by the production and distribution of certain reports and narratives about social realities in parts of Africa. The associations examined in this essay, aiming to raise support for child slaves, relied on religious networks that operated in Germany as well as in various parts of Europe and Africa. It was through these networks that information, ideas, and money circulated. As publishers of periodicals, books, and leaflets, the associations contributed to the production and dissemination of a set of cultural representations, which employed narratives of (anti)slavery from Africa and America and drew on prevalent notions of gender, childhood, vulnerability, and adult–child relationships. Catholic antislavery activists constructed and disseminated the figure of the African child slave that had to be rescued by Catholics in Germany. Indeed, this figure entered the Catholic imagination through narratives of (anti)slavery and acquired mobilizing power. The associations called for social action by promoting both solidarity with child slaves and differentiation from adult Muslims. While they promoted the former as innocent victims in need of foreign assistance, they simultaneously rejected the latter in generalizing terms as cruel slaveholders and traders.

The activities of the associations were indeed significant. They made the involvement with antislavery a quotidian feature for many Catholics in Germany, who not only read about the hardships of slaves in distant Africa (and America) but also regularly prayed and donated money for their liberation. In other words, African slaves (i.e., specific cultural constructions of African slaves) became part of German live worlds, and narratives about the suffering of enslaved children in Africa had the power to mobilize benevolent actions in Germany. Catholic writings, ideas, and practices connected to (anti)slavery and the slave trade entered public and private spaces in Germany. While, in the late nineteenth century, most churches regularly held antislavery collections and the associations organized issue-specific meetings, sermons, and speeches, antislavery literature and media entered also Catholic households. Several people in Germany decided to ransom a slave. They chose names for the children they desired to ransom, and imagined themselves as sponsors, rescuers, or even substitute parents to those children. We may thus well state that Catholic associations emerged as key actors in advancing a specific set of ideas and practices of antislavery to a broad Catholic public in nineteenth-century Germany.

Notes

1. Osterhammel, *Sklaverei*, 7 and 11. However, individual studies have also challenged this argument of the marginal involvement of German traders and manufacturers in the Atlantic slave trade. For instance, see Weber, "Deutschland."
2. Ibid., 11. See also Eckert and Wirz, "Wir nicht, die Anderen auch," 378; Lind, "Africans in Early Modern German Society." A pointed introduction to the ambivalent references to slavery and the slave trade by German (and other) Enlightenment thinkers provides Eckert, "Aufklärung," 243–246.
3. Ribi Forclaz, *Humanitarian Imperialism*; Laqua, "The Tensions." Humanitarian arguments also featured in the Berlin Conference 1884/85. However, as scholars have pointed out, colonial politics with regard to slavery often remained ambivalent, for the European powers also used forced labor and feared social upheavals in the case of a sudden emancipation. See Eckert, "Die Berliner Afrika-Konferenz," 144; Wirz, "Sklavenhandel," 84.
4. Such an approach corresponds to what has been called transnational methods, which, in the words of Isabel Hofmeyr, claim "not simply that historical processes are made in different places but that they are constructed in the movement between places, sites and regions." Bayly et al., "AHR Conversation: On Transnational History," 1444. The analytic value of a transnational approach to German history emphasizes for instance Conrad, "Doppelte Marginalisierung."
5. "Olivieri, die Neger und die Sklavenfrage," 14.
6. Priesching, *Von Menschenfängern*, 1–2; Wirz, "Sklavenhandel," 78.

7. The same has been argued about late nineteenth-century antislavery activists more generally. Laqua, "The Tensions," 707.
8. Carcereri, *Erster ausführlicher Jahresbericht*, 6–7.
9. Priesching, *Von Menschenfängern*, 1–6; Ressel, *Zwischen Sklavenkassen*, 34.
10. For a recent historical and philosophical discussion of the practice of ransoming, see Appiah and Bunzel, *Buying Freedom*.
11. Clarence-Smith, "The Redemption."
12. This shows that, at least theoretically, African converts were assigned key roles in German Catholic institutions. Practically, however, the sources do not tell us much about the roles of native Africans in Catholic antislavery efforts. Still, some German editors published their stories, lauded their contributions, and they never stopped emphasizing the spiritual power of ransomed slaves, who would pray for their liberators during lifetime and act as powerful guardian angels afterwards. However, given that this essay focuses on German involvement with (anti)slavery, the systematic consideration of African agency in this enterprise goes beyond the scope of this essay.
13. In doing so, I broaden the scope of scholarship, which, for a long time, has tended to focus on the figure of the adult male slave. An overview is provided by Campbell, Miers, and Miller, "Editors' Introduction," 1.
14. Slaves were taken to German courts already since the early modern period. Their ambivalent status in the German states, where no legal basis for race-based slavery existed, is discussed by Peter Martin. Martin, *Schwarze Teufel*, 129–181.
15. Osterhammel, *Sklaverei*, 10.
16. Zeller, "Der 'Mohr von Berlin'," 253–260. Besides, African elites also sent their children to Germany for education. See Michels, "West African Families"; Aitken and Rosenhaft, *Black Germany*.
17. See Küppers-Braun, "P. Nicolò Olivieri," 141–144. A study of former slave girls in Bavaria is provided by Zunker, "Drei 'arme Mohrenkinder'."
18. See Küppers-Braun, "P. Nicolò Olivieri," 152–153; Zunker, "Drei 'arme Mohrenkinder'."
19. Sulzbacher, "Beten – dienen – unterhalten," 118–119.
20. Olivieri, *Nona relazione*, 7–8.
21. For an overview on the *Hilfsverein* and its involvement with Olivieri and Verri, see Küppers-Braun, "P. Nicolò Olivieri," 146–151.
22. This was already stated in §1 of the statutes of the association. However, this plan hardly worked out and death rates among the ransomed children were shockingly high. See Küppers-Braun, "P. Nicolò Olivieri," 163. Unfortunately, we know only very little about the lives of the children in Germany. Yet, we know that in 1867 twelve "little Negresses," who had survived the strains of being ransomed, joined an expedition to Cairo, which aimed at rebuilding the Catholic mission in Central Africa. "Bericht über die erste Expedition," 13–39.
23. For instance, in 1856, a promotional article appeared in the *Katholische Wochenschrift*. Besides, in 1870, the *Hilfsverein* published charity appeals in 69 German Catholic journals in Europe and North America. Jonen, Grubenbecher and Bremer, "Verein zur Unterstützung," 389–392; see also "Vorbemerkung," 1–2.
24. Letter from C. Barber to J. von Geissel, Cologne, 19 September 1859. Nachlass Johannes von Geissel, Historisches Archiv des Erzbistums Köln (hereafter AEK), 169.
25. "Rechenschafts-Bericht," 79–92. The development between 1853 and 1864 discusses Küppers-Braun, "P. Nicolò Olivieri," 149–154.
26. Note by I. Baum, July 1917. CR 1 22.19, *AEK*.
27. An excellent survey is provided by McEwan, *A Catholic Sudan*. Even though the mission was in fact started by priests from various countries, its promoters in Germany would soon present it as a German undertaking. See Der Central-Vorstand des Vereines zur Unterstützung der armen Negerkinder. "Aufruf," Cologne, 1870. CR 1 22.19, AEK.
28. See Rohrbacher, "Franz Xaver Logwit-lo-Ladù," 55.
29. For instance, a report of the *Hilfsverein* in 1859 at first openly posed the question, why to aid "the children of this scorned human race, these descendants of Ham, of whom the Holy

Scripture says: [sic] that they should be the servants of the servants of their brothers?" In what followed, the anonymous author deconstructed this view by describing the cruelties of slavery and the suffering of slaves. Eventually, he concluded that God, through his redemptive act had "festively withdrawn" the curse. "Olivieri, die Neger und die Sklavenfrage," 4 and 12. For a more general discussion of this theme, see Priesching, *Von Menschenfängern*, 98–102; Haynes, *Noah's Curse*.

30. An overview is provided by Baer, "Slavery in Nineteenth Century Egypt."
31. Walter Sauer has emphasized the legitimizing function of a rhetoric of antislavery. See Sauer, "Schwarz-Gelb in Afrika," 75.
32. At that time, the ransoming of child slaves also inspired Protestant missionary practice, which likewise related to both missionizing strategies and practices of child saving. See Clarence-Smith, "The Redemption." However, as several studies show, the language of child saving and anti-slavery did not necessarily mean the end of coercion or indentured labor of children. See Koonar, "Using Child Labor." Some studies even state that Christian missionaries also re-sold slave children. See, e.g., Alsheimer, *Zwischen Sklaverei*, 61.
33. The activities and mobilizing campaigns of Daniele Comboni have largely been overlooked by scholars of slavery and abolition in Africa. For instance, Drescher has argued that it was only with Lavigerie's campaign in 1888 that the Catholic hierarchies had started to encourage antislavery action. See Drescher, *Abolition*, 354–355.
34. "Die Erziehungs- und Bildungs-Anstalten," 29.
35. See Comboni, *Piano*; McEwan, *A Catholic Sudan*, 86–99.
36. Ibid.
37. One text introduced Comboni on his visit to Cologne in 1863 admiringly as being a "rare appearance," for he was fluent not only in Italian, Latin, French, German, and Spanish, but also in 13 Arabic and three African dialects and vernaculars. "Die Erziehungs- und Bildungs-Anstalten," 29.
38. In 1866, the *Hilfsverein* printed an essay in which Comboni explained the benefits of his *Piano* against other strategies. Comboni, "Promemoria," 56–57.
39. See Laqua, "The Tensions," 706–7; Miers, *Slavery*, 21.
40. See Ribi Forclaz, *Humanitarian Imperialism*, 17–18.
41. See Clarence-Smith, "The Redemption," 176.
42. Evidence can be found in the annual letters sent by the bishops or nuncios to the Roman Congregation. For instance, in 1901 alone, Cesare Sambucetti, nuncio in Munich, transmitted 2925 marks from the dioceses of Hildesheim, 4100 from Warmia, 450 from Lusatia, and 1417 from Limburg. Besides, he informed Rome that he had forwarded 52,536.69 marks collected in the Bavarian dioceses to the procurator of the Ottilien Congregation. Letters from C. Sambucetti to M. Ledóchowski, Munich, 20 July 1901, Munich, 30 July 1901, Munich, 4 August 1901, St. Ottilien, 16 August 1901 and Munich, 11 November 1901. N.S. (Nuova Serie), The Propaganda Fide Historical Archives (hereafter N.S., APF), Vol. 208, 749, 766, 769, 775 and 820.
43. See letter from B. Lorenzelli to M. Ledóchowski, Munich, 1 July 1898. N.S., APF, Vol. 138, 92.
44. See Egger, "Transnationale Architekturen," 49.
45. The slave market in Zanzibar was closed due to British pressure in 1873. See Glassman, "Racial Violence," 176–7. On (anti)slavery in German East Africa, see Owzar, "The Image," 135–136; Deutsch, *Emancipation*; Mann, *Sahibs*, 67–72.
46. See Bechhaus-Gerst, "'Das finstere Heidenthum'," 113.
47. Ibid., 114.
48. The national and colonial orientation of the *Afrika-Verein* can be observed on basis of the example of its founder Franz Karl Hespers, who demanded the joint intervention of German missionaries and government forces to end slavery in German East Africa. See Horstmann, "Franz Karl Hespers," 117.
49. Although Ledóchowska also knew how to promote the Sodality in national terms, she insisted on its international character and refused to privilege missions of certain national origin. For instance, when some Austrian clergymen attempted to establish an Austrian Missionary Association in 1906 she wholeheartedly argued against it. See letters from M. Th. Ledóchowska

to G. M. Gotti, Rome, 9 February 1906 and Salzburg, 28 June 1906. N.S., APF, Vol. 340, 802–803 and 815–816.
50. The early volumes of the *Echo* contained a rubric entitled "Rundschau" (Review), which informed about antislavery associations all over Europe.
51. For instance, see the Sodality's various annual reports to Rome in N.S., APF, Vol. 340, 804–810; Vol. 484, 173–184; Vol. 586, 456–473.
52. For instance, see "Ueber die heurige Propagandareise."
53. See Sauer, *Expeditionen*, 314–315.
54. See letter from F. Kuefstein to M. Ledóchowski, Viehofen, 27 December 1900. N.S., APF. Vol. 648, 249–251. Moreover, see Laqua, "The Tensions," 708.
55. Ledóchowska, *Die Antisclaverei-Bewegung*, 1.
56. Ibid., 5.
57. Her uncle, Cardinal Ledóchowski, acted as prefect of the Sacred Congregation for the Propagation of the Faith from 1892 to 1902. Besides, her brother Wladimir was a high-ranking Jesuit and her sister Maria Ursula founded a women's congregation. See Bielak, *Maria Theresia Gräfin Ledóchowska*, 5–10.
58. According to a report, in 1918 alone, the Sodality processed 58,937 incoming and 55,034 outgoing letters by/to benefactors (see letter from M. Th. Ledóchowska to W. M. Van Rossum, Zug, 12 April 1919. N.S., APF, Vol. 620, 47). A glimpse of her vast correspondence with individual missionaries in Africa is provided by Gütl, *Adieu*.
59. See Ribi Forclaz, *Humanitarian Imperialism*, 24.
60. See Ledóchowska, *Die Antisclaverei-Bewegung*, 3–4.
61. Ibid., 4.
62. Ibid.
63. See *Die Aufgabe der katholischen Frauen*, 1–2 and 4–5.
64. See letter from M. Th. Ledóchowska to W. M. Van Rossum, Zug, 12 April 1919. N.S., APF, Vol. 620, 47–51.
65. See Ledóchowska, *Der Beruf*, 63.
66. Ibid., 43.
67. *Die Aufgabe der katholischen Frauen*, 12.
68. The reference to the members of the members of the St. Petrus Claver Sodality as "assistant missionaries" (*Hilfsmissionärinnen*) can be found in many publications.
69. Ultimately, she also added her pious and wealthy husband as another feature to this list. Appendix IV, letter from J. Schaaf to M. Ledóchowski, Steyl, 29 April 1893. N.S., APF, Vol. 10, 118.
70. *Die Aufgabe der katholischen Frauen*, 16.
71. For instance, see the reports in "Chronik der St. Petrus Claver-Sodalität," 12–14.
72. See Stornig, "Figli della chiesa," 82–83.
73. Laura Suski has proposed analyzing humanitarianism as both an emotion-based impulse and a simultaneous active response. See Suski, "Children," 210.
74. See Halka, "Das Scapulier," 15–16. Altogether, the story was published in four serial issues of the *Echo aus Africa* in 1891.
75. Ibid., 16.
76. Ibid., 16.
77. The rupture of loving family relationships due to the slave trade plays an important role in Beecher Stowe's *Uncle Tom's Cabin* as well as in many slave narratives, such as for instance, in Harriet Jacobs' *Incidents in the Life of a Slave Girl* (1861). On gendered love in female slave narratives, see Bader-Zaar, "'Why Does the Slave Ever Love?'"
78. "Jetzige Lage," 9.
79. Ibid., 5.
80. Jonen, Grubenbecher, and Bremer, "Verein zur Unterstützung," 390.
81. See Zelizer, *Pricing*, 7–21.
82. Jonen, Grubenbecher, and Bremer, "Verein zur Unterstützung," 390.

83. Such references to African slaves and particularly child slaves were widespread. For instance, see Nöcker, "Biographische Skizzen," 45–46.
84. Carcereri, *Erster ausführlicher Jahresbericht*, 4.
85. For instance, the report from 1863, which contained short biographical accounts of ransomed children, also introduced the story of Joannes Maria Farrag, who was sold to a Turkish man by his father. See Da Casoria, "Biographische Skizzen," 50.
86. "Vorbericht," 4.
87. See Marten, "Family Relationships," 21–23.
88. "Olivieri, die Neger und die Sklavenfrage," 12–13.
89. Ibid., 9.
90. "Vorbericht," 3.
91. "Olivieri, die Neger und die Sklavenfrage," 15.
92. For details on the publishing history of the book, see Parfait, *The Publishing History*.
93. "Olivieri, die Neger und die Sklavenfrage," 14–15. The role of literature in the creation of human rights and humanitarian sentiments has been pointed out by Hunt, *Inventing Human Rights*.
94. See Frevert, *Emotions*, 100–101.
95. See Hausen, "Die Polarisierung."
96. "Olivieri, die Neger und die Sklavenfrage," 14.
97. See Sheller, "Bleeding Humanity," 173; Midgley, *Women Against Slavery*, i.e., 35–36.
98. Sheller, "Bleeding Humanity," 179.
99. Nöcker, "Biographische Skizzen," 57–58.
100. "Beschreibung und Geschichte," 13.
101. See Owzar, "The Image," 135–136.
102. See Laqua, "The Tensions," 712; Ribi Forclaz, *Humanitarian Imperialism*, 17.
103. *Ein Wort an alle*, 9.
104. On the Roman order of Gonfalon, see Priesching, *Von Menschenfängern*.
105. See Ressel, *Zwischen Sklavenkassen*, 38.
106. See Priesching, *Von Menschenfängern*, 8.
107. See Sauer, *Expeditionen*, 29 and 137.
108. "Jetzige Lage," 5.
109. On a practical level, the Pope invited the Trinitarians to carry out collections for Olivieri and to provide logistic support. Ibid., 6.
110. "Die Stiftung," 13.
111. Ibid., 26.
112. For instance, in 1891, the *Echo aus Africa* announced that, in the mission of Lavigerie's *Missionnaires d'Afrique*, the price of slave child was about 30 guilders. In turn, donors had to send about 50 guilders if they sought to ransom a child slave in the Vicariate of Central Africa. See "Verschiedenes," 21.
113. See Comboni, "Bericht," 28.
114. "Das Negerknaben Institut," 54.
115. This was suggested by the second paragraph in the regulations of the *Hilfsverein*.
116. For instance, in 1893, a certain Nikolaus Sieberg from Aachen, by then an important center of the Catholic missionary movement in Germany, had posted 51,09 lire to Rome and requested that the money was to be used for the ransoming of two slave boys who were to be baptized Anton and Sebastian. Letter from M. Rampolla to A. Ciasca, Rome, 25 March 1893. N.S., APF, Vol. 10, 43–44.
117. The *Norddeutsche Missionsgesellschaft* maintained a *Sklavenkasse* (slave fund) with the goal to ransom child slaves who were expected to become a first generation of converts. See Alsheimer, *Zwischen Sklaverei*, 59–64.
118. See Clarence-Smith, "The Redemption," 173–190; Vos, "Child Slaves," 71–91.
119. Numerous examples are provided in the *Echo aus Africa*, the *Kleine Afrika-Bibliothek*, and *Das Negerkind*.

Acknowledgements

The author wishes to thank Esther Möller, the editors of this special issue, and two anonymous reviewers for many helpful comments, critical remarks, and suggestions on earlier drafts of this essay. In addition, thanks are owed to Katharina Wolf and both editors for assisting me with editing and English revisions.

Disclosure statement

No potential conflict of interest was reported by the author.

References

Aitken, Robbie, and Eve Rosenhaft. *Black Germany. The Making and Unmaking of a Diaspora Community*. Cambridge: Cambridge University Press, 2013.

Alsheimer, Rainer. *Zwischen Sklaverei und christlicher Ethnogenese. Die vorkoloniale Missionierung der Ewe in Westafrika (1847–ca.1890)*. Münster: Waxmann, 2007.

Appiah, Kwame Anthony, and Martin Bunzel, eds. *Buying Freedom. The Ethics and Economics of Slave Redemption*. Princeton: Princeton University Press, 2007.

Bader-Zaar, Brigitta. "'Why Does the Slave Ever Love?' Die Liebe in Selbstzeugnissen nordamerikanischer Sklavinnen." In *Liebe und Widerstand. Ambivalenzen historischer Geschlechterbeziehungen*, edited by Ingrid Bauer, Christa Hämmerle, and Gabriela Hauch, 309–327. Wien: Böhlau, 2005.

Baer, Gabriel. "Slavery in Nineteenth Century Egypt." *The Journal of African History* 8, no. 3 (1967): 417–441.

Bayly, Christopher A., Sven Beckert, Matthew Connelly, Isabel Hofmeyr, Wendy Kozol, and Patricia Seed. "AHR Conversation: On Transnational History." *American Historical Review* 111, no. 5 (2006): 1441–1464.

Bechhaus-Gerst, Marianne. "'Das finstere Heidenthum mit seinen Greueln' – Der Afrika-Verein deutscher Katholiken in Köln." In *Köln und der deutsche Kolonialismus. Eine Spurensuche*, edited by Marianne Bechhaus-Gerst and Anne-Kathrin Horstmann, 113–114. Köln: Böhlau, 2013.

"Bericht über die erste Expedition nach Africa." *Fünfzehnter Jahresbericht des Vereines zur Unterstützung der armen Negerkinder* (1868): 13–39.

"Beschreibung und Geschichte eines uralten Herdes der unerhörtesten Sclaverei." *Echo aus Afrika* 14, no. 1 (1902): 11–14.

Bielak, Valerie. *Maria Theresia Gräfin Ledóchowska. Gründerin der St. Petrus Claver-Sodalität für die afrikanischen Missionen und die Befreiung der Sclaven*. Salzburg: Selbstverlag, 1931.

Campbell, Gwyn, Suzanne Miers, and Joseph C. Miller. "Editors' Introduction." In *Children in Slavery Through the Ages*, edited by Gwyn Campbell, Suzanne Miers, and Joseph C. Miller, 1–15. Athens: Ohio University Press, 2009.

Carcereri, Stanislaus. *Erster ausführlicher Jahresbericht über die Neger-Institute von Aegypten, die im Dezember des Jahres 1867 von Don Daniele Comboni gegründet wurden*. Wien: Selbstverlag, 1871.

"Chronik der St. Petrus Claver-Sodalität." *Echo aus Afrika* 11, no. 1 (1899): 12–14.

Clarence-Smith, William G. "The Redemption of Child Slaves by Christian Missionaries in Central Africa, 1878–1914." In *Child Slaves in the Modern World*, edited by Gwyn Campbell, Suzanne Miers, and Joseph C. Miller, 173–190. Athens: Ohio University Press, 2011.

Comboni, Daniele. "Bericht des Herrn Comboni über die Reise nach Africa." *Vierzehnter Jahresbericht des Vereines zur Unterstützung der armen Negerkinder für die Zwecke der central-africanischen Mission* (1866): 7–76.

Comboni, Daniele. *Piano per la rigenerazione dell'Africa proposto da D. Daniele Comboni Missionario Apostolico dell'Africa Centrale*. 4th ed. Rome: Tipografia della S. C. De Propaganda Fide, 1867.

Comboni, Daniele. "Promemoria für Se. Eminenz, den Cardinal Patrizi, Generalvikar von Rom, Protector des Olivieri'schen Werkes der Loskaufung der Negerkinder." *Jahresbericht des Vereines zur Unterstützung der armen Negerkinder* (1866): 55–59.

Conrad, Sebastian. "Doppelte Marginalisierung, Plädoyer für eine transnationale Perspektive auf die deutsche Geschichte." *Geschichte und Gesellschaft* 28, no. 1 (2002): 145–169.

CR 1 22.19. Historisches Archiv des Erzbistums Köln (AEK), Cologne.

Da Casoria, Ludovico. "Biographische Skizzen der Zöglinge des Instituts della Palma in Neapel." *Elfter Jahresbericht des Vereines zur Unterstützung der armen Negerkinder für die central-africanische Mission* (1863): 35–59.

"Das Negerknaben Institut della Palma zum Zwecke der Mission in Central-Afrika." *Jahresbericht des Vereines zur Unterstützung der Armen Negerkinder* (1859): 42–64.

Deutsch, Jan-Georg. *Emancipation Without Abolition in German East Africa c.1884–1914*. Athens: Ohio University Press, 2006.

Die Aufgabe der katholischen Frauen im Missionswerke. Salzburg: Verlag der St. Petrus Claver-Sodalität, 1908.

"Die Erziehungs- und Bildungs-Anstalten für junge Neger und Negerinnen." *Elfter Jahresbericht des Vereines zur Unterstützung der armen Negerkinder für die central-africanische Mission* (1863): 27–30.

"Die Stiftung des 'Ordens der heiligen Dreifaltigkeit zur Erlösung der Gefangenen'." *Elfter Jahresbericht des Vereines zur Unterstützung der armen Negerkinder für die central-africanische Mission* (1863): 12–26.

Drescher, Seymour. *Abolition. A History of Slavery and Antislavery*. Cambridge: Cambridge University Press, 2009.

Eckert, Andreas. "Aufklärung, Sklaverei und Abolition." *Geschichte und Gesellschaft* 23 (2010): 243–262.

Eckert, Andreas. "Die Berliner Afrika-Konferenz (1884/85)." In *Kein Platz an der Sonne. Erinnerungsorte der deutschen Kolonialgeschichte*, edited by Jürgen Zimmerer, 137–149. Frankfurt: Campus, 2013.

Eckert, Andreas, and Albert Wirz. "Wir nicht, die Anderen auch. Deutschland und der Kolonialismus." In *Jenseits des Eurozentrismus. Postkoloniale Perspektiven in den Geschichts- und Kulturwissenschaften*, edited by Sebastian Conrad and Shalini Randeria, 372–392. Frankfurt: Campus, 2002.

Egger, Christine. "Transnationale Architekturen. Benediktinermission, Räume und Repräsentationen." *Österreichische Zeitschrift für Geschichtswissenschaften* 24, no. 2 (2013): 47–69.

Ein Wort an alle, welche der Antisclavereibewegung Österreichs Erfolg wünschen. Wien: Selbstverlag St. Norbertus Druckerei, 1890.

Frevert, Ute. *Emotions in History – Lost and Found*. Budapest: Central European University Press, 2011.

Glassman, Jonathon. "Racial Violence, Universal History, and Echoes of Abolition in Twentieth-Century Zanzibar." In *Abolition and Imperialism in Britain, Africa, and the Atlantic*, edited by Derek R. Peterson, 175–206. Athens: Ohio State University Press, 2010.

Gütl, Clemens, ed. *'Adieu ihr lieben Schwarzen.' Gesammelte Schriften des Tiroler Afrikamissionars Franz Mayr (1865–1914)*. Wien: Böhlau, 2014.

Halka, Alexander. "Das Scapulier des Sclaven." *Echo aus Afrika* 3, no. 1, 2, 3 and 4 (1891): 7–8, 15–16, 23–24, and 30–32.

Hausen, Karin. "Die Polarisierung der 'Geschlechtscharaktere.' Eine Spiegelung der Dissoziation von Erwerbs- und Familienleben." In *Sozialgeschichte der Familie in der Neuzeit Europas: Neue Forschungen*, edited by Werner Conze, 363–393. Stuttgart: Ernst Klett, 1976.

Haynes, Stephen R. *Noah's Curse: The Biblical Justification of American Slavery*. Oxford: Oxford University Press, 2002.
Horstmann, Anne-Kathrin. "Franz Karl Hespers – Domkapitular und Kolonialaktivist." In *Köln und der deutsche Kolonialismus. Eine Spurensuche*, edited by Marianne Bechhaus-Gerst and Anne-Kathrin Horstmann, 115–119. Köln: Böhlau, 2013.
Hunt, Lynn. *Inventing Human Rights: A History*. London: W.W. Norton, 2007.
"Jetzige Lage und fernere Entwicklung des Vereines." *Elfter Jahresbericht des Vereines zur Unterstützung der armen Negerkinder für die central-africanische Mission* (1863): 1–9.
Jonen, P. Jos., L. Grubenbecher, and J. Bremer. "Verein zur Unterstützung armer Negerinnen." *Katholische Wochenschrift* (1856): 389–392.
Koonar, Catherine. "Using Child Labor to Save Souls: The Basel Mission in Colonial Ghana, 1855–1900." *Atlantic Studies* 11, no. 4 (2014): 526–554.
Küppers-Braun, Ute. "P. Nicolò Olivieri und der (Los-)Kauf afrikanischer Sklavenkinder." *Schweizerische Zeitschrift für Religions- und Kulturgeschichte* 105 (2011): 141–166.
Laqua, Daniel. "The Tensions of Internationalism: Transnational Anti-slavery in the 1880s and 1890s." *The International History Review* 33, no. 4 (2011): 705–726.
Ledóchowska, Maria Theresia. *Der Beruf einer Hilfsmissionärin für Afrika*. 4th ed. Salzburg: Verlag der St. Petrus Claver-Sodalität, 1919.
Ledóchowska, Maria Theresia. *Die Antisclaverei-Bewegung und die St. Petrus Claver-Sodalität*. Wien: Selbstverlag, 1900.
Lind, Vera. "Africans in Early Modern German Society: Identity – Difference – Aesthetics – Anthropology." *GHI Washington Bulletin* 28 (2001): 74–82.
Mann, Michael. *Sahibs, Sklaven und Soldaten: Geschichte des Menschenhandels rund um den Indischen Ozean*. Darmstadt: Philipp von Zabern, 2011.
Marten, James. "Family Relationships." In *A Cultural History of Childhood and Family in the Age of Empire*, 2nd ed., edited by Colin Heywood, 19–38. London: Bloomsbury, 2014.
Martin, Peter. *Schwarze Teufel, edle Mohren. Afrikaner in Geschichte und Bewußtsein der Deutschen*. Hamburg: Hamburger Edition, 2001.
McEwan, Dorothea. *A Catholic Sudan – Dream, Mission, Reality. A Study of the Roman Catholic Mission to Central Africa and Its Protection by the Hapsburg Empire from 1846 to 1900 (1914) as Revealed in the Correspondence of the Imperial and Royal Austro-Hungarian Consulate in Khartoum*. Rome: Stabilimento Tipografico Julia, 1987.
Michels, Stefanie. "West African Families Sending Children to German Homes: Duala and Oesterle (1891–1911)." *Genesis. Rivista della Società Italiana delle Storiche* 14, no. 1 (2015): 85–116.
Midgley, Clare. *Women Against Slavery. The British Campaigns 1780–1870*. London: Routledge, 1992.
Miers, Suzanne. *Slavery in the Twentieth Century. The Evolution of a Global Problem*. Oxford: Altamira, 2003.
Nachlass Johannes von Geissel. Historisches Archiv des Erzbistums Köln (AEK), Cologne.
Nöcker, Gottfried. "Biographische Skizzen über die schwarzen Lehrerinnen des ersten Etablissements zu Cairo in Aegypten." *Jahresbericht des Vereines zur Unterstützung der armen Negerkinder* (1869): 43–61.
N.S. (Nuova Serie). The Propaganda Fide Historical Archives. Volumes 10, 138, 208, 340, 484, 586, 620, 648, 749, 766, 769, 775 and 820, Rome.
"Olivieri, die Neger und die Sklavenfrage." *Jahresbericht des Vereines zur Unterstützung der Armen Negerkinder* (1859): 3–27.
Olivieri, Nicolò. *Nona relazione sui progressi della pia opera pel riscatto delle fanciulle more*. Genoa: Stamperia Casamara, 1857.
Osterhammel, Jürgen. *Sklaverei und die Zivilisation des Westens*. Munich: Carl Friedrich von Siemens Stiftung, 2000.
Owzar, Armin. "The Image of Islam in German Missionary Periodicals." In *Missions and Media. The Politics of Missionary Periodicals in the Long Nineteenth Century*, edited by Felicity Jensz and Hanna Acke, 133–150. Stuttgart: Franz Steiner, 2013.
Parfait, Claire. *The Publishing History of Uncle Tom's Cabin, 1852–2002*. Burlington: Ashgate, 2007.

Priesching, Nicole. *Von Menschenfängern und Menschenfischern. Sklaverei und Loskauf im Kirchenstaat des 16.–18. Jahrhunderts*. Hildesheim: Georg Olms Verlag, 2012.

"Rechenschafts-Bericht für das Vereinsjahr 1862–1863." *Elfter Jahresbericht des Vereines zur Unterstützung der armen Negerkinder für die central-africanische Mission* (1863): 77–92.

Ressel, Magnus. *Zwischen Sklavenkassen und Türkenpässen. Nordeuropa und die Barbaresken in der frühen Neuzeit*. Berlin: De Gruyter, 2012.

Ribi Forclaz, Amalia. *Humanitarian Imperialism. The Politics of Anti-slavery Activism 1880–1940*. Oxford: Oxford University Press, 2015.

Rohrbacher, Peter. "Franz Xaver Logwit-lo-Ladù (1848–1866): Seine Bedeutung als afrikanische Gewährsperson in der Frühphase der österreichischen Afrikanistik." In *Afrikanische Deutschland-Studien und deutsche Afrikanistik – Ein Spiegelbild*, edited by Michel Espagne, Pascale Rabault-Feuerhahn, and David Simo, 49–72. Würzburg: Königshausen & Neumann, 2014.

Sauer, Walter. *Expeditionen ins afrikanische Österreich. Ein Reisekaleidoskop*. Wien: Mandelbaum, 2014.

Sauer, Walter. "Schwarz-Gelb in Afrika. Habsburgermonarchie und koloniale Frage." In *k. u. k. kolonial. Habsburgermonarchie und europäische Herrschaft in Afrika*, edited by Walter Sauer, 17–78. Wien: Böhlau, 2002.

Sheller, Mimi. "Bleeding Humanity and Gendered Embodiments: From Antislavery Sugar Boycotts to Ethical Consumers." *Humanity: An International Journal of Human Rights, Humanitarianism, and Development* 2, no. 2 (2011): 171–192.

Stornig, Katharina. "Figli della Chiesa. Riscatti e la globalizzazione del welfare cattolico, 1840–1914." *Genesis. Rivista della Società Italiana delle Storiche* 14, no. 1 (2015): 55–83.

Sulzbacher, Christine. "Beten – dienen – unterhalten. Zur Funktionalisierung von Afrikanern und Afrikanerinnen im 19. Jahrhundert in Österreich." In *Von Soliman zu Omofuma. Afrikanische Diaspora in Österreich. 17. bis 20. Jahrhundert*, edited by Walter Sauer, 99–128. Innsbruck: Studienverlag, 2007.

Suski, Laura. "Children, Suffering, and the Humanitarian Appeal." In *Humanitarianism and Suffering. The Mobilization of Empathy*, edited by Richard Ashby Wilson, 202–222. Cambridge: Cambridge University Press, 2009.

"Ueber die heurige Propagandareise der General-Leiterin der St. Petrus Claver-Sodalität." *Echo aus Afrika* 19, no. 8, 9, and 10 (1907): 125–127, 141–141, and 156–159.

"Verschiedenes." *Echo aus Afrika* 3, no. 3 (1891): 21.

"Vorbericht." *Vierzehnter Jahresbericht des Vereines zur Unterstützung der armen Negerkinder* (1866): 2–4.

"Vorbemerkung." *Jahresbericht des Vereines zur Unterstützung der armen Negerkinder* (1871), 1–2.

Vos, Jelmer. "Child Slaves and Freemen at the Spiritan Mission in Soyo, 1880–1885." *Journal of Family History* 35 (2010): 71–90.

Weber, Klaus. "Deutschland, der atlantische Sklavenhandel und die Plantagenwirtschaft der Neuen Welt (15. bis 19. Jahrhundert)." *Journal of Modern European History* 7, no. 1 (2009): 37–67.

Wirz, Albert. "Sklavenhandel, Sklaverei und legitimer Handel." In *Afrika. Geschichte und Gesellschaft im 19. und 20. Jahrhundert*, edited by Inge Grau, Christian Mährdel, and Walter Schicho, 75–91. Wien: Promedia, 2000.

Zelizer, Viviana A. *Pricing the Priceless Child. The Changing Social Value of Children*. New York: Basic Books, 1985.

Zeller, Joachim. "Der 'Mohr von Berlin.' Abd El Faradj Alias Henry Noël." In *Unbekannte Biographien. Afrikaner im deutschsprachigen Raum von 18. Jahrhundert bis zum Ende des Zweiten Weltkrieges*, edited by Ulrich van der Heyden, 253–260. Werder: Kai Homilius, 2008.

Zunker, Maria Magdalena. "Drei 'arme Mohrenkinder' in der Benediktinerinnenabtei St. Walburg, Eichstätt: Eine Spurensuche." *Studien und Mitteilungen zur Geschichte des Benediktinerordens und seiner Zweige* 114 (2003): 481–532.

Exploring race and gender in Anna Seghers's "The Reintroduction of Slavery in Guadeloupe"

Priscilla Layne

ABSTRACT
After having spent several years in exile in Mexico during World War II, in 1949 German Jewish author Anna Seghers published two novellas set in the Caribbean during the time of transatlantic slavery. In this essay, through an investigation of the novella "Wiedereinführung der Sklaverei in Guadeloupe" ("The Reintroduction of Slavery in Guadeloupe"), I question what Seghers's portrayal of differently gendered and raced characters says about her argument about revolutionary politics. In general, socialists have long been criticized for their tendency to downplay racism as simply a by-effect that would be eliminated with capitalism. In this regard, Seghers seems to differ; rather than overlooking or downplaying race, "The Reintroduction of Slavery in Guadeloupe" has indeed been praised for demonstrating cross-racial solidarity embodied in its white, mulatto, and black male protagonists. As an author who had been active in socialist political circles since the 1920s and who settled in the Soviet-occupied zone upon returning to Germany from exile in 1947, Seghers's interest in minority struggles and postcolonial issues is not surprising. However, I find this claim to cross-racial solidarity in Seghers's text problematic; I will demonstrate my intervention with the story's representation of its female characters. I argue that while the dark-skinned black women of the story are portrayed positively as having revolutionary potential, white and mulatto women are depicted as apolitical, bourgeois, and merely inhibitions to their male partners' political activity. By allowing her white and mulatto female characters this passivity, Seghers's attempt at a postcolonial narrative that encourages readers in socialist East Germany to view their colonial legacy more critically ultimately fails, in part because of the binaries and borders she maintains between women.

Though German Jewish author Anna Seghers is best known for her anti-fascist novels depicting life prior to and during Nazi Germany like *Das Siebte Kreuz* (The Seventh Cross, 1942) and *Transit* (1944), she was also one of the first German authors to contribute to postwar postcolonial literature with the publication of her *Karibische Geschichten* (Caribbean Stories) in 1949,[1] novellas set during slavery. *Caribbean Stories* originally consisted of just two novellas: "Die Hochzeit von Haiti" (The Wedding of Haiti) – a kind of revision of

Heinrich von Kleist's novella "Die Verlobung in St. Domingo" (The Betrothal in St. Domingo, 1811) – and "Die Wiedereinführung der Sklaverei in Guadeloupe" (The Reintroduction of Slavery in Guadeloupe). In 1960 she wrote a third novella, "Das Licht auf dem Galgen" (The Light on the Gallows), which depicts a slave revolt in Jamaica and was eventually made into a film by the official East German film studios, the Deutsche Film-Aktiengesellschaft (DEFA), in 1976.[2]

Seghers was familiar with Kleist's novella and in a letter to Renate Francke from 1963, her acknowledgment that Kleist "didn't know much and didn't understand much about the Negro revolution," suggests that her *Caribbean Stories* were partially an attempt to provide a more nuanced German depiction of transatlantic slavery that goes beyond the simple binaries of white/black and good/evil that one might find in older narratives, such as Kleist's, which is set during the Haitian slave revolt (1791–1804) and is populated with stereotypical black caricatures.[3] For example, Kleist juxtaposes the violent, animalistic black rebel, exotically named Congo Huango, who attempts to lure whites into a deadly trap, with the beautiful, acquiescent tragic mulatto Toni who tries to help a Swiss family fleeing the rebellion.[4] In Seghers's novellas, however, black characters are not portrayed simply as being good only because they are less vengeful or more understanding of their white masters. Rather, in Seghers's novellas, black characters are heroic if they have a greater political awareness of slavery and if they can look past race and work *together* with empathetic whites to end oppression. Nevertheless, as postcolonial scholar Herbert Uerlings argues in his analysis of "The Wedding in Haiti," her narrative is still fraught with an air of Eurocentrism that frames the slave revolts only as an extension of the French Revolution.[5]

Despite these problems, critics have lauded the novellas for Seghers's political awareness and her emphasis on cross-racial cooperation, elements which are rooted in her socialist beliefs. Seghers joined the Communist Party of Germany in 1928 and was also a co-founder of the *Bund Proletarisch-Revolutionärer Schriftsteller* (Association of Proletarian Revolutionary Authors) during that same year. Her communist ties helped her family escape to Mexico during World War II. Following the war, in 1947, Seghers returned to Germany and settled in the Soviet-occupied zone of Berlin, which would eventually become part of the socialist German Democratic Republic (GDR) in 1950.[6]

Seghers wrote her *Caribbean Stories* in the late 1940s, at a time when the GDR was just forming and not all of the ideological and state apparati were in place that would eventually repress the work of authors in the 1960s, 1970s, and 1980s. Nevertheless, as Mary Fulbrook argues, the GDR was a repressive state ruled by a degree of paranoia and insecurity that was present since the nation's founding, which Fulbrook identifies as the first of two major periods of instability.[7] Regarding Seghers, though she had been a member of the Socialist Unity Party (*Sozialistische Einheitspartei Deutschlands*, SED) since she returned to Berlin, she had a tenuous relationship to the state, which I will discuss below. Nevertheless, even if Seghers was not a party hardliner, she did adhere to the notion that class-consciousness would resolve issues of race and this is why cross-racial cooperation is such a focal point of these texts. In order to promote working across racial lines in "The Reintroduction of Slavery in Guadeloupe," the novella focuses on a trio of white (Beauvais), black (Paul Rohan), and mulatto (Berenger) male protagonists working together. Guadeloupe had been a French colony since 1635 and had since then been a part of the transatlantic slave trade. In 1794, Robespierre abolished slavery in Guadeloupe and sent the colonial administrator, Victor Hugues to govern the island. However, in 1798 Napoleon sought to reinstate slavery on the island and as a result, Hugues, who was known for treating both black and white soldiers fairly, was called back to France. The novella begins in 1798 with Beauvais, Berenger, and Paul Rohan anticipating both the arrival of their new commander and the reintroduction of slavery. The three men are committed to resisting these changes, and together with the black female cook Manon, they devise a plan of action. But while Seghers depicts an alliance across race among male characters, it is suspiciously absent from the presentation of her female characters.

A few critics have discussed the issue of femininity in regard to passivity and revolutionary potential in the *Caribbean Stories*, but most of these discourses only pertain to the black female characters. One exception is Herbert Uerlings' analysis of "The Wedding in Haiti," where he does note the passive manner in which both black and white women are portrayed.[8] Interestingly, by restricting *all* the women to the private/non-political realm, "The Wedding in Haiti" is similar to several other socialist realist novels published in the founding years of the GDR. In Julia Hell's analysis of Willi Bredel's *Verwandte und Bekannte* trilogy, for example, she notes that "participation in revolutionary struggle excludes women. Men are real men only *without* women, and outside of what the texts define as the women's sphere."[9]

Considering this pattern of excluding all women from revolutionary struggle in foundational socialist realist narratives, I see the uniqueness of "The Reintroduction of Slavery in Guadeloupe" because not *all* of the women are excluded from politics. While the dark-skinned black women are either active in politics or convey the potential for politicization, white and mulatto women are dismissed as bourgeois, apolitical, and actually a threat to their male partners' political activity. However, this division between dark-skinned activism and light-skin or white passivity allows the European female character to be blissfully ignorant and innocent. I argue that because of the way Seghers portrays her female characters based on race and because of the borders and binaries she maintains between her female characters, Seghers ultimately fails to offer a postcolonial narrative to East German readers that would substantially confront them with a colonial past and their own legacy of racism.

Historically, no matter whether blacks have been viewed positively or negatively, all skin tones have not been treated equally. In the case of transatlantic slavery, on the spectrum of blackness, light-skinned blacks were seen as being closer to a European standard of beauty and because of their preferential treatment, more likely to collaborate with their oppressors than dark-skinned blacks. This assumption is central to Kleist's "The Betrothal in St. Domingo." In Kleist's novella, the Swiss officer Gustav is fleeing from the slave revolt with a group of whites, including some family members.[10] He happens to come upon the household of Congo Huango. Congo Huango has been using the young woman Toni, with whose mother he is in a relationship, in order to lure unsuspecting whites into the house so that they can be killed. Toni is described as a *mestiza*, the child of a mulatto and a white person, and her light skin is what lures white travelers into trusting her. Therefore, a lot of focus in the narrative is placed on the play between light and dark, the visible and the invisible, trust and distrust.[11]

Like many nineteenth-century stories depicting slavery, Kleist's novella values light skin, associating it with European beauty, but also associating it with collaborations with Europeans and the dilemma of the "tragic mulatto."[12] After Toni falls in love with Gustav, she denounces her blackness and wishes to run away with him to Europe, only to be killed by her lover who mistakenly believes she has betrayed him. In contrast to Kleist's story, which privileges light skin over dark skin, colorism affects Seghers's story in the opposite direction. Colorism is "the allocation of privilege and disadvantage to the lightness or darkness of one's skin."[13] For Seghers, a mulatto female character's light skin warrants her to be portrayed just as negatively as the white women. Therefore, she depicts the soldier Berenger's mulatto wife Lucienne as non-political and bourgeois, whereas the dark-skinned female slaves are endowed with a stronger political awareness and potential for revolutionary action. Lucienne's designation to the non-political realm of white women can best be explained by the fact that despite her racial difference, she shares a bourgeois class status with white women that would exempt her from the kind of life experiences of a character like Manon, who is a former slave, cook, wife, mother, and political agitator.

Seghers's colorism in this novella actually aligns her with a contemporaneous praise of dark skin typical for *négritude*, a term coined by Aimé Césaire in the 1930s. Césaire, a Martinican author who was a leading thinker in postcolonial politics, valued dark skin and viewed it as being inherently linked to a unique spirituality shared by black people.[14] Not only was Seghers familiar with Césaire's work, but he had a direct influence on her *Caribbean Stories*, as I will explain below. Yet, by dividing the female characters along the lines of color and presenting dark-skinned female characters as active, Seghers actually not only prohibits the kind of cross-racial alliance she promotes among the male characters, but allows the white and light-skinned women a form of innocent, non-involved, or non-guilty passivity.

On the level of the narrative, this essay is concerned with how the intersection of gender and race informs the character portrayals in Seghers's novella. Analyzing Seghers's portrayals of race, gender, and the politics of slavery offers insight into the socialist politics of depicting race after the Holocaust and within an East German tradition specifically. In contrast to the existing secondary literature on "The Reintroduction of Slavery in Guadeloupe" that merely praises Seghers's male characters, a closer look at the depictions of female characters invites scholars to take a more critical look at how her text constructs its anti-racist argument and what might possibly be forfeited by this construction. Within the field of postcolonial studies, my arguments about "The Reintroduction of Slavery in Guadeloupe" relate to the question of what is a white German author's responsibility when a (post)colonial subject matter is portrayed. Arlene Teraoka has remarked that in Seghers's Caribbean texts, "Latin America was discursively 'made' to serve Seghers's purposes."[15] Keeping this in mind, I question what Seghers's portrayal of differently gendered and raced characters says about her general argument about revolutionary socialist politics. In order to explore this issue, I first contextualize Seghers's postcolonial writing within Germany's entanglement with the legacy of transatlantic slavery and within postwar politics, before giving some background information on the novella and the roots of Seghers's interest in the Caribbean. Second, I discuss the critical reception of the novella and the critics' lack of engagement with intersectionality.[16] Finally, in my analysis of the story, I show how the disproportionately positive portrayal of black female characters ultimately reinforces stereotypes about black women and forecloses cross-racial solidarity for women. Ultimately, I claim that the lacking solidarity between women of different races in the novella means that the story is unable to accomplish what Seghers set out to do, namely to have Germans learn from rather than repeat their racist past.

Germany and slavery

The question of to what extent Germany is entangled in the history of the transatlantic slave trade has only recently become a heavily disputed issue. Scholars across disciplines have begun uncovering and documenting Germany's legacy in the slave trade in order to challenge the widely accepted myth of German general non-involvement.[17] The recent volume *Slavery Hinterland*, edited by Eve Rosenhaft and Felix Brahm, documents both German companies' involvement in and benefit from the slave trade, as well as the presence of individual slaves in Germany who were bought at foreign ports by noblemen.[18]

Raphael-Hernandez offers the following examples of such German involvement:

> individual people, trading companies, and entire branches of production participated in the profit made. Though sometimes indirect, in the larger, macroeconomic context, they contributed to the strengthening of groups of people and of entire regions in German territories. […] A further important point is the intellectual involvement of German thinkers, who are afforded much more importance nowadays compared to before. German authors were, in part, greatly influenced by travelers or traveled themselves as adventurers, researchers, missionaries, sailors, doctors or businessmen. Their reports decisively shaped views about slavery and Africans in the land of poets and thinkers, views that are still mirrored in certain attitudes.[19]

Unless one finds any notes of Seghers on German participation in slavery, it would be difficult to know whether she was aware of these facts. But even prior to these recent discoveries in historical scholarship, German authors still found ways to interrogate their country's involvement in slavery and further brutalities linked to colonialism. Texts like Alfred Andersch's *Weltreise auf deutsche Art* (World Trip in a German Fashion 1949/1958), Hubert Fichte's radio plays *San Padro Claver* (1976) and *Großes Auto für San Pedro Claver* (Great Act for San Pedro Claver, 1980) and Uwe Timm's historical montage novel *Morenga* (1978) take varying approaches to challenging Germans' colonial memory – either by depicting former German colonies or by placing German characters as witnesses to postcolonial settings abroad.[20] Fichte, for example, circumvented an alleged lack of German perpetrators by experimenting with literary genres in order to include German characters in other roles.[21]

Remarkably, while Seghers's Nazi-era writings are very critical of German culture and society, in her *Caribbean Stories* the villains are *not* German, but British, French, and Swiss. Seghers wrote her *Caribbean Stories* after World War II during a period wrought with postcolonial resistance and marked by Europeans' introspective criticism of their countries' legacies.[22] Despite Seghers's honorable goals that her *Caribbean Stories* help teach Germans more empathy for people of other races and keep Germans from repeating the horrors of the Holocaust, the absence of German characters in her Antillean texts represents a disturbing similarity shared with earlier colonial texts, like Kleist's "Betrothal in St. Domingo."

As Susanne Zantop argues in *Colonial Fantasies*, prior to acquiring colonies in the late nineteenth century, Germans had already engaged in colonial fantasies, viewing themselves as the benevolent colonial masters, compared to the British and the French.[23] In order to fit this ideological goal, a text would not necessarily need to have a benevolent German character. Rather, simply omitting German actors from a colonial setting sufficed for Germans to criticize their neighbors without having to reflect on *German* involvements in slavery and colonialism. Thus, one could make an argument for a correlation between the omission of German actors and an author's ideological belief in the superiority of German humanism. Furthermore, one must wonder whether avoiding the question of *German* implications in slavery points to a larger problem of German authors' failure to recognize their own prejudices about race. I intend to explore the latter issue vis-à-vis Seghers's *Caribbean Stories*.

Seghers's politics and the politics of race

Seghers first fled Nazi Germany in 1940, heading for France, hoping to find refuge from persecution. But when Hitler's army entered Paris that very same year, it became too dangerous to stay and the North American Writers Association provided her and her family with financial support to escape, while the Mexican government offered her asylum.[24] When Seghers set off for Mexico, reaching her ultimate destination was made difficult by the political situation of the time and Seghers was forced to make several stops throughout the Caribbean including stopping in St. Domingo in Haiti and on Martinique.

If we are to believe that, as Hannah Arendt claims in *The Origins of Totalitarianism*, the horrors of colonialism are a precursor to the Holocaust, then it is easy to imagine that someone like Seghers, who was persecuted by the Nazis and forced to flee the country, might be interested in the history of the Caribbean.[25] In the aforementioned letter to Renate Francke, Seghers claimed that her intentions to write the novellas may have emerged during her trip to the Caribbean, but they certainly solidified when she returned to Germany and "often thought about the countries and islands [she] had left."[26] Over the years, scholars have offered several explanations for why Seghers wrote her Antillean novellas. Initial scholarship in the GDR read the stories as "a portrayal of the 'first great attempts' at emancipation on the Antilles" or as an "echo of the French Revolution in the colonies."[27] In more recent scholarship, Thomas Mast claims Seghers wished to "open up post-World War II German society to the cultural and historical heritage of Latin America."[28] A further suggestion is that her Antillean stories were an attempt to frame Caribbean blacks' fight for freedom from slavery as part of a larger universal struggle for freedom from exploitation, which, as John Pizer points out, is demonstrated in 'The Reintroduction of Slavery in Guadeloupe" in the clear equation of "Napoleon and Napoleonic France with Hitler and Nazi Germany in the wake of the Weimar Republic."[29] A third proposal is that as someone who had experienced racial hatred herself, she perhaps sought to provide more positive representations of blacks that broke from previous stereotypes found in German literature, for, as Arlene Teraoka states, there was "emotional and moral debt to be repaid to the continent that had saved her, her husband and her children and hundreds of other German communists."[30]

It is entirely possible that Seghers was motivated by any one of these intentions or a combination of them, for they do not negate each other. In this essay, I focus on one motivation in particular: the suggestion that Seghers wrote the *Caribbean Stories* to teach Germans something about the history of this part of the world. Christiane Zehl Romero suggests that Seghers's interest in depicting the Caribbean was always tied to how these depictions could be instrumentalized for *Germans*. While Seghers still lived in Mexico, she suffered an unfortunate car accident that led to a period of inactivity. Romero claims that once Seghers began writing again, she turned to exploring material about the Caribbean, precisely *because* she intended to return to Europe and wanted to consider what role her writing would play after her return to a postwar Germany. Romero writes:

> Though it might sound like a paradox, at the same time as she prepared for her return to Europe she began to become more interested with Latin America, more specifically the Caribbean, and to consider what especially interested her and what she would want to convey to Europe.[31]

Furthermore, Romero points out that when Seghers returned to Europe and settled in the Soviet-occupied zone of Berlin, her concentration on the Caribbean in fact intensified, because of the alienation she felt towards this new Germany:

> She [Seghers] found it difficult, even as a writer, to mold a contemporary German reality … for this reason, and because she found it important, in the first years [since her return] she focused on topics from which Germans should learn from foreign cultures, in order to build a "bridge to other peoples," which is the goal she had set for herself at the end of her exile.[32]

But the question remains, *what* were Germans actually supposed to learn from these Caribbean stories? What was to be the purpose of this "bridge to other peoples"? Upon returning to Europe, Seghers stated,

> I came back, so I can do the most for the people whom I know at their best and their worst. With the books I will write here, I want to help hinder that the mistakes of the past can ever be repeated.[33]

One can imagine that for Seghers, the mistakes of the past include the rise of fascism, the Holocaust, and the spread of racist ideologies and laws. Therefore, I suggest that with the Caribbean stories, Seghers wanted to teach Germans how to empathize with blacks' struggle for freedom and envision a future where cross-racial cooperation is possible. But even if this was Seghers's goal, I see a discrepancy between the revolutionary potential assigned to white and mulatto female characters on the one hand and to black female characters on the other hand. This discrepancy eventually endangered Seghers's goal to make Germans empathize with blacks and understand how blacks' struggle might actually relate to them.

In East Germany, Seghers co-founded the *Akademie der Künste* (Academy of Arts) in 1950; in addition, she became a member of the *Schriftstellerverband*, the national writers' association.[34] Nevertheless, Seghers's politics and relationship to the state were not uncomplicated. Unlike other German exiles who had also been politically active in the German Communist Party while still in Mexico, Seghers did not become directly involved in German politics when she returned, preferring instead to contain her activity to moral and educational representations in her writing.[35] Despite her decades-long participation in communist organizations both in Germany and in exile, she often faced criticism that her writing did not strictly adhere to socialist realist expectations.[36] Seghers intended to have an international audience for her work. She did not want to write only for an East German audience or an audience restricted to the Soviet Bloc. For all of these reasons, she actually traveled quite a bit abroad after her return to Europe, but this high degree of travel to the West caused her to be viewed with a degree of suspicion by the East German authorities.[37] In general, during the early years of the GDR, writers were criticized or praised according to whether they adhered to Socialist realism. While

Seghers was not a dogmatic member of the East German Socialist Unity Party towing the party line within her work, her writing was clearly influenced by her individual socialist beliefs. Still, one of the novels that came under scrutiny in these early years was her *Die Toten bleiben jung* (The Dead Stay Young, 1949), which was criticized for its socialist figures not being interesting enough literary figures.[38] This shows that Seghers's work was not entirely free from criticism; therefore, if we are to consider Seghers's portrayal of race and gender in "The Reintroduction of Slavery in Guadeloupe," we must consider both how her individual politics and how political pressure from others may have informed her portrayals.

On a theoretical level, East Germany adhered to a Marxist–Leninist ideology which demanded that differences based on race, gender, and sexuality among others were to be downplayed due to the belief that capitalism and its class divide was the sole root cause of discrimination. As Quinn Slobodian writes, "The East German leadership felt that elites used racism in both its scientific and cultural forms as a means of misleading the majority."[39] He cites as an example Politburo Central Committee member Fred Oelssner who claimed racism could be used to transform "class resentments into the willingness for war."[40] However, as Slobodian continues, in reality East Germany had a much more complicated relationship with race.

During the early years of the newly founded GDR, East German politicians "followed the UNESCO statement [from 1950] in discarding racial hierarchy while preserving the kernel of hereditary racial difference," but by maintaining the existence of *some* racial difference, this left the door open for old prejudices, fears and white supremacist beliefs to be maintained.[41] Despite East Germany's then-president Walter Ulbricht's claim in 1950 that "there is no longer any racial hatred in the German Democratic Republic," latent acts of racism by East German citizens were expressed in everyday encounters with foreigners throughout the entire history of the GDR.[42] Nevertheless, since Seghers's published "The Reintroduction of Slavery in Guadeloupe" fairly early in the GDR's existence and she already felt alienated towards her fellow Germans at this time, rather than a reflection of GDR policies or everyday life, Seghers's opinion on race was more likely influenced by a pre-war experience of German communism that was linked to anti-racist internationalism in the Weimar Republic. According to Jonathan Derrick, the Weimar Republic was an "important base for radical anti-colonial activity," and communists were incredibly active in these efforts.[43]

Background to the novella and critical reception

"The Reintroduction of Slavery in Guadeloupe" is based on Seghers's research of the history of the island. While the majority of her exile was spent in Mexico, en route to Mexico she made several stops throughout the Caribbean.[44] It is during this time that she became interested in a central figure for Guadeloupe's slavery history, Victor Hugues. As I mentioned in the introduction, Hugues was the former commander of the island who had been tasked with implementing the emancipation decree that freed the slaves in February 1794; he ruled there until 1798. According to historian H. J. K. Jenkins, Hugues was a rather divisive figure. His politics on race were very progressive for the time period. Hugues substituted "military discipline for the old servitude. Turning the whole island into a vast armed camp [...]. All inhabitants, of whatever racial origin, found themselves subject to martial law."[45] Thus, by treating the island's inhabitants like soldiers, Hugues did away with preferential treatment based on race. This aspect of Hugues' rule might have intrigued Seghers because she creates a fictional cross-racial solidarity for her three male protagonists; with these three men and their friendship to each other and their devotion to Hugues, she represents the possibility for racial harmony.

In 1949, two years after returning to Europe, Seghers followed up on her interest in Hugues by consulting the Bibliothèque Nationale de France[46] and speaking with Aimé Césaire, whom she had met previously in 1948 at a conference in Wroclaw.[47] Seghers's estate at the Academy of Arts in Berlin includes hand-written notes that Seghers made about Victor Hugues during her research in the Bibliothèque Nationale de France in Paris.[48] Whatever sparked her initial interest in Hugues, her curiosity about Guadeloupe would be supported by Césaire, with whose help she was able to conduct background research for the story.[49] Seghers first encountered Césaire's work when she read his introduction to Victor Schoelcher's book *Esclavage et colonisation*.[50] While in Martinique, Seghers had seen a monument for Schoelcher, who had helped during the 1848 revolution to free the slaves in the French West Indies.[51] Seghers was given a copy of *Esclavage et colonisation* by a French friend while she was in Warsaw.[52] After initially meeting in 1948, Seghers and Césaire met again in 1949 in Paris, where Césaire was working as a representative of Martinique and Guadeloupe in the French National Assembly. It is during this second meeting in Paris that Seghers asked Césaire what he knew about the liberation of the slaves in Guadeloupe and about Hugues, and Césaire gave her several books, the titles of which are not mentioned.[53]

I mentioned above, Seghers's novella is set after Hugues' departure from the island and it focuses on three male protagonists: the (white) French soldier Beauvais, the mulatto soldier Berenger, and the former slave Paul Rohan. In past interpretations of "The Reintroduction of Slavery in Guadeloupe," scholars tend to focus on Seghers's representation of the three male protagonists. Thomas Mast's analysis of Seghers's *Caribbean Stories*, for example, is mainly concerned with rescuing the novellas from postcolonial criticism that as a white, intellectual, European woman, Seghers cannot effectively convey the experience of oppressed peoples in the Caribbean.[54] Therefore, he lauds "The Reintroduction of Slavery in Guadeloupe" for its depiction of race that breaks the black/white, victim/perpetrator binary by offering a black–white–mulatto constellation. According to Mast, these men of diverse racial backgrounds are an embodiment of the French tricolor and exemplify the possibility of different races working together.[55] John Milfull makes a similar claim; since Beauvais, Berenger, and Paul Rohan are "revolutionary representatives of three groups (whites, mulattoes, and blacks)," they constitute Seghers's "most convincing example of cooperation."[56] John Pizer also praises Seghers's cross-racial cooperation.[57] Andreas Schrade, too, claims that only Berenger, Beauvais, and Paul Rohan are "those who carry the action."[58] In order to make their arguments, all these scholars have to ignore the key figure of the female former slave Manon.[59] However, Manon's importance for the story is evident from the very beginning. The novella opens with all four protagonists, Berenger, Beauvais, Rohan, and Manon, conspiring together at dinner. During this scene, Manon is clearly just as important as the three male protagonists, an observation on which I will elaborate below.

If one reinstates Manon's importance for the story, Seghers's model of cross-racial cooperation is called into question, because significant differences become apparent not only between white and black female characters, but among the black women of which there are three altogether: Manon, Claire (Paul Rohan's wife), and Suzanne (Paul Rohan's sister-in-law). Both, the differences between black and white women in the novella as well as the differences among black women, allow me to show the problem with Seghers's approach and the way she makes gender and race operate in the novella.

Nurturing the revolution: Seghers's portrayal of black women

In order to properly consider how black women are portrayed in Seghers's novella, it is necessary to first contextualize her characters within a larger history of representations of black women in German literature and in particular, consider the effect the transatlantic slave trade had on these representations. In *Schwarze Teufel, edle Mohren*, historian Peter Martin observes that Germans' opinions of blacks have not remained static through time. Prior to the transatlantic slave trade, when Germans encountered Africans, they were usually Ethiopians, who, due to their Christianity, were not considered heathens, but simply exotic, "Oriental" and in fact, cultivated. However, the image of the black as cultivated "Oriental" Ethiopian servant changed with the onset of the transatlantic slave trade. At this time, Germans began to see blacks as something primitive and barely human, a belief system that helped justify slavery during a period when German philosophers became more and more concerned solely with liberating white men from the metaphorical slavery of tyranny.[60]

As part of this intellectual construct, black women held a special place; they were seen as sexual objects that could be conquered along with the land. This fantasy led to the image of the hypersexual black woman who was overzealously eager to please European men. The happy union between the German explorer and his black female lover served as an excuse for German attempts to conquer foreign bodies and lands.[61] This trope is included in Kleist's "The Betrothal in St. Domingo," as represented by Toni and Gustav's attraction to one another. However, while the couple does consummate their union, Kleist only allows its permanence to be achieved in untimely early death.[62]

German authors like Kleist were engaged in fantasies of cross-racial unions prior to Germans actually acquiring colonies, yet the reality of such unions hit home when in the early days of German colonialism in the 1880s and 1890s in Western, Southwestern, and Eastern Africa, quite a few German men had sex with and sometimes married African women. At first, any children born to these unions could claim German citizenship, but the government soon put a stop to this with a law passed in 1905.[63] Negative depictions of black women as unattractive and domineering were employed during this time with the purpose of deterring German soldiers and settlers from having sex with local black women. This is the case in Gustav Frenssen's colonial novel about the German war against the Herero, *Peter Moors Fahrt nach Südwest* (Peter Moor's Journey to Southwest Germany, 1906), in which black women are portrayed as murderous and ugly.[64]

In contrast to these previous German depictions of black women that present them in a negative light as either hypersexual objects or hideous and unfeminine, in Seghers's *Caribbean Stories*, all dark-skinned black women are portrayed positively and as having value for the revolution, though not all of them are actively involved in the resistance. Looking at the diversity of Seghers's black female characters will stress even more how disproportionately negative Seghers's depiction of the white and mulatto women is, for Seghers does not allow the white and mulatto women the same diverse roles in helping the revolution.

Claire is a former slave and Paul Rohan's wife, and her importance lies solely in her role as his wife. What seems to make Paul's relationship unique compared to his co-conspirators, is that Paul and Claire's union is portrayed as an act of resistance. We are told by the narrator that Paul had loved his wife even during the days of slavery, however, the two had not been allowed to marry, because their owner had wanted the freedom to sell her off if he so desired, which he had done. As Teroaoka points out, Paul and Claire's marriage to each other after slavery ended could be seen as an act of resistance, simply because their previous slave master had intended to keep them apart. In contrast, Beauvais' and Berenger's marriages have more to do with bourgeois tradition and the transfer of inheritance than revolutionary politics. Thus, there are potentially two reasons why Paul Rohan's marriage is not depicted as posing a conflict with his political efforts. First, as a former slave, his black wife has experienced the same oppression that drives his political involvement. Second, due to their race and class, Paul's marriage exists outside of the petit bourgeois conventions that mark the other marriages.

A second black female character is Paul Rohan's sister-in-law Suzanne. Not only is Suzanne not actively engaged in politics, but she actually occupies the role of the black woman as the exotic Other, similar to the depictions found prior in German colonial fantasies. In past analyses of the *Caribbean Stories*, while scholars have not addressed all of the gender issues that arise in the texts, they *have* discussed the objectification and exotification of the black female characters. Suzanne would be a prime example thereof due to her treatment as an exotic "fruit" that Beauvais desires. While Beauvais and Berenger both express ambivalence towards their romantic relationships for fear their relationships will hinder their political work, in contrast there is a degree of enthusiasm towards a romantic relationship with Suzanne expressed in Beauvais' interiority, even though Suzanne does not appear to be any more political than the white and mulatto female characters. At one point in the story, Beauvais is dreaming of his fiancée, when an image of Suzanne pleasantly chases her away. One can read:

> He tried hard to hang on to something blond and white; but then it disappeared in the darkness as if dissolving in water, into a time that was no longer his own. Suzanne remained hard and shiny like the core of the fruit she was peeling for him. The fruit of the country. Red, yellow, violet and green, sometimes with black seeds. He loved the pink inner surface of her hand more than the blond and white smoke. It was a part of something, that suffered, was threatened and needed more love than one person could spare. That which had tormented him no longer mattered. Suzanne was happy that he kept looking at her.[65]

Seghers's representation of Beauvais and his fantasy of Suzanne is very problematic in how it fetishizes the black woman. On the one hand, Suzanne is real and concrete, in contrast to Beauvais's fiancée who is described as more ephemeral, "blond and white smoke."[66] However, the physical presence he grants Suzanne is tied to her being both a passive object – a victim who must be saved – and someone who waits on him. Thus, his desire for Suzanne seems linked to a savior complex – his refusal to abandon the revolution. His comparison between her and the fruits or seeds of the island also stresses her fertility and solidifies her role as sexual being and bearer of local culture. Beauvais' desire for Suzanne seems to confirm Hortense Spillers's argument that a series of imposed meanings often come into play when white men encounter black, enslaved women, Spillers writes:

> 1) the captive body becomes the source of an irresistible, destructive sensuality; 2) at the same time – in stunning contradiction – the captive body reduces to a thing, becoming *being* for the captor; 3) in this *absence* from a subject position, the captured sexualities provide a physical and biological expression of "otherness" [...].[67]

According to Spillers's observations, it is inherently racist when, in an interracial relationship, the white man objectifies the black woman and views her as at once hypersexual and helpless – therefore creating a masochist sexual fantasy for the white man. Keeping Spillers's point in mind, Seghers clearly reproduces the logic of the white man in her construction of Beauvais' thoughts about Suzanne. Beauvais might be an anti-racist character who fights for the slaves' freedom, but by viewing Suzanne as both the fertile "fruit" of the island and the suffering victim for him to save, his desire for her is clearly tied to issues of power, gender, and race that place him in the role of captor and her in the role of captive. It is for this reason that Teraoka reads Seghers's *Caribbean Stories* as recreating simplified binaries where white men are rational revolutionaries and black women are merely passionate sexual beings.[68] This definitely seems to be the case for Beauvais and Suzanne. But Manon clearly does not fit Teraoka's generalization.

Of the three black female protagonists in "The Reintroduction of Slavery in Guadeloupe," Manon is the most positive, because she neither conforms to previous stereotypes of the hypersexual submissive black woman nor the unattractive aggressor.[69] Furthermore, Manon's political involvement does not come into conflict with her roles as wife and mother. In addition to being a wife and mother who runs a restaurant, she is also an important political agitator. From the very beginning of the story, it is clear that the narrator positions Manon and the male protagonists on equal footing. This is first apparent, when the four main protagonists are introduced. During the opening scene the narrator uses descriptions of shadows and light in order to stress the characters' similarities despite their belonging to separate racial categories like *Negerin* (negress) and *Mulatte* (mulatto). Although Manon is initially described as simply a *Negerin*, the narrator elaborates by saying "her face looked silver in the moonlight" which is then compared to Beauvais and Berenger who "were paler except for the metal pieces of their uniforms."[70] This sentence both acknowledges that the mulatto Berenger and the white Frenchman Beauvais are lighter in complexion than Manon; however, all three are united by a silver coloring which perhaps denotes their common politics and their loyalty. Although Manon does not wear a uniform, her silver coloring in the moonlight stands in for this. Finally, the narrator states that "all three shadows were the same, dull and close together" (67) thus lumping Manon, Beauvais, and Berenger together, despite their racial and gender differences. The fact that Seghers associates Manon with the male protagonists in this way underscores that in the novella, it is not a woman's gender that would prohibit her from playing an active role in the revolution. Rather, as a dark-skinned black woman and a former slave, Manon has the right racial identity that would allow for her politicization.

Not only is Manon political, but she takes on a dominant role in her household, which possibly endangers Seghers's depiction of reproducing stereotypes of aggressive, unfeminine black women. Since Manon is married, one would expect her husband to be the head of the household due to the novella's historical setting. However, the narrator treats Manon as if she were the head of the household, despite the presence of men there: "They were about fifteen, men and children, sons-in-law and grandchildren" (67). Her family is described as "Manon's family, big and small" (67); her black husband, Baptiste, does not get a name until several pages into the story. Instead of the customary "women and children," it is significant that the narrator lists them as "*men and children*, sons-in-law und grandchildren" (67, my emphasis). In this way, the men are associated with the children, while Manon stands apart as the one in control. It is also notable that there are only sons-in-law and no daughters or daughters-in-law present, suggesting that Manon's household is dominated by a sole female matriarch. At the start of the novella, when Beauvais, Berenger, and Paul join Manon at dinner to discuss their political strategy, Manon's family hungrily rushes towards the food. She repeatedly pushes them away, a motion mentioned by the narrator twice (67–68). This demonstrates not only that Manon is clearly in control, but also that she puts politics before family. Feeding her co-conspirators – feeding the revolution – takes precedence over feeding her family.

Manon is also described as more intuitive than her husband. When Paul Rohan is worried he and Beauvais will not be able to get the former slaves organized before the new administrator arrives, Manon can tell that the political stakes are in danger and that she will be a key part of the plan, all without having to discuss it; one reads: "She [Manon] could sense better than her husband, who was outwardly quicker but inwardly duller than she was, that everything which tortured these three men somehow in some incomprehensible way had to do with her" (71). Manon scolds her husband for not properly understanding politics and after giving a passionate speech in which she attempts to motivate the former slaves to return to work, her husband suggests she should have gone along with Beauvais to organize the other former slaves.

Despite her depiction as a dominant matriarch in these scenes, what saves Seghers's depiction of Manon from just reproducing negative tropes of aggressive, unfeminine black women, is that Manon is not portrayed as undesirable. In fact, when the resistance to the reintroduction of slavery on the island ensues, we are told that a French officer makes advance at Manon leading her to fatally stab him. This minor incident conveys a great deal about Manon's character. Arguably, of all the women in the novella, she is granted the most complexity. Not only is she capable of being a revolutionary and a mother, but her political toughness does not negate her femininity. And by fatally stabbing the white French officer, she both confirms her political views *and* refuses to become the fetishized object of white men.[71]

White and mulatto women and the confines of marriage

When compared to Manon, it becomes even more apparent how little agency the white and mulatto women in the story have. Beauvais' fiancée Claudine is not even present in Guadeloupe; rather she anxiously awaits his return in France. Thus, the only knowledge we have about her is conveyed through Beauvais' thoughts about her, about their relationship and his impending return to France. Berenger's wife Lucienne arrives on the island near the beginning of the novella, but afterwards she is confined to their residence, and rather than hearing about her from herself, we hear only Berenger's concerned thoughts about how her arrival will change his life. Thus, in order to better understand how the white and mulatto female characters of the novella are portrayed, it is ultimately necessary to closely examine the men's relationships to them.

A reoccurring motif in the story is that Beauvais and Berenger both lament their relationships with women. Beauvais keeps postponing his wedding date each time he finds a reason to remain on the island. When the new commander arrives, Beauvais once again fears he will have to return to France. However, it just so happens that the new commander had to leave his assistant in Haiti due to illness, buying Beauvais some time because he can remain on the island and assist the new commander. In fact, Beauvais is so resistant to return to France to marry that before his trip, he is stricken with an inexplicable, seemingly psychosomatic illness that makes it impossible for him to travel.

At the end of the first chapter, when Beauvais laments having to leave Paul and Berenger behind, each of his thoughts about the individual men is preceded by "Beauvais thought": "Beauvais thought: This might be my last trip with him [Paul]. [...] Beauvais thought: Berenger will remain on the island. One man can support the other" (72). After his lamentations about Paul and Berenger, a third "Beauvais thought" introduces his thoughts about his fiancée, "Beauvais thought: The ship definitely brought mail for me. Claudine awaits my return daily" (72). The fact that the phrase "Beauvais thought" appears three times here seems significant. It appears to draw an equivalence between the three people who mean the most in his life, his two male friends and his fiancée. The conclusion of this first chapter clearly shows that Beauvais is torn over to whom he should be most loyal. One learns that "[w]hat happened on this island was confusing and vague, and it didn't let him go. What kept him there was just as strong as what pulled him home" (72). The fact that Beauvais feels torn between his political loyalties on the island and his future marriage to Claudine shows that he does not feel he can reconcile his politics with his love of a white woman. In contrast, this conflict between politics and love is not an issue vis-à-vis his attraction to the black woman Suzanne. In fact, as his attraction to Suzanne grows, it becomes clear that his loyalty to the island and to his commitment to his political engagements outweigh his loyalty to Claudine.

In contrast to Beauvais, who is only engaged, Berenger has a wife, Lucienne, and a child, whom he is not happy to see arrive on the island. When Berenger is confronted with his wife and child debarking a ship, the narrator describes their love for him as "forceful" (75). Heinz Neugebauer simply interprets Berenger's reaction as "reservations, because they [he and Beauvais] are worried about freedom. That's why he [Berenger] is more stunned than happy about the unexpected arrival of his wife and child."[72] It is unclear whether Neugebauer believes Berenger and Beauvais are worried about the slaves' freedom, their own freedom, or both. Either way, Berenger's discomfort with the presence of his family indicates that just like in Beauvais' case, Berenger feels he cannot reconcile his political commitments with his love to a mulatto woman.

The notion that his wife and child's presence constricts him also comes across in the narrator's depiction of their living quarters. At the fort where the family resides, the rooms of Berenger's family "did not look out onto the sea. They looked out onto a small courtyard" (77). In contrast to the freedom represented by the sea, Berenger's wife and child are associated with the interiority and confinement of the courtyard.

This feeling of being cut off from freedom is reinforced by how his daughter's playful laughter and the sounds of the fountain in the courtyard are so loud "that you couldn't hear the sea, everything was a memory of a lively dream" (77). These same metaphors for captivity and entrapment surface, when Berenger tells Beauvais of his family's arrival: He tells Beauvais, "In the meantime, Lucienne has nested. Brown and gray pigeons amuse themselves outside of their cages with the wild birds with whom they otherwise would not play" (85). In her analysis of the story, Gertraud Gutzmann claims that here Seghers associates mulatto women with flowers and birds, thus adding to the exotification of women of color.[73] But I argue that in this scene, Lucienne and her daughter are actually represented by the brown and gray pigeons that have been newly freed from their cages. Thus, Berenger draws a comparison between his wife and the pigeons by describing her setting up house as *einnisten*, the German word for nesting. His wife and child are the plain brown and gray pigeons who now mingle with his colorful life on the island represented by the wild birds. During this scene, Beauvais, who just happens to be visiting, becomes lost in his own thoughts and fears that his Claudine would never mingle with the wild nature there: "Claudine suddenly seemed tougher and harder to him. She would never let her life waste away in a courtyard with so many flowers and birds."[74] Thus, on the one hand, Berenger's mulatto wife, who is darker, is depicted as more open to the life on the island, while Beauvais cannot imagine his white fiancé being happy there. On the other hand, both Berenger's mulatto wife Lucienne and Beauvais' white French fiancée Claudine are depicted as a distraction, as too domestic and irreconcilable with the men's life and political engagement on the island. It is clear from the men's thoughts of their significant others that neither can imagine reconciling married life with their political engagement on the island. While the black female characters are allowed a variety of roles, from nurturer and wife to exotic female Other and active resistor, the white women are merely depicted as a bourgeois nuisance hindering their husbands' freedom and therefore hindering progress towards the men's political goals.

It is certainly possible that by limiting white and mulatto women to the domestic realm, Seghers is not conveying her own opinions, but showing us these female characters through the eyes of their men. The white and mulatto women are not given any interiority; therefore, we have no knowledge of what their opinions about politics or race might be. Thus, when Seghers gives us the men's negative opinions about their wives and fiancés, she could be critiquing the men's inability to see any political potential in their wives. However, by not giving us any access to the women's thoughts or experience themselves, it is unclear whether this is Seghers's position. Within the narrative, black female characters either express an interest in politics or the narrator tells us what their experiences of slavery and racism have been. In contrast, the white and mulatto women express no interest in oppressed minorities, we are told nothing of their lives and their husbands and fiancés have very little interest in them. This is, of course, a problematic depiction of white and mulatto women that bars them from public space and any potential for politicization. Seghers's depiction not only ignores these women's potential oppression under patriarchy, but it also ignores a long history of white female abolitionists active during the nineteenth century and it denies the fact that mulatto women were also subjected to racism and racist violence throughout history.

Conclusion: The ghosts of colonialism

In "The Reintroduction of Slavery in Guadeloupe," Seghers ultimately argues that in order for the enslaved to triumph over their oppressors, it is necessary for people of color to fight together with white allies. Seghers puts forth an alliance that not only cuts across race – uniting a white Frenchman, a mulatto officer, and a black slave – it also cuts across gender if one reinstates Manon's key role in this fight. However, while the male characters can unite across race and they can also work together with black women, the exclusion of white and mulatto women from this alliance ultimately maintains the very borders Seghers is trying to undo. This becomes evident at the conclusion of the story when a framing device of storytelling is introduced.

The final chapter of the novella introduces us to a military colonel who fought against the slave rebellion in Guadeloupe and now, a year after the conflict, is visiting his family near the French-Swiss border. The colonel tells his family about his experience in Guadeloupe. Although only a year has passed since the slaves' resistance, one can still sense that everything that has happened on the island seems to be part of a distant past for those living in Europe. This sense that the occurrences in the colonies are not part of their own, current lives anymore is also present in the discussion of the event that triggers the colonel's memory: the death of Touissant, leader of the slave revolt in Haiti. When a comrade tells the colonel that Touissant has passed, he responds, "You don't say! Was he still alive?" (124). Therefore, even though, in the form of Touissant imprisoned in France, the colonial remnants were now also within Europe, they were denied a mental and intellectual presence. The colonel's story of how he and the French soldiers violently struck down the rebellion of the slaves is interrupted by his disapproving wife who, we can assume, does not find the subject matter appropriate for the family setting. However, the narrator of the story picks up where the colonel leaves off. After we have learned the deadly fates of Berenger, Paul, and Manon, the only story that remains is that of Beauvais whose body was burned along with the other "Neger":

> They'd been throwing the niggers onto a pile. Then suddenly someone had shouted, hey, he's white! You can only imagine their astonishment. A single white man in the mass of blacks. Should someone pull him out? Bury him separately? Nonsense, his friend said. Let him celebrate the resurrection with them. (125–6)

The colonel's audience responds to the subject matter as if it were a gripping thriller: "The mother-in-law rattled with her knitting needles. She never dropped her knitting into her lap, because she was so excited" (120). Nevertheless, the most important member of the audience is a young boy who is particularly impressed by the story. With this narrative strategy, Seghers shows the importance of storytelling for keeping the colonial project going. As Edward Said famously argues in *Orientalism*, Orientalism is two-pronged: latent and manifest. While manifest Orientalism refers to concrete acts to take control of and govern a foreign country, latent Orientalism consists of terms, ideas, literature, art, and a host of other vehicles for spreading ideology that contrasts a Western "us" against the Other and perpetuates the racist and chauvinist thinking necessary for the colonial project to be supported.[75] One can certainly make the same arguments about colonialism, which also depends on both ideological and physical violence against the colonized population. In this sense, the colonel's story is meant to transfer his racist ideas, a sense for adventure and a desire to conquer to this young boy, who in turn would eventually take his place.

What is most important about this ending is that the young boy is not impressed by the colonel, but by Beauvais. Therefore, rather than being drawn to fantasies of conquest, he is more interested in Beauvais' empathy for the slaves and why he would give his life for them. One reads about the young boy:

> The strange man had sacrificed his life for something that didn't have anything to do with the kind of fame, that one talked about here. The kind of fame that fascinated the young people. The fame of triumphal arches and medals, the fame of drum rolls and flags sunk over graves. The fame of the strange man consisted of a chill, that trickled down the boy's spine. (126)

Just as Beauvais' actions serve as an intervention within the colonel's story, Seghers's story is intended to serve as a counternarrative that can change the way Germans think about Europe's colonial past. The problem with this ending, however, is once again a problem of intersectionality. The European boy is touched by the story of the slave revolt not necessarily because he recognizes the humanity of the slaves, but because he can relate to the white revolutionary Beauvais – the one person in the story who shares his race and gender. If such commonalities are necessary for this kind of identification, then not only does a white audience require a white hero against the backdrop of a black slave rebellion, but there is no way for white *girls* to identify with Beauvais' counter example within the colonel's story or with Seghers's text, for none of the white female characters exhibit the same political activity and sympathy with the slaves. Thus, this ending to the story does not really indicate a break with past Western portrayals of slavery and resistance, because Seghers's portrayal of white and mulatto women maintains the kind of dichotomy which juxtaposes a feminine, non-active, and apolitical domestic space with a masculine, active, political foreign space. Such a dichotomy is bound to recreate the same male desiring subject who wants to go abroad to fulfill his desires that can be found throughout German colonial narratives.[76] Thus, Seghers's attempt at a postcolonial narrative that encourages East German readers to view the colonial project more critically ultimately fails, in part because of the binaries and borders she maintains between women. When "The Reintroduction of Slavery in Guadeloupe," is contextualized within Seghers's sociohistorical condition as a Socialist author writing in the GDR, this shortcoming is not surprising. Despite the anti-racist and anti-sexist position of the East German state, racism and sexism still plagued the everyday reality of the GDR. In Seghers's narrative, the missing alliances between women and the exoticization and sexualization of Suzanne demonstrate that East German Socialist authors of Seghers's generation still struggled to conceptualize a world free of oppression. This warrants taking another look at the nuances of East German portrayals of "Third World" revolutions; for rather than mere anti-Western propaganda, chances are these texts will reveal latent patriarchal, racist ideas that did not just disappear in the Eastern zone's transition from National Socialism to Socialism.

Notes

1. There is actually a long tradition of Germans writing about the Caribbean: from Alexander von Humboldt's *Views of the Cordilleras* and *Political Essay on the Island of Cuba*, which was originally published between 1810 and 1813, to Hans Christoph Buch's *Die Scheidung von San Domingo* (The Separation of San Domingo, 1976) and *Die Hochzeit von Port-au-Prince* (The

Wedding of Port-au-Prince, 1984) to the more recent Daniel Kehlmann's *Die Vermessung der Welt* (*Measuring the World*, 2005) which depicts Humboldt's exploration of South America and his encounters with Native Americans and African slaves. Herbert Uerlings discusses the history of German authors' depictions of Haiti in *Poetiken der Interkulturalität*.
2. Hilzinger, *Anna Seghers*, 152.
3. Seghers, "Zur Entstehen der Antillen-Novellen," 254.
4. Kleist, "Die Verlobung in St. Domingo."
5. Uerlings, *Poetiken der Interkulturalität*, 60.
6. Romero, *Anna Seghers*, 94–97.
7. Fullbrook, *Anatomy of a Dictatorship*, 31.
8. Uerlings, *Poetiken der Interkulturalität*, 72–93.
9. Hell, "At the Center," 30.
10. For a discussion of Swiss ideas about blackness during the nineteenth century, see also Jeroen Dewulf's article on the portrayal of African characters in Swiss author Gottfried Keller's *Don Correa*. Dewulf, "Mirroring Zambo in an Atlantic Context."
11. Kleist, "Die Verlobung in St. Domingo," 75–79.
12. Judith Martin writes that nineteenth-century German fiction addressing slavery and gender employed female mulatto characters and "romantic melodrama to permit white audiences to identify with the sexual vulnerability of the slave woman involved making concessions to the prejudices of the audience in the white skin and genteel moral standards of the heroine." J. Martin, "The 'Tragic Mulatto'," 358.
13. Burke, "Colorism," 17.
14. Pizer, "Négritude in East German Literature," 23.
15. Teraoka, *East, West, and Others*, 9.
16. Intersectionality is a feminist term stemming from legal scholar Kimberlé Crenshaw. Crenshaw defines intersectionality as a concept that "denote[s] the various ways in which race and gender interact to shape the multiple dimensions of Black women's employment experiences" (1244). Since Crenshaw's initial theorization of the term, further categories of identification, such as sexuality and disability, have been taken into consideration. Furthermore, it is acknowledged that not only does intersectionality affect a variety of people besides black women, but it can have an effect on all aspects of life beyond the work environment.
17. Some of the scholars who have published on German involvement in the transatlantic slave trade are African-American scholar Saidiya Hartman, German scholars in African Studies Nadja Ofuatey-Alazard, and two German scholars in American Studies Sabine Broeck and Heike Raphael-Hernandez.
18. Brahm and Rosenhaft, *Slavery Hinterland*.
19. Raphael-Hernandez, "Deutsche Verwicklungen," 35. My translation. In line with this work of reinscribing German perpetrators in the narrative of transatlantic slavery, Sabine Broeck has started a project with high-school students in Bremen called Denkwerk, which involves the students in recuperating their city's involvement in the slave trade.
20. For a discussion of German postcolonial writings concerning Africa, see Göttsche, *Remembering Africa*. For a discussion of the discourse on colonialism in the postwar German media and in literary texts, see Albrecht, *Europa ist nicht die Welt*.
21. See, for example, Fichte's radio play *San Padro Claver*, about a Spanish missionary's implications in the abuse of slaves. Fichte is able to bypass a lack of German perpetrators present for Claver's original acts by introducing several layers of performance. Instead of perpetrators who directly abuse the slave, the Germans are introduced as tourists who watch a reenactment of the historic setting.
22. A few examples of such writing are Memmi, *The Colonizer and the Colonized* and Sartre, "Black Orpheus."
23. See Zantop, *Colonial Fantasies*. The kind of chauvinism vis-à-vis colonialism that Zantop describes was not only prevalent in the eighteenth and nineteenth centuries. Even after World War II, in the midst of postcolonial debates and long after Germany had lost its colonies, according to Monika Albecht, Germans did not feel they had the "burden of colonial deeds."

Albrecht, who rejects the notion that postcolonial debates were absent in Germany in the 1950s and 1960s, insists instead that what Germans rejected was not "German participation in the colonial system [...] but rather, more so Germany's failure in the area of colonial civilization." See, Albrecht, *Europa ist nicht die Welt*, 117.
24. Seghers, "Gespräch mit Anna Seghers," 269.
25. Arendt, *Origins of Totalitarianism*, 123.
26. Seghers, "Zur Enstehung der Antillen-Novellen," 254.
27. According to Sonja Hilzinger, West German critics responded negatively to the stories because of "the Eurocentric perspective on the Revolution and the people." See Hilzinger, "From the Revolution," 166. While West Germany certainly had its own problems with racism in the postwar period, West German critiques of Seghers's Antillean novellas at least reflect *some* awareness of contemporary postcolonial critiques of representation and the desire for a non-Western perspective. It is also possible that West Germans were more critical about Seghers's work, because she was an East German writer. For a discussion of the relevance of postcolonial arguments in West Germany, see Albrecht, *Europa ist nicht die Welt*.
28. Mast, "Representing the Colonized," 26.
29. Pizer, "Négritude in East German Literature," 32.
30. Teraoka, *East, West, and Others*, 9.
31. Romero, *Anna Seghers: 1900–1947*, 423.
32. Romero, *Anna Seghers: 1947–1983*, 16.
33. Ibid., 22.
34. The *Schriftstellerverband* had a history of expelling authors whose work did not conform to the party line of the Sozialistische Einheitspartei Deutschlands (Socialist Unity Party).
35. Bernstorff, *Fluchtorte*, 47.
36. See Brockmann, "Postwar Restoration," 84.
37. Bernstorff, *Fluchtorte*, 47.
38. Brockmann, "Postwar Restoration," 84.
39. Slobodian, "Socialist Chromatism," 27.
40. Ibid., 27. Rather than referring to an actual war between countries, Oelssner's comments can be understood as describing how race is used to create disputes among the working-class in order to redirect anger that would otherwise be directed against capitalists. For example, racism in America is often used to redirect the economic frustrations of working-class whites so that they believe immigrants are to blame for their poverty.
41. Ibid., 25–27.
42. Ulbricht as quoted in Slobodian, "Socialist Chromatism," 31.
43. Derrick, *Africa's "Agitators,"* 259.
44. Seghers, *Briefe 1953–1983*, 25–27.
45. Jenkins, "The Colonial Robespierre," 736.
46. Seghers, *Briefe 1953–1983*, 127.
47. Of the books she receives from Cesaire, Seghers merely says, "He gave me a few notebooks from his library," Seghers, *Briefe 1953–1983*, 127.
48. Seghers, Anna-Seghers-Archiv, Nr. 598/1.
49. Seghers also had a number Césaire's works in her library. Uehrlings, 50–51, note 72.
50. Seghers recounts how she became familiar with Césaire in "Zur Enstehung der Antillen-Novellen," 254–255.
51. Seghers, *Briefe 1953–1983*, 126–127.
52. Ibid.
53. Ibid.
54. This is one of Viebke Rützou Petersen's main critiques of the novellas in "Revolution or Colonization," 43–44.
55. Mast, "Representing the Colonized," 34.
56. Milfull, "Juden, Frauen, Mulatten, Neger," 51
57. Pizer, "Négritude in East German Literature," 29.
58. Schrade, *Anna Seghers*, 92.

59. Milfull does not ignore Manon altogether. He does note that she is the one black female character in Seghers's Antillean stories that has the capacity to not just act in accordance with the revolution but articulate her intentions as well. Milfull, "Juden, Frauen, Mulatten, Neger," 52.
60. See Buck-Morss, "Hegel and Haiti."
61. Zantop, *Colonial Fantasies*, 3.
62. Kleist, "Die Verlobung in St. Domingo," 93, 117.
63. Reich, "Racially Mixed Marriages," 160.
64. Frenssen, *Peter Moors Fahrt*, 45.
65. Seghers, *Karibische Geschichten*, 101.
66. Ibid.
67. Spillers, "Mama's Baby," 67.
68. Petersen also discusses Seghers's sexualization and exotification of her black female protagonists. Petersen, "Revolution or Colonization," 399–400.
69. In order to make this point, it would be helpful to know Manon's age. For while younger, female black characters were often fit within the mold of the hypersexual Jezebel, older female black characters were typically portrayed as maternal, non-sexual "mammy" figures. However, as readers we are never told Manon's age. This is not unusual, since none of the characters' ages are explicitly mentioned *and* it was typical for slaves to not know their real age because they had no record of their birth.
70. Seghers, *Karibische Geschichten*, 67.
71. Ibid., 118.
72. Neugebauer, *Anna Seghers*, 121.
73. Gutzmann, "Eurozentrisches Welt- und Menschenbild," 201.
74. Seghers, *Karibische Geschichten*, 85.
75. Said, *Orientalism*, 201–225.
76. See Bowersox, *Raising Germans in the Age of Empire*.

Acknowledgements

I would like to thank both the editors, the reviewers, and Michael Palm (University of North Carolina at Chapel Hill) for their comments on previous drafts of this essay.

Disclosure statement

No potential conflict of interest was reported by the author.

ORCID

Priscilla Layne ⓘ http://orcid.org/0000-0002-3542-8686

Bibliography

Albrecht, Monika. *Europa ist nicht die Welt: (Post)Kolonialismus in Literatur und Geschichte der westdeutschen Nachkriegszeit*. Bielefeld: Aisthesis, 2008.
Arendt, Hannah. *The Origins of Totalitarianism*. New York: Harvest Book, 1976.
Bernstorff, Wiebke von. *Fluchtorte: Die mexikanischen und karibischen Erzählungen von Anna Seghers*. Göttingen: Wallstein, 2006.
Bowersox, Jeff. *Raising Germans in the Age of Empire: Youth and Colonial Culture, 1871–1914*. Oxford: Oxford University Press, 2013.
Brahm, Felix, and Eve Rosenhaft, eds. *Slavery Hinterland: Transatlantic Slavery and Continental Europe, 1680–1850*. Woodbridge, UK: The Boydell Press, 2016.
Brockmann, Stephen. "The Postwar Restoration in East and West." *New German Critique* 42, no. 3 (2015): 69–90.
Buch, Hans Christoph. *Die Scheidung von San Domingo: Wie die Negersklaven von Haiti Robespierre beim Wort nahmen*. Berlin: Wagenbach, 1976.
Buch, Hans Christoph. *The Wedding of Port-au-Prince*. San Diego: Harcourt Brace Jovanovich, 1986.
Buck-Morss, Susan. "Hegel and Haiti." *Critical Inquiry* 26, no. 4 (2000): 821–865.
Burke, Meghan. "Colorism." In *International Encyclopedia of the Social Sciences*, edited by William Darity, Jr., 17–19. Detroit: Macmillan, 2008.
Crenshaw, Kimberlé. "Mapping the Margins: Intersectionality, Identity Politics, and Violence Against Women of Color." *Stanford Law Review* 43, no. 6 (1991): 1241–1299.
Derrick, Jonathan. *Africa's "Agitators": Militant Anti-colonialism in Africa and the West, 1918–1939*. London: Hurst, 2008.
Dewulf, Jeroen. "Mirroring Zambo in an Atlantic Context: The Open Wound of Slavery in Gottfried Keller's Don Correa (1881)." *Atlantic Studies* 10, no. 2 (2013): 247–267.
Fichte, Hubert. *Schulfunk: Hörspiele*. Frankfurt am Main: S. Fischer, 1988.
Frenssen, Gustav. *Peter Moors Fahrt nach Südwest: Ein Feldzugsbericht*. Berlin: G. Grote'sche Verlagsbuchhandlung, 1944.
Fulbrook, Mary. *Anatomy of a Dictatorship: Inside the GDR, 1949–1989*. Oxford: Oxford University Press, 1995.
Göttsche, Dirk. *Remembering Africa: The Rediscovery of Colonialism in Contemporary German Literature*. Rochester, NY: Camden House, 2013.
Gutzmann, Gertraud. "Eurozentrisches Welt- und Menschenbild in Anna Seghers' Karibischen Geschichten." In *Frauen Literatur Politik*, edited by Annegret Pelz and Sabine Broeck, 189–204. Hamburg: Argument, 1988.
Hell, Julia. "At the Center an Absence: Foundational Narratives of the GDR and the Legitimatory Discourse of Antifascism." *Monatshefte* 84, no. 1 (1992): 23–45.
Hilzinger, Sonja. *Anna Seghers*. Leipzig: Reclam, 2000.
Hilzinger, Sonja. "From the Revolution Lost to the Revolution Betrayed: Anna Seghers's Karibische Geschichten." In *Anna Seghers in Perspective*, edited by Ian Wallace, 165–173. Amsterdam: Rodopi, 1998.
Humboldt, Alexander von. *Views of the Cordilleras and Monuments of the Indigenous Peoples of the Americas and Political Essay on the Island of Cuba*. Edited and translated by Vera M. Kutzinski and Ottmar Ette. Chicago: University of Chicago Press, 2012.
Jenkins, H. J. K. "The Colonial Robespierre: Victor Hugues on Guadeloupe 1794–98." *History Today* 27, no. 11 (1977): 734–740.
Kehlmann, Daniel. *Measuring the World*. Translated by Carol Brown Janeway. New York: Pantheon, 2006.
Kleist, Heinrich von. *Das Erdbeben in Chili, Die Marquise von O . . ., Die Verlobung in St. Domingo*. Frankfurt am Main: Suhrkamp, 2009.

Martin, Peter. *Schwarze Teufel, Edle Mohren: Afrikaner in Geschichte und Bewußtsein der Deutschen.* Hamburg: Hamburger Edition, 2001.

Martin, Judith E. "The 'Tragic Mulatto' in Three Nineteenth-Century German Antislavery Texts." *German Studies Review* 37, no. 2 (2009): 357–376.

Mast, Thomas. "Representing the Colonized/Understanding the Other? Rereading of Anna Seghers' *Karibische Geschichten*." *Colloquia Germanica* 30, no. 1 (1997): 25–45.

Memmi, Albert. *The Colonizer and the Colonized.* London: Earthscan, 1990.

Milfull, John. "Juden, Frauen, Mulatten, Neger: Probleme der Emanzipation in Anna Seghers Karibische Erzählungen." In *Frauenliteratur: Autorinnen – Perspektiven – Konzepte*, edited by Manfred Jurgensen, 45–56. Bern: Peter Lang, 1983.

Neugebauer, Heinz. *Anna Seghers: Leben und Werk.* West Berlin: Verlag das europäische Buch, 1978.

Petersen, Viebke Rützou. "Revolution or Colonization: Anna Seghers's Drei Frauen aus Haiti." *The German Quarterly* 65, nos. 3/4 (1992): 396–406.

Pizer, John. "Négritude in East German Literature: Anna Seghers, Heiner Müller and the Haitian Revolution." *Comparatist* 35 (May 2011): 19–39.

Raphael-Hernandez, Heike. "Deutsche Verwicklungen in den transatlantischen Sklavenhandel." *Aus Politik und Zeitgeschichte* 50–51 (2015). Accessed August 4, 2017. http://www.bpb.de/apuz/216485/deutsche-verwicklungen-in-den-transatlantischen-sklavenhandel?p=all.

Reich, Kathleen J. "Racially Mixed Marriages in Colonial Namibia." In *Crosscurrents: African Americans, Africa, and Germany in the Modern World*, edited by David McBride, Leroy Hopkins, and Carol Blackshire-Belay, 159–164. Columbia, SC: Camden House, 1998.

Romero, Christiane Zehl. *Anna Seghers: Eine Biographie, 1900–1947.* Berlin: Aufbau, 2000.

Romero, Christiane Zehl. *Anna Seghers: Eine Biographie, 1947–1983.* Berlin: Aufbau, 2003.

Said, Edward. *Orientalism.* New York: Vintage Books, 1994.

Sartre, Jean-Paul. *Black Orpheus.* Translated by S. W. Allen. Paris: Présence africaine, 1976.

Schrade, Andreas. *Anna Seghers.* Stuttgart: Metzlersche Verlagsbuchhandlung, 1993.

Seghers, Anna. Anna-Seghers-Archiv, Akademie der Künste, Berlin, Nr. 598/1.

Seghers, Anna. *Briefe 1953–1983.* Berlin: Aufbau, 2000.

Seghers, Anna. *Das Siebte Kreuz: Roman.* Darmstadt: Luchterhand, 1982.

Seghers, Anna. "Gespräch mit Anna Seghers: [Gekürzte Rückübersetzung eines im Mai 1943 in der mexikanischen Zeitung 'Futuro' erschienen Gesprächs]." In *Sinn und Form: Beiträge zur Literatur* 38 (1986): 268–273.

Seghers, Anna. *Karibische Geschichten.* Berlin: Aufbau, 2000.

Seghers, Anna. *Transit: Roman.* Berlin: Aufbau, 2000.

Seghers, Anna. "Zur Enstehung der Antillen-Novellen." In *Karibische Geschichten*, 251–256. Berlin: Aufbau, 2000.

Slobodian, Quinn. "Socialist Chromatism: Race, Racism, and the Racial Rainbow in East Germany." In *Comrades of Color: East Germany in the Cold War World*, edited by Quinn Slobodian, 23–39. New York: Berghahn, 2015.

Spillers, Hortense. "Mama's Baby, Papa's Maybe: An American Grammar Book." *Diacritics* 17, no. 2 (1987): 64–81.

Teraoka, Arlene. *East, West, and Others: The Third World in Postwar German Literature.* Lincoln: University of Nebraska Press, 1996.

Uerlings, Herbert. *Poetiken der Interkulturalität: Haiti bei Kleist, Seghers, Müller, Buch und Fichte.* Tübingen: Max Niemeyer, 1997.

Zantop, Susan. *Colonial Fantasies: Conquest, Family and Nation in Precolonial Germany, 1770–1870.* Durham, NC: Duke University Press, 1997.

Index

Note: *page numbers followed by "n" denote endnotes.*

Acker, Pater Amandus 88
Acosta de Samper, Soledad 18
Adelsverein 67
Africa-based missionaries 105, 107
Africa Society of German Catholics 83
Afrika-Verein deutscher Katholiken 107
Afro-Moravian members 48, 49, 50
Alfinger, Ambrosius 21, 22
America: christian slavery in 103; Civil War 92; slavery 9, 47
America Anti-Slavery Society 60
Andersch, Alfred 129
Anglo-American culture 62
Anneke, Mathilde Franziska 8, 11, 59
Anti-Slavery Congress in Cologne 85
anti-slavery policy 80
anti-slavery societies 60, 80
anti-slave-trade bill 86
anti-slave-trading platform 84
"Arab Revolt" 81
Arendt, Hannah 130
Atlantic slave trade 101
Atlantic Studies 63
Atlas of the Transatlantic Slave Trade 2
Ayim, May 5

Basker, James G. 60
Beckles, Hilary McD 39, 40, 54n41
Bergquist, James 67
Berlin, colonial exhibition in 5
Berlin Missionary Society (Berlin I) 82
Bible-reading slaves 46
Biografías de Hombres Ilustres ó Notables 18
Biographies of Famous or Notable Men 25
Bismarck, Otto von 2, 81–5, 93
Bloch, Ernst 41, 43
Blumenbach, Johann Friedrich 8
Booth, Sherman 67
Bradford, William 64
Brahm, Felix 3, 129
Brandenburgisch-Afrikanische Compagnie 5

Bredel, Willi 127
Brevísima relación de la destrucción de las Indias 25
Brinkmann, Tobias 67
Brother Michler 49, 50
Brown, John 40, 68
Brussels Conference Act 86, 87
Buchanan, James 61
Bund Proletarisch-Revolutionärer Schriftsteller 126

Caribbean: Christian theology 42; fight for freedom 130; Moravian missionary 40, 42; plantation economies of 12, 13n19; slavery, German involvements 11
Caribbean Stories 125–7, 129, 130, 133, 134
Catholic missionary associations 82, 88, 89; African slaves and aid practices 113–15; antislavery activism, formation of 102, 104–8; freed children education 106; in gender 108–13; roles of 102; social dependency in 103
Césaire, Aimé 128, 133
Charles V 19, 20, 23, 32n25
Chicago Tribune 67
"Christian civilisation" 81, 82
Christian theology 42
Christian VI 48
Christian worship 49
church community: cross-racial and cross-class equality 41, 44; inside and outside interactions 44; "spiritual-cum-secular" 46
Church Missionary Society 80
"civilising project" 91
Civil Rights Marches 44
collective existence 43
Collegi dei moretti 106
colonial advocacy groups 84, 91
"colonial amnesia of Germans" 2, 5
Colonial Congress: in 1902 88; in 1905 90; in 1910 91
Colonial Fantasies (Zantop) 129
Comboni, Daniele 106

INDEX

Conzen, Kathleen Neils 62
Crenshaw, Kimberlé 142n16
Cuban slave plantations 6
"cultural value" of Islam 90
Cuon, Albert 23

Daniel Webster's Fugitive Slave Law of 1850 61
Danish West Indies 40, 42
Das Siebte Kreuz 125
de Las Casas, Bartolomé 25
Denzer, Jörg 25
de Samper, Soledad Acosta 25
Deutsche Frauen-Zeitung 63
Deutsche Kolonialgesellschaft 81
Deutsche Kolonialzeitung 82, 83, 85, 88
Deutscher Katholikentag 107
Deutsch-Ostafrikanische Zeitung 90
diarium 48, 49, 51
The Dictionary of Literary Biography 62
Die Toten bleiben jung 132
Dittmann, Wilhelm 92
Dober, Leonard 42, 45, 49, 51
Douai, Adolf 61, 62
Douglass, Frederick 47, 61, 68
Dutch West India Company 5

economic bliss 8
Edward Robinson, Orientalist 63
Efford, Alison Clark 59
Ehinger, Heinrich 23
Ehinger, Jörg 22
Eltis, David 2
"Emin Pasha Expedition" 82
"entangled histories of uneven modernities" 20
Erzberger, Matthias 91, 92
Esclavage et colonisation (Schoelcher) 133
Essai politique sur l'île de Cuba 6, 61
Essay on the Island of Cuba 6
Estévez, Álvarez 23
European-Christian civilizing mission in Africa 113
Evangelical Africa Society 87
Evangelical Mission Society for German East Africa in Berlin (Berlin III) 82
The Exiles (Talvj) 11, 59, 63, 67

Fabri, Friedrich 82, 85
Federmann, Arnold 25
Federmann, Nicolaus 21, 25
Fichte, Hubert 129
Fischer-Hornung, Dorothea 13n15
A Five Years Expedition 53n13
Follen, Charles 61
Forclaz, Amalia Ribi 102
Frederick V, Denmark 5
"free labourers" 89
Frémont, John C. 61
Frenssen, Gustav 134

Freundlich, Matthäus 42
Frey, Sylvia 43
Friedrich Wilhelm I, Prussian 5
Froberger, Joseph 90
Fugger and Welser companies 5
Fugitive Slave Act of 1850 6
Fulbrook, Mary 126
Fünf Jahre deutscher Kolonialpolitik:Rück-und Ausblicke 84

Garrison, William Lloyd 60, 61
GDR *see* German Democratic Republic (GDR)
German American women writers: antislavery and immigration 60–3; antislavery fiction 62; political and literary work 67; utopian communities 66–71; women's views 62
German colonization 19
German Democratic Republic (GDR) 132, 141
German East Africa: acquisitions in 81; anti-slavery movement 85; "Arab Revolt" 81; Centre Party 83–7, 91; colonial acquisitions in 80; colonial governance 84–8; gubernatorial policy in 88; "Islamic danger" and slavery 88–93; muslim children education 85–6; realpolitik reasons 83; slavery and the slave trade 80, 81; translocal slave trade 79
German East Africa Company 81
Germany: antislavery sentiments 63–6; black legends 25–7; Catholic antislavery activism in 104–8; colonial foundational myths 25–30; competitive memories and claims 30–1; economic entanglement 4; Holocaust 1–2; humanitarian mission 5; ideological groundwork for 7; immigrant women 62; involvements, slavery trade 4–10; memory culture 1–2, 4; micro- to macro-economic level 4; in New World slavery 3; political refugees 61; "poor Negresses" 104; private capital conquest 20–1; products and profits 22–5; revolutionary activities of 64; slave children 104; slave economies 10–12; and slavery 129–30
Germany and the Black Diaspora 13n7
Gerstäcker, Friedrich 8, 62
Geschichte der Mission der evangelischen Brüder 53n11
Goethe, Johann Wolfgang 63
"guerilla gangs" 68
Gutzmann, Gertraud 129

Harzig, Christiane 62
Hausen, Karin 112
Haustein, Jörg 11
Hegel, Georg Wilhelm Friedrich 8
Hell, Julia 127
Herrnhuter community 41
Hilfsverein zur Unterstützung der armen Negerkinder 104, 105

INDEX

Hilzinger, Sonja 143n27
Historie der caribischen Inseln 47
History of the Mission of the Evangelical Brethren 53n11
Holocaust 1–2
Holy Roman Empire 10
"Holy War" 92
Honeck, Mischa 59, 61
Hopkins, Daniel 13n10
Hubert, Franz 63
Hugues, Victor 127, 132–3
human right to freedom: awareness of 41; eternal slavery and white superiority 50–1; historical background 41–3; ideological insistence on the 52; literacy as weapon 46–8; political consciousness 43–6; political visions of 43; protest, encouragement to 48–50
Humboldt, Alexander von 6, 61, 62
Humboldt on Slavery 13n23
Hus, Jan 41

Illinois Staatsanzeiger 59, 67
intersectionality 128, 141, 142n16

Jenkins, H. J. K. 132
Johannes, Samuel 45

Kaiserreich 107
Kansas-Nebraska act of 1857 70, 75n61
Kant, Immanuel 8
Katholische Wochenschrift 111
Keil, Hartmut 59
Kleist, Heinrich von 126; "The Betrothal in St. Domingo" 127, 134
Koloniale Zeitschrift 90, 92
Korten, Johann Abraham 5
Kosmos (von Humboldt) 58
Kossuth, Louis 60

Lampe, Armando 43
"Las Indias Occidentales" 21
Lavigerie, Cardinal 106
Lavigerie, Charles 82
Lavigerie's campaign 107
Layne, Priscilla 12
Ledóchowska, Maria Theresia 107–9
Levine, Bruce 59
The Light on the Gallows (Seghers) 126
Lincoln's Republican Party 61
literacy, slavery 46–8
Livingstone, David 85
Livingstonia missionaries, Nyasaland 82
Lüderitz, Adolf 2

MacDaniel, Caleb 60–1
Martin, Friedrich 42
Martin, Judith 142n12

Martin, Peter 134
Marxist–Leninist ideology 132
"maturing political consciousness" 39, 40
Mazzini, Joseph 60
"Mecca letter affair" 91
Meinecke, Gustav 82
Merensky, Alexander 82, 87, 88
"middle way" 62
Milfull, John 133
"military fortification" 68
Mintz, Sidney 20
Missionnaires d'Afrique 106
"Mohammedan" 88
Möllhausen, Balduin 8
Moravian missionary 10, 40, 42; children education 47; contradictory attitudes of 10; enslaved Africans 40; fierce opposition to 49; harassment and mistreatment 48; secular political awareness 50; white *vs.* black people 50
Morenga (Timm) 129
"Muhammadan fanaticism" 83
Münchener Allgemeine Zeitung 88
Muslim children education 85–6, 88

National Anti-Slavery Standard 13n23
New World slavery, history of 2, 3, 4, 11
The New York Times 72n19
Nietzsche, Friedrich 8
Nitschmann, David 42, 51
non-Christian antislavery activists 103
not yet: Bloch's theory of 52n7; church community 44; collective existence 43; pre-appearance 43; revolutionary interest 43; secular political imagination 46; vision of 41, 43–6, 50

O'Donnell, Joseph 60
Oelssner, Fred 132, 143n40
Orientalism (Said) 140
The Origins of Totalitarianism (Arendt) 130
Osterhammel, Jürgen 101
Ottilien Congregation 107, 118n42

pan-Islamic dimension 83
Pascual, Guzmán 23
Pasha, Emin 85
The Passage to Cosmos 13n23
Patterson, Orlando 46
Peter Moors Fahrt nach Südwest (Frenssen) 134
Peters, Carl 2, 9, 80, 82
Piano per la rigenerazione dell'Africa 106
Pius IX 114
Pizer, John 130, 133
planter society 49
Pope Leo XIII 106, 107
Pribić, Nikola R. 73n36

INDEX

pro-slavery agenda 6
Protten, Rebecca 44
Prussian protestant 89
Prussian rule 83

Qādirīya 80

Raboteau, Albert J. 44
Ramiya, Sheikh 80
Randeria, Shalini 19, 20
Randolph, John 70
Raphael-Hernandez, Heike 10, 11, 59, 129
Rehlingen, Konrad von 5
The Reintroduction of Slavery in Guadeloupe 12, 126, 127, 132, 136, 140
"Religious and Cultural Conditions" 88
revolutionary interest 43
Rhenish Missionary Society 82
Richards, Helen 46
Richardson, David 2
Richter, Julius 90
Roman Sacred Congregation 107
Romero, Christiane Zehl 130–1
Rosenhaft, Eve 3, 129
Roth, Julia 10, 11

Said, Edward 140
St. Paul's spiritual statement 41, 50
St. Petrus Claver Sodality 107, 108, 113
San Padro Claver 142n21
Schaff, Phillip 58
Schoelcher, Victor 133
Schrade, Andreas 133
Schulte Beerbühl, Margrit 5
Schurz, Carl 61
Scottish missionary 85
Seghers, Anna 125–6; "Beauvais thought" 138; *Caribbean Stories* 125–7, 129, 130, 133, 134; Caribbean texts 128; Césaire's work 128, 133; on colorism 128; cross-racial cooperation 133; Germany and slavery 129–30; ghosts of colonialism 140–1; Manon's importance for story 133–4, 136–7, 144n69; Nazi-era writings 129; politics and the politics of race 130–2; portrayal of black women 134–7; "The Reintroduction of Slavery in Guadeloupe" 126, 127, 132, 136, 140; white and mulatto women 137–9
"Self-Liberation Ethos of Enslaved Blacks" 39
Sensbach, Jon 43
sexual exploitation 51
"shared and divided" history 20
slavery: American women's attitudes 64; economies transnational character of 3; equality, radical theology of 52n6; influence of 62; Islam, conflation of 88–93; letter to Christian VI 48; literacy 46–8; political interest 87; post-conquest policy 87; in Qur'ān 87; regulation of 87; revolt 47; secular class/race division 48; secular empowerment 50; sexual exploitation 51; "transitional measure" 87
Slavery Hinterland:Transatlantic Slavery and Continental Europe 3, 129
Slobodian, Quinn 132
Smith, Gerrit 68
"social death" 46
South Sea Company 5
Spangenberg (Bishop) 49, 50
Spillers, Hortense 136
"spiritual-cum-secular" 41, 46, 48, 50
Sprengel, Matthias Christian 6
Squanto, Wampanoag 64
Ständegesellschaft 40
Steffen, Anka 13n10
Stornig, Katharina 11
Strubberg, Friedrich Armand 62
Suriname: Africans, sold to planters in 53n13; Dutch colony of 40; indigenous people in 49; large slave community 42–3; literacy 47; mission in 42; planter society, local laws of 49; slaveholders in 49

"Talvj" *see also* Therese Robinson, Albertine Louise von Jakob
Tanganyika, slave trade in 79
Taylor, Bayard 61
Teraoka, Arlene 128
Tetzel, Johann 23
Therese Robinson, Albertine Louise von Jakob 11, 59, 63, 73n34
Thrasher, John S. 72n19
Timm, Uwe 129
"tragic mulatta" 70
transatlantic slavery 2, 4
Transit (Seghers) 125
translocal slave trade 87
transnational slave trade 22, 31n8
Trasher, John Sidney 6

Uerlings, Herbert 126, 127
Uganda 83
Uhland in Texas (Anneke) 9, 11, 59
Uhland, Ludwig 67
Ulbricht, Walter 132
UMCA missionaries 84
United States of America (USA): cult of German womanhood 63–6; cultural and political isolationism 62; German immigration 62; transnational entanglements of 60

von der Groeben, Otto Friedrich 5
von Humboldt, Alexander 58
von Hutten, Philipp 21
von Kotzebue, August 61

INDEX

von Mallinckrodt, Rebekka 13n10
von Rohr, Philip Benjamin Julius 13n10
von Sack, Baron Albert 7
von Schimmelmann, Heinrich Carl 5
von Soden, Julius 89
von Speyer, Georg Hohermuth 21
von Württemberg, Johann Friedrich 5
von Zinzendorf, Ludwig 41, 42, 45, 46, 51
Vormärz 68, 72n13

Wallach, Martha Kaarsberg 62
Wallenstein, Carl von 67, 75n56
Walls, Laura Dassow 13n23, 61
We Are the Revolutionists (Honeck) 12n7
Weber, Georg 49
Weber, Klaus 3, 13n10

"The Wedding in Haiti" 126, 127
Welser company 21
Werner, Theodor Gustav 24
white superiority 50–1
Wiegmink, Pia 11
Wilhelm II 5
Windthorst Resolution 84
Wissmann, Hermann 2, 85, 88
Wood, Betty 43
World Council of the Moravian Church 52n6

Zander, Johannes Wilhem 48
Zantop, Susanne 20, 129
Zeuske, Michael 24
Zimmerer, Jürgen 2
Zimmerman, Andrew 7